THE HENNING FAMILY

Lynn Griffith Ester

HERITAGE BOOKS
2012

HERITAGE BOOKS
AN IMPRINT OF HERITAGE BOOKS, INC.

Books, CDs, and more—Worldwide

For our listing of thousands of titles see our website
at
www.HeritageBooks.com

Published 2012 by
HERITAGE BOOKS, INC.
Publishing Division
100 Railroad Ave. #104
Westminster, Maryland 21157

International Standard Book Numbers
Paperbound: 978-0-7884-1627-9
Clothbound: 978-0-7884-9124-5

For Michael.

Without your love and encouragement
none of this would have been possible.

***

There is no king who has not had a slave among his ancestors,

and no slave who has not had a king among his.

Helen Keller

Contents

Preface

Many times I am asked if I am "working on a famous family," to which I reply, "No, just your average poor dirt farmers." In retrospect I now regret those casual remarks. No one is insignificant. No one has a right to "grade" a family until they have walked in their footsteps. Everyone has those moments when they wonder how they will be remembered in a backward glance.

The origins of this book were conceived over twenty years ago while I was working on another related family. The Hennings, while not famous, are an interesting bunch. Certainly not average or "run of the mill." This book is largely a genealogy of the Henning family in America. The Henning patriarch was Johann Adam Henning. Johann Adam was a Hessian soldier who deserted at Shallow Ford (a narrow crossing on the Yadkin River), just prior to the Battle of Guilford Court House, in Guilford County, North Carolina.

During the American Revolution England did not have enough men to meet her military commitments. So she "engaged" organized troop units from Germany. In other words, Germany sold these men to England for the sole purpose of being mercenaries. According to Bruce E. Burgoyne's book, *Enemy Views The American Revolutionary War as Recorded by the Hessian Participants*, this group made up about one-third of the total number of soldiers sent to America (xiv).

War has never been fun, but every once in a while it affords opportunities which, when seized upon, can make all the difference in one's life. This was never truer than in the life of Johann Adam Henning. While many stories have been passed down through the generations, the bottom line is that Johann Adam Henning did make full use of the term Carpe Diem! He seized the day, the moment, and the opportunity to obtain his freedom just prior to the Battle of Guilford Court House. He ran.

Many will say, "What's so special about Henning? After all, there were thousands of deserters." What is so special about Johann Adam Henning is he obviously planned and executed his departure. This was not happenstance.

Henning could not speak English. Perhaps he had picked up a few words here and there, but for the most part he never spoke nor understood English well. There were many places to just slip away during his regiment's move toward Guilford Court House. But for a man who could not speak the language of the countryside, life would indeed be difficult at best. Henning chose a place where he could assimilate into the area. He could blend and become a part of the community without causing too much attention. There was a strong enclave of German speaking people in the area of what is today Yadkin, Stokes, and Forsyth Counties, North Carolina. Many of these people were Moravians. This was a pacifist group who believed in helping all peoples whether they were Patriots, Tories or Hessian soldiers.

The end result of Johann Adam's desertion is that he stayed. He was through running. He prospered, and eventually became a landowner. He probably worked as a farm laborer until he saved up enough money to buy two hundred acres. His twelve children were an interesting lot. Some did extremely well. Others were considered social deviants. But were it not for this one deserter, over 2400 people would have lived very different lives.

This book picks up with Johann Adam Henning's arrival in Yadkin County, North Carolina and covers his family from 1781 to 1999. John Adam Henning (the anglicized version of his name) married a lady named Elizabeth. There are no documents verifying their marriage. This union produced twelve children and many descendants (some legitimate and some not). The Hennings will dispel any ideas the reader might have of a prim and proper antebellum or Victorian society, and of the "good old days."

Henning was a poor man who raised his twelve children in what appears to be a one room log cabin with a loft. After laboring for about eighteen years, he eventually scrapes together 100 pounds to purchase 200 acres in 1799. Henning's farm must have been one of those hard scrabble farms cut out of the woods. There is a creek at the bottom of a steep hill which afforded the family and livestock water. Probably only a few acres were ever cleared. By 1850 the Forsyth County, North Carolina Census shows the Henning properties were worth between $30 to $78.

The daughters and sons of John Adam Henning were probably given a great deal of freedom. Starting in 1812 and continuing until 1843, five of John Adam's children were issued Bastardy Bonds in Stokes County, North Carolina. The children and grandchildren continued in the "family" tradition with the last Bastardy Bond being issued to Rosa Henning in 1878 in Yadkin County, North Carolina. Not because the family suddenly became "moral" in 1878, but because the state was getting away from publishing these bonds.

However, we must not be too harsh on these children. As Bill Cecil-Fronsman points out in his book, *Common Whites Class and Culture in Antebellum North Carolina*, " . . . when poor parents hired out their daughters, many blandishments are thus cast in their way to seduce them from modesty and virtue to shame and misery" (17). Some even "became the rural equivalent to street prostitutes" (17). Several Henning children were "hired" out to people in the surrounding area.

Times were hard and the Henning women had few resources. According to the 1850 Forsyth County, North Carolina Agricultural Schedule some cash was made by selling their surplus home manufacturing. Cecil-Fronsman indicates many of these duties were assigned to black women, i.e., laundering and sewing. But those women "with greater levels of desperation, fewer options, or few scruples about these things might turn to prostitution" (144).

The 1870 Yadkin County, North Carolina Census shows Amanda Hinning (sp.), age 36 and her five children living together in the Forbush Township. The oldest child is nineteen and the youngest is four. Amanda has no occupation listed other than keeping house. The

1880 Census shows her sister Tiney (Pearlina), age 44, living with five children in the Liberty Township. Tiney is a washer woman, her daughter Rosa is doing millinery and a third daughter, Mary J. is "at home." There are three other small children living in the house. One is Anna born about 1879 (the last Bastardy Bond recipient) the daughter of Rosa.

The stories of personal tragedy continue. One lady was accidently burned to death while she cooked over an open hearth. Still another Henning was charged with bigamy and sent to prison when he married two different women. Perhaps the saddest incident in the whole family is that of Mary Anna Henning and her sister, Catherine Henning. Both are daughters of John Adam Henning. Mary Anna Henning married Peter Cline. While Mary Anna was having children by Peter, her sister Catherine was also having children by Peter Cline. One in 1812 and another in 1818. One can only imagine the humiliation and heartache Mary Anna Henning Cline suffered.

This is essentially the story of a poor white immigrant who just managed to eke out a living on a rock infested farm while housing his family of fourteen in a one room log cabin. The reader may ask, "What in this world could this man's descendants have to offer?" No one can go back and change the past, however we can learn by embracing it. The Hennings struggled to pull themselves out of poverty. Each life has a story to tell. Each is significant. From these "humble" beginnings came doctors, nurses, lawyers, teachers, college professors, business people, ministers, and writers. Not bad for such precarious beginnings. Each person chose to seize an opportunity. Sometimes they made the correct choice, sometimes they didn't. But at least they seized the day. They chose to act. Many "ran" for a goal set before them. Thank you Johann Adam Henning for starting the race. Carpe Diem!

Much of the research for this book was made possible through the generous contributions of fellow researchers and Henning family members. I am particularly indebted to Geraldine "Jerry" Cline Brinegar and Charles Edgar "Ed" Hennings for their tireless assistance. Without them there would be no book.

To Kay Fulp Hauser, thank you for the friendship and the many laughs. You were a true source of encouragement and inspiration.

And to Julie Painter Pittman who contacted me through the Internet and connected me to the west coast Hennings. Without her help and friendship these "cousins" would have been completely left out of this work.

To the archival staff at the North Carolina Department of Resources in Raleigh, North Carolina. These individuals provided the help and assistance I needed to put this project together. They carted and carried so many boxes of precious papers out of the stacks for me to dig through. Whenever I was at a dead end they offered guidance and suggestions which proved fruitful. Those in the microfilm room guided me to the right drawers, helped me load film onto machines and taught me to do a soundex code. Thank you all.

Descendants of John Adam Henning

Generation No. 1

1. **John Adam[1] Henning** was born Abt. 1759 in Hesse, Germany[1], and died January 5, 1824 in Stokes County, NC. He is buried in the Hessian Cemetery on Bashavia Dr., in what is now Forsyth County, NC.[2] He married a woman named **Elizabeth**[3], her last name is unknown. She was born Abt. 1770[4] and died November 20, 1858. She is buried in the Hessian Cemetery, Bashavia Dr., Forsyth County, NC.[5]

John Adam Henning before settling in Stokes County, was probably known in Germany as Johann. However, he was known as "John Adam" and "Adam;" not to be confused with his son who was also named Adam.

A story of the Shallow Ford Crossing is found in <u>The Journal of the Yadkin County Historical Society</u>, Vol. 17, No. 2, June, 1998, p. 307. A copy of General Joseph Graham's paper concerning the crossing is dated Feb. 5, 1781.

"March 16, 1781 a Hessian rifle-man arrived. He had run away at the beginning of a battle and did not know how it had ended and he could only say that yesterday for three hours he heard heavy firing after he left the army."[6]

"According to family tradition, Adam Henning was a deserter from one of the Hessian regiments hired by King George III to help fight his battles in America."[7]

Eugene Moore Conrad, born in 1892, told the following story: "Right down the river here a piece, there's a Shallowford Road that goes across the river there, just above where the Shallow Ford used to be. And Cornwallis came up from down beside the river, came up the road there, and crossed over the Shallow Ford with his army. The river was up, down below there, and he had to come up there across it. And there's some people over there now on the other side of the river who are descendants of a man who got away then. He lost his pot. What he cooked in you know? They all had their own old pots, and he lost his off his horse coming across the river. When they got on this side, he got off his horse and went back and waded out in the river and picked up his pot and got it. And now there's a road where this man settled there. He just took off and deserted the army . . . "[8]

Another story told by George L. Doub of Pfafftown: "He heard from his father that Henning was Cornwallis' orderly when Cornwallis made his famous trail through parts of Forsyth County. 'Henning was a short fellow, and when Cornwallis and his troops cross the Yadkin River at the Shallowford Cross Henning lost Cornwallis' gold teakettle in the rushing water. Well, Cornwallis liked to beat him to death for losing his gold kettle. After that, Henning deserted and settled down here.'"[9]

The following information was submitted by Phronica Hill: "I found something at Fort Wayne about the 5 Henrina Volumes, by Clifford Neal Smith on Hessian soldiers. I wrote to Ernest Thode of the Thode Translations for information as he has all the volumes, and will search for a fee. He informed me that, based on what information I had, our John Adam Henning, born ca. 1759, was undoubtedly identical with Adam Henning, born ca. 1755, in present day DDR-5901, (Fortha (with two little dots over the "o") near Eisenach found in Vol. II, entries #5179. He [Henning] was a private in the von BOSE Regiment, 2nd Co., under the immediate command of Col. Karl Ernst von BISCHHAUSEN. He was recruited in Sept. 1779 and reported as deserted in Feb. 1781. The von BOSE Regiment took part in the battles of Fort Clinton, Springfield, Guilford Court House, Green Spring Yorktown. He said this fitted the description of a desertion at Guilford Court House. He may have served Cornwallis, just as all Continental troops served Washington."[10]

John Adam Henning was in Surry County, NC by 1785. He appears on the tax list for Capt. Krouse's District for that year. He was also found on the Stokes County, NC tax lists beginning in 1792. In 1793 and 1794 Henning listed 100 acres.[11]

2

The 1799 Stokes County, NC Property Valuations listed Adam Henning as living in the Binkleys District of Stokes County, having two buildings on the property valued at $90, and two hundred acres of land valued at $290.[12]

On September 8, 1808, Adam Henning purchased 200 acres of land for 100 pounds from Jacob Salmon. The land was located 'on the waters of the big Yadkin River' in what was then Stokes County, NC. Jacob Salmon/Solomon was deeded the land by Isaac Nelson, "late high sheriff of said county" on February 18, 1799.[13]

"Jan. 5 Br. V. V. [Carl Anton Van Vleck] visited our neighbor Henning, who has been sick for months and has wasted until he looks like a skeleton. The Methodists have held service in his house several times, but in the English language, which the old man (born in Hesse) did not understand well. He had asked therefore for a visit from a minister who could speak German. In the Days of health he often attended our church in Bethania. That evening Mr. Henning departed this life. His funeral was held on the 7th by the Methodist preacher Jean."[14]

In a letter dated May 20, 1982 from Irene Choplin to Jeffrey Coltrane, Jr., Mrs. Choplin indicated she had received a letter from the Commission on Archives and History of the United Methodist Church indicating they had found a note on William Jean, Jr. as being of Guilford County, NC in 1785. Jean was living in Stokes County, NC during the 1799 Property Valuations, & he is listed in the 1820 Stokes Census. A William Jean witnessed the will of John Adam Henning [dated 1823] and spoke at his funeral [1824].

There is a Will for John Adam Henning dated November 17, 1823 in Stokes County, NC which lists his wife, twelve children, and two grandchildren. Witnesses are: William Doub, Jacob Spainhour and William Jean.

Children of John Adam Henning and Elizabeth are:

+ 2 i. **Simon² Henning,**[15] born 1787 in Stokes
Cty., NC.
3 ii. **Christina Magdalene Henning**[16], born Abt.
1790 in NC. She married **Peter Hufffman**[17].
Peter and Christina Henning were married prior
to 1823 as they were listed in John Adam
Henning's will dated 1823.
+ 4 iii. **Mary Anna Henning**[15] born Abt. 1790 in NC;
died May 12, 1845 in NC.
+ 5 iv. **Catherine Henning**[16] born Abt. 1791 NC; died
Abt. 1870 in Forsyth Cty, NC.
6. v. **Michael Henning**[17] born 1796 in NC.
+ 7. vi. **Susanna Henning**[18] born Abt. 1798 in NC.
+ 8. vii. **Christian C. Henning**[19] born Feb. 14, 1800 in
NC; died Oct. 15, 1875 in Yadkin County, NC.
Buried at Forbush Baptist Church, Yadkin Cty.,
NC.
+ 9. viii. **Adam Henning**[20] born Jan. 1, 1804 in NC;
died July 4, 1883 in Anderson Cty., TN. Buried
at New Hope Cem., Oak Ridge, Anderson Cty.,
TN.
+ 10. ix. **Gabriel Henning**[21] born 1808 in Stokes Cty.,
NC; died Abt. 1871 in Yakin Cty., NC.
11. x. **William Henning**[22]

According to Jerry Brinegar, William Henning
had a speech impediment. Jerry's grandmother,
Carrie Mae Henning said William could not
pronounce "Carrie" so called her "Mamie."
William never married and lived with his nieces
and nephews throughout his adult life.

The 1830 Stokes County, NC Census, 1850
Forsyth Cty., NC Census, & the 1870 Forsyth

Cty., NC Census all show that William could
not read nor write and was a farm laborer.

+   12.   xi.   **Anna Henning**[23] born 1815 in Stokes Cty.,
NC.

   13.   xii.   **Sally Henning**[24] born Abt. 1820 in Stokes
County, NC, died Abt. 1880 in Anderson Cty.,
TN.[25] No record of Sally could be found after
1880.

Jeffrey Coltrane, Jr. found a journal at Duke
University written by Rev. Michael Doub from
1826 to 1856. A list of class members for 1829
included Sally Henning, who was single and
baptized. In 1832 Sally Henning was "expelled
[sp.] for non-attendance."

Rev. Michael Doub was licensed to preach in
1827. Methodist services were being held in
Michael's father's home - John Doub. John
Doub was licensed to preach in 1802. Doub's
Chapel Methodist Church near Pfafftown is an
outgrowth of these meetings.

Sallie [sp.] Henning, age 50-60, single, is listed
as the sister of Adam Henning living in
Anderson County, TN in the 1880 Federal
Census, 8th Civil District, p. 13, dwelling 112,
family 112, Reel #T9-1244.

Generation No. 2

2. Simon[2] Henning (John Adam[1]) was born 1787 in NC.[26] He
married **(1) Maria Magdalene Sailor** on Aug. 16, 1821. Their
marriage bond was dated Aug. 2, 1821. Maria was born 1782 in NC,

and died Jan. 18, 1847. She is buried at God's Acre, Forsyth Cty., NC.[27]

A letter at Duke University from Michael Doub to his brother Peter Doub dated August 9, 1821 in which he wrote, "Simon Henning is to be married this day week to Lena Saler as she is called." A week from August 9th would place the marriage on August 16, 1821. We can assume Michael Doub married Simon and Magdalena.[28]

Simon Henning married (2) **Catherine Chitty** on Sept. 27, 1850.[29] A Marriage Bond was issued in Forsyth County, NC on Sept. 27, 1850 to Simon Henning. No perspective wife was listed. Jerry Brinegar found a will of Catherine Heckerdom which lists Catharina Chitty as Simon's wife.[30]

Jeffrey Coltrane, Jr. found Simon Henning on a tax list in Stokes County, NC in 1814, but he was not listed as owning any land.

Simon Henning was a bondsman on the Bastardy Bond of Margaret Huffman, dated Nov. 18, 1842 in Stokes County, NC. Margaret Huffman refused to identify the father of her child, but Simon paid the bond.[31]

Simon Henning was listed in the following: 1830 Stokes Cty., NC Census, p. 227, the 1840 Stokes Cty., NC Census, Bethabara District, p. 166, the 1850 Forsyth Cty., NC Census, p. 262, dwelling 940, family 954. The 1850 Forsyth County Agricultural Schedule lists Simon as owning 34 acres valued at $150.

Children of Simon Henning and Maria Sailor are:

14	i.	<Unnamed>
15	ii.	<Unnamed>
16	iii.	<Unnamed>
17	iv.	**Amanda Levina Henning** born September 4, 1830 and died October 13, 1886. She is buried at Forbush Baptist Church, East Bend, NC.[32]

In the 1850 Forsyth County, NC Census, Amanda Henning (age 22) is living with her father Simon Henning (age 63). There is no proof that Simon is Amanda's father, but since she is living with him in the 1850 census, we will assume she is his daughter.

Amanda Henning cannot be located in the 1860 Forsyth, Stokes, Surry, or Yadkin County census'.

The 1870 Yadkin Cty., NC census, Forbush township, Huntsville Post Office, shows Amanda "Hinning" as head of household Henry and Mahalia living with her, along with a Sarah Henning, Elizabeth Henning, and Benjamin Henning.

A Bastardy Bond was issued in Yadkin County, NC on April 9, 1855 to Amanda Henning. She refused to name the father of her illegitimate child. **Thomas Norman** was the bondsman on the bond dated September 10, 1856.

Another Bastardy Bond was issued in Yadkin County, NC on May 21, 1859 to Amanda Henning. She named **Thomas Patterson** as the father of her child..

4. Mary Anna[2] Henning (John Adams[1]) was born in 1790[33] and died May 12, 1845 in NC.[34] She married **Peter Cline**[35] who was born Abt. 1779.[36]

Notes for Mary Anna Henning:
Kay Hauser's e-mail of Feb. 16, 1999, indicated that <u>The Records of the Moravians in North Carolina</u>, p. 4871, Bethania, May 12, 1845

read as follows: "Visited Peter Klein whose wife had died this morning after a short sickness. Undertook to hold the funeral service in Dutch Meeting House. The Klein family is such an abandoned one, as one can just imagine."

Sometimes the name, Cline, was spelled Kline or Klein which means "little" in German.

There should be three (3) more children listed under the union of Peter and Mary Anna Henning Cline as per Jerry Brinegar. Maybe these were his illegitimate children? However, according to the 1850 Forsyth County, NC Census, Peter Cline, age 71, was living with his daughter, Nancy Cline Conrad. Also living with Nancy is someone named Solomon Cline, age 37. For now this writer is listing Solomon Cline as another child of Peter and Mary Anna Cline.

Kay Hauser wrote that Peter and his wife had eight (8) children listed in the 1840 Stokes Cty., NC Census, Yadkin District.

Peter Cline fathered two illegitimate children by Catherine Henning (sister of Mary Anna Henning). These children were born in 1812 (Rachel Henning); and 1818 (Elizabeth "Betsy") Henning.[37]

Children of Mary Anna Henning and Peter Cline are:

+	18	i.	Nancy[3] Cline, born June 29, 1811 in NC; died June 7, 1852. Buried Doub's Chapel Methodist Church, Vienna, NC.
+	19	ii.	Peter Solomon Cline, born 1815 in NC; died in Forsyth County, NC.
+	20	iii.	Eli Cline, born June 4, 1822 in Stokes Cty., NC; died June 1, 1905 in Forsyth Cty., NC. Buried Shiloh Lutheran Cemetery, Forsyth Cty., NC.
	21	iv.	Henry Cline[38] born Abt. 1833 in Stokes Cty., NC.[39] He married Betsy Anne McBride on

August 6, 1856 in Forsyth Cty., NC. **Robert Church** was the bondsman on the marriage bond.[40]

Henry Cline was working an an apprentice for **Emanual Pfaff**, a blacksmith, in the 1850 Forsyth County, NC Census.[41]

22   v.   **Edwin Cline**[42] born Abt. 1836 in Stokes Cty., NC. Married **Phetiten Masecup** on Sept. 30, 1860 in Forsyth Cty., NC.[43]

Edwin Cline was living at the home of **Philip H. Pfaff** in the 1850 Forsyth County, NC Census.[44]

5. Catherine[2] Henning (John Adam[1])[45] was born Abt. 1791 in NC[46], and died Abt. 1870 in Forsyth Cty., NC.[47]

Catherine Henning never married but she did have two (2) illegitimate children by Peter Cline.[48] Peter was married to Catherine's sister, Mary Anna, while he fathered these two children.

Children of Catherine Henning are:

+   23   i.   **Rachel[3] Henning** born 1815 in NC.[49]
+   24   ii.   **Elizabeth Cline** born 1818 in NC,[50] died September 29, 1846 in Stokes Cty., NC.[51]

7. Susanna[2] Henning (John Adam[1])[52] was born in 1798 in NC.[53] A marriage bond was issued to **Joseph Seiler**[54] on Sept. 4, 1821 in Stokes Cty., NC. The bondsman was Simon Henning.[55] Joseph was born Aug. 23, 1793 in Stokes Cty., NC and died Abt. 1840.[56] He was the son of **John Seiler** and **Anna Strupe**.[57]

Children of Susanna Henning and Joseph Seiler are:

25	i.	**William Heinrich**[3] **Seiler** born Sept. 28, 1822, died April 9, 1844.[58]
26	ii.	**Maria Matilda Seiler** born Aug. 1, 1824 in Bethania, NC.[59] Maria Matilda Seiler was baptized Nov. 7, 1824 in Bethania, NC.[60] She married **Elisha Stoltz** on Aug. 29, 1852 in Forsyth Cty., NC.[61]
27	iii.	**Alfred Parminio Seiler** born Oct. 15, 1826.[62]
28	iv.	**Louis White Seiler** born June 20, 1836.[63]
29	v.	**Joseph Wesley Seiler** born April 30, 1842.[64]

8. Christian C.[2] **Henning** (John Adam[1])[65] born Feb. 14, 1800 in NC, and died Oct. 15, 1875 in Yadkin Cty., NC. Buried Forbush Baptist Church, Yadkin Cty., NC.[66] Christian married **Nancy Deitz**. A marriage bond was issued in Stokes Cty., NC on Feb. 20, 1826. Nancy was the daughter of **John & Charity Deitz**. She died Abt. 1849.

Christian C. Henning can be found in the following: The 1830 Stokes Cty., NC Census, p. 247; the 1840 Stokes Cty., NC Census, Bethania District, p. 145; the 1860 Yadkin Cty., NC Census, dwelling 310, family 296, Forbush Township, p. 271; and the 1870 Yadkin Cty., NC Census, dwelling 185, Liberty Township, p. 26. All the census records indicate Christian could not read nor write. He was a farm laborer all his life. Many of his children settled in the Flint Hill section of East Bend in Yadkin County, NC.[67]

Children of Christian Henning and Nancy Deitz are:

+	30	i.	**Pearlina M.**[3] **Henning** born July 6, 1829, died April 30, 1917. She is buried at Forbush Baptist Church, Yadkin Cty., NC.[68]
+	31	ii.	**Amanda Sarah Henning** born Sept. 4, 1830 in NC, died Oct. 13, 1886. Buried Forbush Baptist Church, Yadkin Cty., NC.[69]

+	32	iii.	**Josiah Tyson Henning** born Feb. 13, 1833 in NC, died Feb. 13, 1908. Buried Stony Knoll Methodist Church, East Bend, NC.[70]
+	33	iv.	**Edward T. Henning** born July 10, 1835 in Stokes Cty., NC, died Jan. 5, 1904 in Forsyth Cty., NC. Buried Bethabara Moravian Church, Forsyth Cty., NC.[71]
	34	v.	**Mary Frances Henning** born Abt. 1847 in NC.[72] She married **John S. Colbert** on Aug. 8, 1862 in Yadkin Cty., NC.[73]

It is not known for sure if Mary Frances Henning is the daughter or granddaughter of Christian Henning. She is listed as living with Christian in the 1860 Yadkin County Census, Forbush Township, dwelling 310, family 296, p. 271.

9. Adam[2] Henning (John Adam[1])[74] born Jan. 1, 1804 in NC, died July 4, 1883 in Anderston Cty., TN. He is buried at New Hope Cemetery, Oak Ridge, Anderson Cty., TN.[75] A Marriage Bond was issued in Surry Cty., NC on March 17, 1832 to **Ansora Ann Webster**.[76] She was the daughter of **James Webster** and **Nancy Lambert**. Ansora was born May 31, 1815 in NC, died Jan. 26, 1887 in Anderson Cty., NC. She is buried at New Hope Cemetery, Oak Ridge, Anderson Cty., TN.[77]

Adam Henning was a bondsman who paid 20 pounds on a Bastardy Bond for Lena Shaub on Nov. 12, 1828 in Stokes Cty., NC. **Lena Shaub** did not name the father of her child. The other two bondsmen listed were **Jacob and Magdalena Shaub** (most like her parents). All indications are that Adam was the father of Lena's child.

Children of Adam Henning and Ansora Webster are:

+	35	i.	**Martha A. E.[3] Henning** born 1834 in Surry Cty., NC, died 1913 in Washington State.[78]

	36	ii.	**Nancy Henning** born 1835. Died in infancy.[79]
+	37	iii.	**Archibald G. Henning** born 1839, died 1921 in Thornton, WA.[80]
	38	iv.	**Sarah Jane Henning** born 1842, died Abt. 1924 in Washington State.[81] She married **James Bagley** on July 5, 1885 in Anderson Cty., TN by J. W. Key, Justice of the Peace.[82]
	39	v.	**Naoma Ruth Henning** born Abt. 1846.[83]

The census record for the 1850 Surry Cty., NC Census was hard to read. Naoma could have been "Norma."

+	40	vi.	**John W. Henning** born Abt. 1848 in Surry County, NC, died 1893.[84]
+	41	vii.	**Elvina or Elvira B. Henning** born May 11, 1851 in TN, died Feb. 28, 1889. Buried New Hope Cem., Oak Ridge, Anderson Cty., TN.[85]
+	42	viii.	**Santford Ivan Henning** born Oct. 11, 1854 in TN, died May 30, 1927 in Thornton, Whitman Cty., WA.[86]
+	43	ix.	**William Gabriel Henning** born Abt. 1856 in TN.[87]

10. Gabriel[2] Henning (John Adam[1])[88] was born 1808 in Stokes Cty., NC and died Abt. 1871 in Yadkin Cty., NC.[89] He married **(1) Christina Charlotte Aust**.[90] She was the daughter of **Johann George Aust** and **Delilah Morris**. Christina was born Dec. 9, 1813 in NC, died Aug. 12, 1841 in NC.[91] Gabriel then married **(2) Celia Barber**. A Marriage Bond was issued in Stokes County, NC on July 28, 1842. Celia was born Abt. 1820.

Gabriel Henning purchased land from **John G. Aust** (his father-in-law) in 1832.[92]

In the 1840 Stokes Cty., NC Census, Gabriel is living in the Bethabra District.

Gabriel Henning's name was listed in the ledger of **A. P. and R. C. Poindexter's** general store in Flint Hill, NC (Yadkin County). The store operated during the mid-1800's.[93]

In the 1850 Forsyth County Agricultural Schedule, Gabriel owned 135 acres, and his property was valued at $400.

The 1860 Yadkin County, NC Census listed Gabriel living in the Forbush Township. He is listed as a farm laborer. By 1870 Gabriel is living in the Richmond Hill District of Yadkin Cty., NC. The census records indicate Gabriel could not read nor write. There is no further record of him after the 1870 census.

Notes for Christina Aust Henning:
Jeffrey S. Coltrane, Jr. found a journal at Duke University which Michael Doub kept from 1826 to 1856. On August 13, 1841 Michael "preached Gab. Henning's wife's funeral." He "rode 20 miles, preached on the text Job 22:26-27 and baptized three people."

Children of Gabriel Henning and Christina Aust are:

+   44   i.   **Delilah Louise[3] Henning** born July 15, 1833 in NC, died March 25, 1904. She is buried at Bethabara Moravian Church in Forsyth County, NC.[94]

+   45   ii.   **Julia Mary Ann Henning** born Sept. 12, 1835, died Dec. 22, 1880. She is buried at Deep Creek Friends Church, Yadkin Cty., NC.[95]

+   46   iii.   **Rebecca Catherine Henning** born Feb. 19, 1837 in NC, died Feb. 9, 1873. She is buried at Mt. Tabor Methodist Church, Forsyth Cty., NC.[96]

+   47   iv.   **Lauretta Elizabeth Henning** born March 24, 1839 in Stokes Cty., NC, died Nov. 10, 1915 in Boone Cty., IN. Buried Pleasant View Cem., Whitestown, IN.[97]

Children of Gabriel Henning and Celia Barber are:

	48.	i.	Fanny B.[3] Henning born Abt. 1843.[98]
+	49	ii.	Clemmentine Henning born Abt. 1846.[99]
+	50	iii.	Isaac T. Henning born May, 1849.[100]
+	51	iv.	Adam L. Henning born Abt. 1854.[101]
	52	v.	Emily C. Henning born Abt. 1858.[102]

12. Anna[2] Henning (John Adam[1])[103] was born in 1815 in Stokes Cty., NC.[104] She married **Moses Lewis** on Jan. 19, 1833.[105] Moses was born Abt. 1800 in NC.[106]

The 1860 Forsyth County, NC Census indicates neither Moses nor his wife, Anna, could read or write.

Children of Anna Henning and Moses Lewis are:

53	i.	**Isaac Lewis** born 1835, died 1907. Buried Woodland Cemetery, Forsyth Cty., NC.[107] Isaac married **Julia Ann Knott**[108] on Feb. 15, 1866. Julia is buried at Woodland Cemetery but there are no dates on her tombstone.
54	ii.	**William Lewis** born Abt. 1839.[109]
55.	iii.	**Jane Lewis** born Abt. 1843.[110]
56	iv.	**Sarah Lewis** born about 1847.[111]
57	v.	**Edward Lewis** born Abt. 1848.[112]
58	vi.	**Walter Lewis** born Abt. 1850.[113]

Generation No. 3

18. Nancy[3] Cline (Mary Anna[2] Henning, John Adam[1]) was born June 29, 1811, died June 7, 1852 and is buried in Doub's Chapel Methodist Church, Vienna, NC.[114] She married **William Conrad** on September 23, 1833 in Stokes Cty., NC.[115]

William Conrad and his family can be found in the following: The 1850 Forsyth County, NC Census, dwelling 1185, family 1202; and the 1860 Forsyth County, NC Census, Old Town Township, p. 601.

William Conrad ran a liquor still with the help of Peter and Peter Solomon Cline.[116]

Children of Nancy Cline and William Conrad are:

+	59	i.	**Julia A.**[4] **Conrad** born Feb. 22, 183?, died April 20, 1902. She is buried at Pfafftown Christian Church, Rural Hall, NC.[117]
	60	ii.	**Emily S. Conrad** born 1833.[118]
	61	iii.	**Catherine A. Conrad** born 1835.[119]
	62	iv.	**Clementine R. Conrad** born 1837.[120]
	63	v.	**Felicia Conrad** born 1839.[121]
	64	vi.	**Louisa M. Conrad** born 1841.[122]
	65	vii.	**Permelia M. Conrad** born 1847.[123]
	66	viii.	**Augustine E. B. Conrad** born 1849.[124]

19. Peter Solomon[3] **Cline** (Mary Anna[2] Henning, John Adam[1]) was born in 1815, died in Forsyth Cty., NC. He married **Martha Rebecca [Patsy] Pfaff**, daughter of Christian Pfaff and Elizabeth Doll.[125]

Kay Hauser indicates she believes Soloman's whole name was "Peter Soloman Cline." She also gives the following from <u>The Records of the Moravians in North Carolina</u>, 1856 Bethania Congregation, Sept. 21, 1856: "We drove to Spanish Grove, where first there was infant baptism

(Sol. Klein's) at 10:00 and then preaching service II Pet. 1:10). Alspaugh closed the meeting."

Ms. Hauser also wrote the following: "That Soloman and his Dad, Peter, work for **William Conrad**, Peter's son-in-law and Soloman's brother-in-law (married Nancy). They worked at his [Conrad's] still making liquor and carrying off sour mash. This could explain why they [Soloman & Peter] were listed in the 1850 census as living at the home of William Conrad. See 1850 Forsyth County, NC Census, dwelling 1185, family 1202.

Children of Peter Cline and Martha Pfaff are:

	67	i.	**Julius**[4] **Cline** born in Forsyth Cty, NC.[126]
	68	ii.	**Mattie Cline** born in Forsyth Cty, NC.[127] Mattie had several illegitimate children.[128]
+	69	iii.	**James Nathan Cline** born April 20, 1851 in Forsyth Cty, NC.[129]
	70	iv.	**Lisetta Catherine Cline** born 1852 in Bethania, NC, died Aug. 25, 1926 in Forsyth Cty, NC. Lisetta was baptized on Nov. 6, 1852 at Spanish Grove.[130]
	71	v.	**Peter Cline** born Dec. 1, 1852 in Forsyth Cty, NC.[131]
+	72	vi.	**Charles Christian Cline** born Jan. 4, 1854 in Vienna Township, Pfafftown, NC, died Dec. 27, 1936 in Pfafftown, NC.[132]
	73	vii.	**Jennie Cline** born Nov. 7, 1869 in Forsyth Cty., NC.[133]

20. Eli[3] **Cline** (Mary Anna[2] Henning, John Adam[1]) was born June 4, 1822 in Stokes Cty., NC, died June 1, 1905 in Forsyth Cty., NC. Buried Shiloh Lutheran Cemetery, Forsyth Cty., NC. He married **(1) Nancy**

Shelton in North Carolina. She was born Abt. 1829, died Abt.

1869. He married (2) Jane Elizabeth Davenport September 30, 1869. She was born Feb. 9, 1849 in Halifax Cty., NC, died Oct. 28, 1924 in NC.[134]

Eli and Nancy were living together in Forsyth Cty., NC in 1850 with no children. Eli was working as a laborer.[135]

Children of Eli Cline and Nancy Shelton are:

74	i.	Sarah[4] Cline born Abt. 1851, died Feb. 2, 1918. She married Fredrick Hix, born 1847.[136]
+ 75	ii.	Peter S. Cline born Jan. 12, 1852, died May 15, 1932 in Forsyth Cty., NC. Buried Pfafftown Christian Church, Pfafftown, NC.[137]
76	iii.	Melvina Cline born 1855.[138] She married James Livingston on May 18, 1876 in Forsyth Cty., NC.[139]
77	iv.	Richard Cline born 1856.[140]
+ 78	v.	Augustine C. Cline born 1857 in NC, died 1946 in Forsyth Cty., NC. Buried Crews Methodist Church, Forsyth Cty., NC.[141]
79	vi.	Sanford Cline born 1858.[142]
80	vii.	Laura Cline born 1862.[143]
81	viii.	Isaac Cline born 1867.[144]

Children of Eli Cline and Jane Davenport are:

82	i.	Lewis W.[4] Cline born 1867 in NC.[145] Married Ellen W. George born Oct. 1, 1873 in NC, died Dec. 20, 1927. She is buried at Pfafftown Christian Church, Forsyth Cty., NC.[146]
+ 83	ii.	Pleas David Cline born May 13, 1883 in Lewisville, NC, died July 17, 1948. He is buried at Woodland Cemetery, Forsyth Cty., NC.[147]

84   iii.   **Early Cline** born April 19, 1885 in Forsyth County, NC, died July 9, 1967 in Forsyth Cty., NC. He is buried at Pfafftown Christian Church, Pfaftown, NC.[148] Married **Mary Jane Spainhour** on Feb. 2, 1908.[149] She was born Feb. 19, 1883, died Nov. 25, 1941. She is buried at Mt. Pleasant Methodist Church, Tobaccoville, NC.[150]

85   iv.   **J. Harrison Cline** born Nov. 22, 1888 in NC, died July 31, 1909 and buried at Pfafftown Christian Church, Forsyth Cty., NC.[151] He married **Minnie Gordon** Dec. 17, 1908. She was born in 1889 in N.C.[152]

23. Rachel[3] Henning (Catherine[2], John Adam[1]) was born 1815.[153] She married **Edmond Wood** on Jan. 17, 1840 in Davidson Cty., NC.[154] Edmond was born Abt. 1821.[155]

Rachel Henning was given $5.00 by her grandfather, John Adam Henning.[156]

Jeffrey Coltrane, Jr. found a journal at Duke University which was kept by **Rev. Michael Doub** from 1826 to 1856. A list of class members for 1829 includes Rachel Henning who was single and baptized.

Children of Rachel Henning and Edmond Wood are:

86.   i.   **Henry[4] Wood** born 1842.[157]
87   ii.   **John Wood** born 1844.[158]
88   iii. **Alexander Wood** born 1845.[159]
89   iv.   **Amanda J. Wood** born 1847.[160]

24. Elizabeth[3] Cline (Catherine[2] Henning, John Adam[1]) was born 1818 in NC.[161] She died Sept. 29, 1846 in Stokes Cty., NC.[162]

Elizabeth Henning was also given $5.00 in the will of her grandfather, John Adam Henning.[163]

Jeffrey Coltrane, Jr. found a journal at Duke University written by
Rev. Michael Doub which spanned the years 1826 - 1856. On
September 30, 1846 Rev. Doub preached Betsy Henning's funeral and
rode 16 miles. He text was Luke 13:5, "I tell you, No; but unless you
repent you will all likewise perish."

Children of Elizabeth Cline are:

90.   i.   **Child⁴ Henning** born Abt. July, 1840 in Stokes
           Cty., NC.[165]

+   91   ii.   **Lavina Melvina Henning** born Abt. Dec.,
              1843 in Stokes Cty., NC, died Jan. 9, 1918 in
              Forsyth Cty., NC. She is buried at Pfafftown
              Cemetery, Forsyth Cty., NC.[166]

   92   iii.   **Uriah W. Cline** born Abt. 1848.[167]

30. Pearlina M.³ Henning (Christian C.², John Adam¹) was born
July 6, 1829 in NC, died April 30l, 1917. She is buried at Forbush
Baptist Church, Yadkin Cty., NC.[168]

Pearlina never married but had three illegitimate children.

Pearlina, sometimes called Polina and Paulina in the census', was living
with her father, Christian, in the 1870 Yadkin Cty., NC Census in the
Liberty Township. She had two children living with her, Rose and
Mary Jo. In the 1880 Yadkin Cty., NC Census, Pearlina is known as
"Tiney". She was a washer woman.

Pearlina died of Sclerosis of the liver.[169]

Children of Pearlina M. Henning are:

+   93   i.   **Rosa⁴ Henning** born Aug. 10, 1857 in Yadkin
             Cty., NC, died April 11, 1889. She is buried at
             Forbush Bapt. Church, Yadkin Cty., NC.[170]

Children of Pearlina M. Henning are:

+   93   i.   Rosa[4] Henning born Aug. 10, 1857 in Yadkin Cty., NC, died April 11, 1889. She is buried at Forbush Bapt. Church, Yadkin Cty., NC.[170]

       94   ii.   Mary Jo Henning born Abt. 1863.[171]

       95   iii.   Dault Henning born July 10, 1870 in Yadkin Cty., NC, died Sept. 12, 1889 and is buried at Forbush Bapt. Church, Yadkin Cty., NC.[172]

There is no way of proving that Dault "Bub" Henning was the son of Pearlina Henning instead of Rosa. The reason this writer is calling him the son of Pearlina, is because Rosa would have been only 13 years old in 1870.

31. Amanda Sarah[3] Henning (Christian C.[2], John Adam[1])[173] was born Sept. 4, 1830 in NC, and died Oct. 13, 1886. She is buried at Forbush Bapt. Church, Yadkin Cty., NC.[174]

Children Amanda Sarah Henning are:

       96   i.   Sarah A.[4] Henning born Abt. 1850 in Yadkin Cty., NC.[175]
While Sarah is the illegitimate daughter of Amanda Henning, there is no Bastardy Bond for Sarah.

       97   ii.   Louisa M. Henning born Abt. 1855.[176]
Louisa was the illegitimate daughter of Amanda Henning. A Bastardy Bond was issued on April 9, 1855 in Yadkin Cty., NC to Amanda Hening [sp.] and Thomas Norman. Amanda refused to name the father of her unborn child.

+   98   iii.   Henry T. Henning born Abt. 1856.[177]
Henry was the illegitimate child of Thomas Norman. See Bastardy Bond issued in Yadkin County, NC on Sept. 10, 1856.

+   99   iv.   **John Kenyon Henning** born July 6, 1858 in Yadkin Cty., NC, died Dec. 25, 1924. He is buried in Salem Cemetery, Forsyth Cty., NC.[178]

    100   v.   **Rosanah M. Henning** born Abt. 1859.[179] It should be noted the 1860 Yadkin County, NC Census lists a twin sister, Mahalia.[180]

    101   vi.   **Mahalia Henning** born Abt. 1859 in Yadkin Cty., NC. See information listed above re twin sister, Rosanah.

Mahalia & Rosanah were the illegitimate daughters of Amanda Henning and **Thomas Patterson**: See Bastardy Bond dated May 16, 1859 in Yadkin County, NC where Amanda named Patterson as the father of her unborn children.

    102   vii.   **Elizabeth Henning** born Abt. 1861.[181]

32. Josiah Tyson[3] Henning (Christian C.[2], John Adam[1]) was born Feb. 13, 1833 in NC, died Feb. 13, 1908 and is burid at Stony Knoll Methodist Church, East Bend, NC.[182] He married **Edith Columbia Norman** on Sept. 7, 1856 in Yadkin Cty., NC. She was the daughter of **John Norman** and **Elizabeth Alred** was born Dec. 18, 1837 in NC, and died Feb. 25, 1917. Buried Stony Knoll Methodist Church, East Bend, NC.[183]

The name Tyson Henning was listed in a ledger at A.P. & R.C. Poindexter's general store in Flint Hill, NC (Yadkin County). The store operated during the mid 1800's.[184]

The 1860 Yadkin County, NC Census, shows Tyson as a farm laborer. By 1870, Tyson was a farmer and cobbler living in East Bend, NC.

Children of Josiah Tyson Henning and Edith Norman are:

+   103   i.   **William Turner[4] Hennings** born Aug. 4, 1857

in Yadkin Cty., NC, died Aug. 13, 1938. He is
buried at Stony Knoll Methodist Church, East
Bend, NC.[185]

+ 104 ii. **Lewis Hiram Hennings** born May 30, 1859 in
NC, died Dec. 15, 1945. He is buried at
Baltimore M.E. Church, Yadkin Cty., NC.[186]

+ 105 iii. **Joseph Manasseh Hennings** born April 10,
1862 in NC, died Oct. 5, 1926. He is buried at
Stony Knoll Meth. Church, East Bend, NC.[187]

33. Edward T.[3] Henning (Christian C.[2], John Adam[1]) was born
July 10, 1835 in Stokes Cty., NC, died Jan. 5, 1904 in Forsyth Cty.,
NC. Buried Bethabara Moravian Church, Forsyth Cty., NC.[188]

A Marriage Bond was issued in Forsyth County, NC on Oct. 18, 1866
to **Delilah Louise Henning**. She was born July 15, 1833 in NC, and
died March 25, 1904. She is buried at Bethabara Moravian Church,
Forsyth Cty., NC.[189] Delilah was the daughter of Gabriel Henning and
Christina Aust.

In the 1850 Forsyth County, NC Census, Edward Henning was 12
years old and living with his grandfather, **John Deets [Deitz,** age 55,
farmer].[190]

The following information was copied from North Carolina Troops
1861-1865 A Roster, by Weymouth T. Jordon, Jr., 1983, Vol. IX,
Division of Archives and History, Raleigh, NC.

"Edward H. [T.] Henning, Private, Co. G., Regiment 33.
Resided in Forsyth County where he enlisted at age 30, July
15, 1862, for the war. Present or accounted for through
October, 1863. Reported absent without leave on or about
December 26, 1863. Returned to duty on May-June, 1864.
Present or accounted for through February, 1865; however he
reported absent sick during most of that period. Captured in
hospital at Richmond, Va., April 3, 1865. Transferred

to Newport News, Va., April 23, 1865. Released at Newport News on June 30, 1865, after taking Oath of Allegiance. (North Carolina pension records indicate he was wounded at Fredericksburg, Va., December 13, 1862)."

Edward T. Henning and Delilah Henning [Styers] were first cousins.

June 1, 1874 - "Br. Greider reported that Edward Hennig [sp.] and wife have applied for permission to unite with the congregation at Bethabra, . . ."[191]

Children of Edward Henning and Delilah Henning are:

106   i.   **Paul Jackson[4] Henning** born Sept. 20, 1867 in Forsyth Cty., NC, died Oct. 10, 1930 in Bassett, VA.[192]

Paul Henning owned and operated *Halbrook and Henning Saloon* in Winston-Salem, NC. Family tradition tells us when the workers at R. J. Reynolds Tobacco Company received their pay, many would stop by the *Halbrook and Henning Saloon* on their way home. The bartender would gladly serve the men until they were drunk. Then the bouncer would take them out back in the alley, beat them up and take their money.[193]

At the time of his death in 1930, Paul Henning owned a farm on Old Pfafftown Road and Bethania Road which included 42.34 acres.[194]

On August 2, 1999, Jeff Coltrane copied the following articles from microfilm at the Forsyth County Public Library in Winston-Salem, NC:

"Paul J. Hennings is Dead at Bassett, Va. P. J. Hennings, 64, passed away at Bassett, Va. about 6 o'clock last night following an illness of several weeks, according to a message received from that city. The body will be brought to Winston-Salem today and after its arrival complete details regarding the funeral will be announced. Facts regarding the survivors are not available last night. The deceased was a resident of the Old Town Community. He was not married."[195]

"P. J. Henning to be buried today. Funeral will be conducted at Old Town Moravian Church. Funeral services for P. J. Henning, 64 of Winston-Salem, Route 1 who passed away Friday at Bassett, Va. will be held this afternoon at 3 o'clock at Old Town Moravian Church. Rev. Howard Foltz and Dr. Clay Lilly will conduct the service. Interment will follow in the church graveyard.

The funeral party will leave Manual Funeral Home at 2:15 p.m.

Pallbearers will be Nat Bullard, Orville Smith, H. W. Coltrane, John Henning, Hoke Bullard, Albert Smith, G. S. Bullard, Morris Henning, and P. M. Henning. Honary pallbearers will be Freeman Dancy, Sam Craft, Gray Henning, Tom Gough, George Dilworth, and George Doub.
Surviving is a half-sister, Mrs. J. W. Bullard of this city."[196]

At the time of his death, there was speculation that Paul Henning was living with a woman in Bassett, Virginia and had fathered a child by her. A thorough search has been made for a Death Certificate both in Virginia and North Carolina. None can be found. Obviously the newspaper account did not list the woman nor a child.

Another family story is that Paul weighed about 400 pounds at the time of his death and that is why it took nine (9) men to carry his casket and they had a hard go of it.

35. Martha A. E.[3] Henning (Adam[2], John Adam[1]) was born 1834 in Surry Cty., NC, died 1913 in Washington State.[197] She married **Lewis B. Phillips** on Sept. 28, 1854 by **R. S. Phillips** in Yadkin Cty., NC.[198]

Lewis Phillips died in the Civil War and Martha, lived with her son, Abe, a bachelor in Tennessee. In 1911 Martha moved to Washington State with **John and Bettie Massengale**.[199]

Children of Martha Henning and Lewis Phillips are:

	107	i.	Abe[4] Phillips born in TN, died 1901 in TN.[200]
+	108	ii.	**Sarah Ann Phillips** born 1857.[201]
+	109	iii.	**Bettie Jean Phillips** born 1859, died 1916 in Thornton, WA.[202]

37. Archibald G.[3] Henning (Adam[2], John Adam[1]) was born 1839 in Yadkin Cty., NC, died 1921 in Thornton, WA.[203] He married **N. Ann Galbreath** on Dec. 13, 1865 in Anderson Cty., TN by **R. M. Dail**, J.P.[204] Ann was born in 1844 in Knoxville, TN, and died in 1909 in Thornton, WA.[205]

Arch and Ann Henning moved from Tennessee to the Washington
Territory in 1888. They lived with **Joe Roberts** and his family until
they could rent some land. Eventually they bought what is now known
as the Howard Rambo Farm. It was railroad land and the Henning's
paid $7.50 for 360 acres.[206]

Children of Archibald Henning and Ann Galbreath are:

110.   i.   **Pulaski**[4] **Henning** born May 1, 1867 in TN,
died 1944 in Thornton, WA.[207]

+   111.   ii.   **Iris Henning** born 1868, died 1936 in
Thornton, WA.

+   112.   iii.   **Cordelia Henning** born 1870 in TN, died 1958
in Washington.[208]

+   113   iv.   **Arvel Henning** born 1872 in Robertsville, TN,
died Jan. 1971 in Thornton, Whitman Cty., WA.

114   v.   **Therod Henning** born 1874, died 1936 in
Thornton, WA.[209]

115   vi.   **Frederick Henning** born 1881, died 1959 in
Thornton, WA.[210] He married **Ethel
Clementine Crowe**, born Dec. 17, 1899 in
Glade Springs, VA.[211] Ethel died Dec. 29, 1989
in Thornton, WA. She is buried in Thornton
Cemetery.[212]

40. John W.[3] **Henning** (Adam[2], John Adam[1]) was born Abt. 1848
in Surry Cty., NC,[213] died 1893.[214] John married (1) **Anna
Galbraith.**[215] Anna died in 1933.[216] John then married (2) **Annie
Wright** on Dec. 3, 1882 in Anderson Cty., TN by **G. H. Young,**
Minister of the Gospel. Annie was born Abt. 1862 in PA.[217]

Children of John Henning and Anna Galbraith are:

116   i.   **John W.**[4] **Henning, Jr.** born 1884, died
1885.[218]

117   ii.   **Luther Henning** born 1886, died 1901.[219]

118   iii.   William G. Henning born 1890. Married
                Elizabeth Holt on Aug. 30, 1911.[220]

41. Elvina or Elvira B.[3] Henning (Adam[2], John Adam[1]) born May
11, 1851 in TN, died Feb. 28, 1889. She is buried at New Hope
Cemetery, Oak Ridge, Anderson Cty., TN. She married **Bradford
DeMarcus Long** on Nov. 12, 1881 in Anderson Cty., NC.[221]

Child of Elvina/Elvira Henning and Bradford Long is:

119   i.   **Webster Kenneth[4] Long.**[222]

42. Santford Ivan[3] Henning (Adam[2], John Adam[1]) born Oct. 11,
1854 in TN,[223] died May 30, 1927 in Thornton, Whitman Cty., WA.[224]
He died of a stroke. Santford married **(1) Elizabeth F. Johnson** on
Oct. 11, 1874 in Anderson County, TN by **John Webster**, Minister of
the Gospel at New Hope Church. She is the daughter of **Elijah
Johnson** and **Rose French.**[225] Elizabeth was born Abt. 1851 in TN,
and died Aug. 24, 1886.[226] Santford married **(2) Happy Elizabeth
Hooks** Feb. 9, 1888 in Anderson County, TN by **J. B. Carden**, Justice
of the Peace. Happy was the daughter of **George Hooks** and **Martha
Brock.**[227] Happy died Abt. 1901 of smallpox.[228]

The 1880 Tennessee Census, Anderson County, listed **Eliza
Scarborough** as a white servant, age 14, who was helping Elizabeth
Henning.

Children of Santford Henning and Elizabeth Johnson are:

+   120   i.   **William Lafayette[4] Henning** born Feb. 9,
                  1876 in Clinton, Anderson Cty., TN, died Feb.
                  22, 1956 in Clinton, Anderson Cty., TN.[229]
     121   ii.   **Elijah John Henning** born Aug. 28, 1877 in
                  Clinton, Anderson Cty., TN.[230] He died July 4,
                  1948 in Pine City, WA. He married **(1) Edith**

			Davis, who died 1928. He later married (2) Lula Curtis.[231]
	122	iii.	James David Henning born Aug. 14, 1879 in Clinton, Anderson Cty., TN, died Jan. 3, 1958. Buried in Thornton, WA. Never married.[232]
+	123	iv.	Julius Adam Henning born Setp. 26, 1881 in Clinton, Anderson Cty., TN, died Aug. 16, 1962 in Rosalia, Whitman Cty., WA.[233]
+	124	v.	John Thomas Henning born Oct. 23, 1884 in Clinton, Anderson Cty., TN; died Jan. 6, 1952 in St. John, WA.[234]

Children of Santford Henning and Happy Hooks are:

+	125	i.	Fred Henry[4] Henning born Jan. 31, 1889 in Clinton, TN, died Feb. 3, 1969.[235]
+	126	ii.	Daniel Webster Henning born May 20, 1890 in Clinton, TN, died Aug. 25, 1959 in Pine City, WA.[236]
+	127	iii.	George Washington Henning born Oct. 12, 1892 in TN, died 1952 in Colfax, WA.[237]
	128	iv.	Martha Anzora Henning born March 31, 1894 in TN, died May 13, 1973.[238] She married (1) Lloyd Squires.[239] Later she married (2) Edgar Parrish born Aug. 18, 1896, died July, 1975.[240]
+	129	v.	Dora Henning born Nov. 21, 1900; died April, 1979 in WA.[241]

43. William Gabriel[3] Henning (Adam[2], John Adam[1]) was born Abt. 1856 in Anderson Cty., TN.[242] Married **Betty Tunnel/Roberts** on Aug. 4, 1881 in Anderson Cty., TN by J. W. Key, Justice of the Peace. She was born Abt. 1853 in TN.[243]

Betty was called Betty Tunnel and Betty Roberts on the marriage license.

Children of William Gabriel Henning and Betty Tunnel/Roberts:

    130   i.   Sam[4] Henning.[244]
    131   ii.   Will Henning.[245]

44. Delilah Louise[3] Henning (Gabriel[2], John Adam[1]) born July 15, 1833 in NC, died March 25, 1904. Buried Bethabara Moravian Church, Forsyth Cty., NC.[246] Delilah was named after her grandmother, **Delilah Morris Aust.**

She married (1) **Nathaniel Richard Styers.** A Marriage bond was issued on Sept. 4, 1859 in Forsyth Cty., NC.[247] Nathaniel was the son of **Samuel Styers** and **Martha Wall.** He was born in 1836 in NC, and died 1864 in VA.[248]

Family tradition tells us that Nathaniel was killed in the *Battle of the Pines* around Petersburg, VA in April, 1864. However, correspondence with the National Archives disproves this theory. A copy of a Receipt Roll for Clothing for N. R. Styers, Co. D, 21 N. C. Inf. dated, June, 1864. Nathaniel's estate papers are dated Oct., 1864.

Military records from the United States Archives Compiled Service Records, 21st Infantry, Reel F.6.338P, does not show a record of Nathaniel's death.

"N. R. Styers, Private, Co. D., Reg. 21. Resided in Forsyth County and enlisted at age 23, July 8, 1862 for the war. Present or accounted for through Aug. 3, 1863. No further records." Copied from North Carolina Troops 1861-1865 A Roster, by Weymouth T. Jordan, Jr., Division of Archives and History, 1977, Vol. VI, p. 572.

It seems as though Nathaniel enlisted just seventeen (17) days prior to the birth of his daughter, Mary Lutency (July 24, 1862).

Nathaniel must have been very musical. His estate papers listed a dulcimer valued at $10 and a fiddle with box, valued at $6. His wife, Delilah, kept the dulcimer.

Children of Delilah Henning and Nathaniel Styers are:

+   132   i.   Martha Ophelia[4] Styers born March 30, 1861 in Forsyth Cty., NC, died June 23, 1940. She is buried at Salem Cemetery, Forsyth Cty., NC.[249]

+   133   Mary Lutency Styers born July 24, 1862 in NC, died July 19, 1920. She is buried at God's Acre, Bethabara, Forsyth Cty., NC.[250]

Delilah married (2) **Edward T. Henning**. A Marriage Bond was issued in Forsyth County, NC on Oct. 18, 1866.[251] Edward was the son of **Christian Henning** and **Nancy Deitz**. He was born July 10, 1835 in Stokes Cty., NC, died Jan. 5, 1904 in Forsyth Cty., NC. He is buried at Bethabara Moravian Church, Forsyth Cty., NC.[252]

Edward and Delilah were first cousins.

The following information was copied from North Carolina Troops 1861-1865 A Roster, by Weymouth T. Jordan, Jr., Vol. IX, Division of Archives and History, 1983:

"Edward H. [T.] Henning, Private, Co. G., Regiment 33. Resided in Forsyth County where he enlisted at age 30, July 15, 1862, for the war. Present or accounted for through October, 1863. Reported absent without leave on or about December 26, 1863. Returned to duty on May-June, 1864. Present or accounted for through February, 1865; however he reported absent sick during most of that period. Captured in hospital at Richmond, Va., April 3, 1865. Transferred to Newport News, Va., April 23, 1865. Released at Newport News on June 30, 1865, after taking Oath of Allegiance. (North Carolina pension records indicate he was wounded at Fredericksburg, Va., December 13, 1862)."

Records of the Moravians in North Carolina, Vol. 11, p. 6143:

June 1, 1874 - "Br. Greider reported that Edward Hennig [sp.] and wife have applied for permission to unite with the congregation at Bethabra, . . . "

Children of Delilah Henning Styers and Edward T. Henning are listed under #33.

45. Julia Mary Ann[3] Henning (Gabriel[2,] John Adam[1]) was born Sept. 12, 1835,[253] died Dec. 22, 1880 and is buried at Deep Creek Friends Church, Yadkin Cty., NC.[254] She married **John Irvin/Ervin Shore** Sept. 20, 1860, son of **Jacob Shore** and **Susan Stoltz**. He was born Abt. 1833, and died Abt. 1863 in the Civil War.[255]

On March 7, 1864, Julia Henning Shore sold her father, Gabriel Henning, twenty-two and one half acres of land for $125. The reason for this sale was Julia was the Administrator of her late husband's estate. On the same day, Gabriel and Julia sold the same piece of land (22 ½) acres to **James Reed** for $600.[256]

A John Shore, age 7, was living with Gabriel and Celia Henning in the 1870 Yadkin County, NC Census. This would mean the child was born around 1863. I am going to assume that since Julia is Gabriel's daughter, this is probably her child and/or Gab's grandchild.

+   134   I.   **John Irvin[4] Shore, Jr.**, born Nov. 5, 1862, died March 1, 1932. Buried Union Cross Friends, Yadkin Cty., NC.[257]

46. Rebecca Catherine[3] Henning (Gabriel[2], John Adam[1]) was born Feb. 19, 1837 in NC, died Feb. 9, 1873. Buried Mt. Tabor Methodist Church, Forsyth Cty., NC.[258] A Marriage Bond was issued in Forsyth Cty., NC on Nov. 30, 1856 to **Timothy Boose** and Rebecca. Rebecca was Timothy's second wife.[259] Timothy was born July 22, 2832l, died

Oct. 2, 1903. He is buried at Mt. Tabor Methodist Church, Forsyth Cty., NC.[260]

Children of Rebecca Henning and Timothy Boose are:

+ 135   i.   **Edward T.**[4]**Boose** born Sept. 15, 1858 in NC, died March 23, 1936. Buried Mt. Tabor Methodist Church, Forsyth Cty., NC.[261]

     136   ii.   **Lauretta Boose** born 1861 in NC.[262]

+ 137   iii.   **George Gabriel Boose** born Feb. 28, 1863 in NC, died June 2, 1950. Buried Mt. Tabor Methodist Church, Forsyth Cty., NC.[263]

+ 138   iv.   **Sanford N. Boose** born May 8, 1865 in NC, died Feb. 3, 1954. Buried Mt. Tabor Methodist Church, Forsyth Cty., NC.

     139   v.   **Francis Wesley Boose** born May 30, 1867 in NC, died April 2, 1953. Buried Wachovia Arbor Moravian Church.[264] Married **Hattie E.** who was born Jan. 2, 1869, died July 29, 1916 and is buried at Wachovia Arbor Moravian Church, Forsyth Cty., NC.[265]

     140   vi.   **Delilah Boose** born Nov. 27, 1869 in NC, died Feb. 27, 1953. Buried Mt. Tabor Methodist Church, Forsyth Cty., NC.[266] Married **Permanie S. Pfaff** born June 1, 1861 in NC, died Nov. 4, 1903 and is buried Mt. Tabor Methodist Church, Forsyth Cty., NC.[267]

     141   vii.   **Emily Boose** born Jan. 27, 1872 in NC, died Dec. 22, 1952. Buried Mt. Tabor Methodist Church, Forsyth Cty., NC.[268] Married **Isaac Jerome Shamel.**[269] Isaac was born Sept. 8, 1870 in NC, died Dec. 20, 1906 and is buried at Mt. Tabor Methodist Church, Forsyth Cty., NC.[270]

47. Lauretta Elizabeth[3] Henning (Gabriel[2], John Adam[1]) born March 24, 1839 in Stokes Cty., NC, died Nov. 10, 1915 in Boone Cty., IN. Buried Pleasant View Cem., Whitestown, IN. Married **John Fleming Snipes** on Sept. 2, 1865 in Forsyth County, NC. He was the son of **James Snipes** and **Martha Thomason**. John was born June 15, 1840, and died Feb. 16, 1916 in Boone Cty., IN. Buried Pleasant View Cem., Whitestown, IN.[271] John Fleming Snipes died in the county poor farm.[272]

In the 1850 Forsyth County, NC Census, dwelling 1432, family 13447, p. 295, Lucetta [sp.] Henning, age 15, was living with Richard Wall's family.

Child of Lauretta Henning and John Snipes is:

+   142   i.   **Lewis Edwin[4] Snipes** born Jun 1, 1866 in Milledgville, Boone Cty., IN, died June 30, 1899 in Tipton Cty., IN.[273]

49. Clemmentine[3] Henning (Gabriel[2], John Adam[1]) was born Abt. 1846.[274] Married **Samuel Hutchens** in 1870,[275] son of **Patrick Hutchens** and **Nancy Welch**. He was born in 1837.[276]

Child of Clemmentine Henning and Samuel Hutchens:

    143   i.   **John[4] Hutchens**.[277]

50. Isaac T.[3] Henning (Gabriel[2], John Adam[1]) was born May 1849 in NC. He married **Rhoda (Luda) Boose**. She was born Oct. 1847.[278]

The name of Isaac's wife, Rhoda, and her date of birth Oct., 1847, came from a family work sheet provided by Irene Choplin. She gave no reference for this other than the Yadkin County Census. The name of the children, Evan and Hughy L., also did not have a reference, nor did their dates of birth.

Children of Isaac Henning and Rhoda Boose are:

> 144   i.   **Evan[4] Henning** born March, ?.
> 145   ii.   **Hughy L. Henning** born 1877. Ms. Choplin's notes indicated Hughy "died before 1880."

51. Adam L.[3] Henning (Gabriel[2], John Adam[1]) was born Abt. 1854 in NC.[279] He married **Mary Groce** on March 27, 1877. Mary was born in 1853.[280]

Children of Adam Henning and Mary Groce are:

> 146   i.   **Lewis[4] Henning** born Abt. 1878.[281]
> 147   ii.   **Jane D. Henning** born Abt. 1880.[282]

Generation No. 4

59. Julia A.[4] Conrad (Nancy[3] Cline, Mary Anna[2] Henning, John Adam[1]) born Feb. 22, 183?, died April 20, 1902 and is buried at Pfafftown Christian Church, Rural Hall, NC.[283] Julia married on June 11, 1850[284] to **Julius A. Transou** born Jan. 1, 1832, died June 21, 1930 and is buried Pfafftown Christian Church, Rural Hall, NC.[285]

Children of Julia Conrad and Julius Transou are:

> 148   i.   **Stephen[5] Transou** born Feb. 24, 1856, died Sept. 10, 1932. Buried Pfafftown Christian Church, Rural Hall, NC.
> 149   ii.   **Isabella Transou** born July 17, 1860, died Nov. 6, 1875. Buried Pfafftown Christian Church, Rural Hall, NC.[286]
> 150   iii.   **Mary Transou** born Abt. 1862.[287]
> 151   iv.   **Caroline Transou** born Abt. 1863.[288]

69. James Nathan⁴ Cline (Peter Solomon³, Mary Anna² Henning, John Adam¹) was born April 20, 1851 in Forsyth County, NC.[289] He married **Rebecca George**.[290]

Records of the Moravians in North Carolina, Bethania Congregation, 1851, May 31, 1851: "In the afternoon I rode to Pfafftown, and after visiting old Mother Pfaff preached the monthly sermon on I Tim. 2:5 as customary in Miicke Schoolhouse. Prior to preaching service a little son (James Nathan) was baptized into death of Jesus. Following a visit I went with Bro. Shouse and the Widow Miicke, the old mother in Pfafftown, though she was unconscious, was giving blessing preparatory to her home going."[291]

Child of James Cline and Rebecca George is:

+   152   i.   **Charlie Earnest⁵ Cline.**

72. Charles Christian⁴ Cline (Peter Solomon³, Mary Anna² Henning, John Adam¹) was born Jan. 4, 1854 in Vienna Township, Pfafftown, NC, died Dec. 27, 1936 in Pfafftown, NC. Married **Cornelia Fulk** on June 6, 1876 in Southfork Township, Forsyth Cty., NC by **Franklin Brindle**, Justice of the Peace. **J. W. Flynt** applied for their License for Marriage. Witnesses were **Antionette Brindle, Wink Brown**, and **James A. Bruer**.[292] Cornelia Fulk was the daughter of **Augustus Fulk** and **Legusta Hauser**. She was born Abt. 1861, died April 28, 1942 in Pfafftown, NC.[293]

Charles Cline's death certificate shows him to be 82 yrs. old at the time of his death. He was a farmer. He died of Angina Pectoris, neuralgia of the heart.[294]

Children of Charles Cline and Cornelia Fulk are:

       153   i.   **Maggie⁵ Cline** died in Zionsville, IN. Married **Sherman Shields**.[295]

154	ii.	Sudie Cline died in Ramseur, NC. Married Roscoe Ashburn.[296]
155.	iii.	Karl Cline.[297]
156.	iv.	Annie Laura Cline born in Pfafftown, NC, died in Rural Hall, NC.[298] She married Oscar Smith born Nov. 11, 1899, died April, 1979.[299]
157	v.	Maude Cline born June 18, 1884 in Pfafftown, NC, died Oct., 1973 in Eden, NC. Married Ralph W. McKinney.[300]
+ 158	vi.	Mattie Beatrice Cline born July 2, 1885 in Pfafftown, NC, died Oct. 4, 1957 in Winston-Salem, NC.[301]
159	vii.	Mertie Cline born Feb. 14, 1894 in Pfafftown, NC, died Jan., 1970. Married Claude Davis.[302]
+ 160	viii.	Howard Olin Cline born Dec. 14, 1894 in Pfafftown, NC, died April 15, 1964 in Pfafftown, NC.[303]

75. Peter S.[4] Cline (Eli[3], Mary Anna[2] Henning, John Adam[1]) was born Jan. 12, 1852, died May 15, 1932 in Forsyth Cty., NC. Buried Pfafftown Christian Church, Pfafftown, NC.[304] He married **Amanda Binkley** March 7, 1878 in Forsyth Cty., NC. She was born June 8, 1861 in NC, and died Nov. 5, 1923 in Forsyth Cty., NC. Buried Pfafftown Christian Church, Pfafftown, NC.[305]

A Bastardy Bond was issued in Forsyth County, NC on May 15, 1877 to **Amanda George**, mother, and Peter Cline, father. See Forsyth County Bastardy Bonds, 1874-1879, Reel C.038.10003, NC State Archives, Jones St., Raleigh, NC.

On the Marriage Bond of Amanda Binklely her last name was spelled "Bonkley." Amanda and Peter were married on the same day the bond was issued, March 7, 1878 by J. R. Lehman.

Children of Peter Cline and Amanda Binkley are:

161	i.	Stella[5] Cline born June, 1884.[306]
+ 162	ii.	Everett Odel Cline born July, 1889[307]
163	iii.	Clarence Cline born Dec. 20, 1891, died Dec. 1971 in Winston-Salem, NC.[308] Married Gertrude Staley on Dec. 9, 1916 in Forsyth Cty., NC.[309]

78. Augustine C.[4] Cline (Eli[3], Mary Anna[2] Henning, John Adam[1]) born 1857 in NC, died 1946 in Forsyth County, NC. Buried Crews Methodist Church, Forsyth County, NC.[310] Married **Rosa J**. Rosa was born 1868 in NC, died 1946 and is buried at Crews Methodist Church.[311]

Children of Augustine Cline and Rosa J. are:

164	i.	Walter B.[5] Cline born 1889. Married Madie Whicker on June 10, 1909 in Forsyth County, NC. Madie was born in 1890.[312]
165	ii.	Augustine S. Cline born Aug. 19, 1889, died Aug. 9, 1964 in Forsyth Cty., NC. He is buried at Mt. Pleasant Church.[313] Married Martha Jane born June 19, 1910.[314]
166	iii.	Jamie B. Cline born 1890. Married Naamah E. Morris on Feb. 18, 1912. Naamah was born in 1891.[315]

83. Pleas David[4] Cline (Eli[3], Mary Anna[2] Henning, John Adam[1]) was born May 13, 1883 in Lewisville, NC, died July 17, 1948. Buried Woodland Cemetery, Forsyth Cty., NC. Married **Carrie Mae Henning** on Feb. 11, 1903 in Forsyth Cty., NC, daughter of **Lavina Melvina Henning**. Carried was born March 17, 1883 in Pfafftown, Forsyth Cty., NC, died May 9, 1976 in Rowan Cty., NC.[316] Buried Woodland Cem., Forsyth Cty., NC.[317]

Pleas David Cline was a carpenter.[318]

Children of Pleas Cline and Carrie Henning are:

> 167   i.   **Flossie Irene**[5] **Cline** born Aug. 8, 1903 in Forsyth Cty., NC, died July 1, 1992 in Durham, NC. She married on April 16, 1923 **Charles Frederick Reeves** in Forsyth Cty., NC.[319]
>
> +   168   ii.   **Raymond Arthur Cline** born Oct. 16, 1904 in Forsyth Cty., NC, died July 6, 1969 in Forsyth Cty., NC. Buried Woodland Cemetery, Forsyth Cty., NC.[320]
>
> 169   iii.   **Virginia Dare Cline** born Abt. 1905 in Forsyth Cty., NC. Died Abt. 1905 in Forsyth Cty., NC.[321]
>
> 170   iv.   **Nellie Mae Cline** born Dec. 28, 1906 in Forsyth Cty., NC. Married (1) **Ira Weaver**. She married (2) **Paul Weaver** on Dec. 20, 1926. Paul and Ira were brothers.[322]
>
> 171   v.   **Myrtle Louise Cline** born May 9, 1910 in Forsyth Cty., NC, died April 22, 1994 in Okeechobee Cty., FL. Buried Homestead, Dade Cty., FL. Married (1) **Mervin Reiquam**. Married (2) **George Tiabe**.[323]
>
> 172   vi.   **Carlton Clinton Cline** born Oct. 20, 1914 in Forsyth Cty., NC, died Nov. 28, 1914 in Forsyth Cty., NC.[324]
>
> 173   vii.   **Grady Oscar Cline** born March 21, 1916 in Forsyth Cty., NC, died Nov. 29, 1979 in Forsyth Cty., NC. Buried Parklawn Cem., Forsyth Cty., NC. Married **Mary Cummings** on Feb. 9, 1935 in Forsyth Cty., NC.[325]
>
> 174   viii.   **Gurney Lee Cline** born Nov. 28, 1917 in Forsyth Cty., NC, died June 24, 1992. Married (1) **Katherine (?)**. Married (2) **Billie Link** in Davidson Cty., NC.[326] Gurney Lee Cline

received the Purple Heart in World War II.[327]

175   ix.   **Dallas David Cline** born Oct. 20, 1920 in
Forsyth Cty., NC. Married (1) **Helen Scott** on
Dec. 25, 1941. Married (2) **Betina Marable** on
Aug. 2, 1951.[328]

91. Lavina Melvina[4] Henning (Elizabeth[3] Cline, Catherine[2] Henning, John Adam[1]) born Abt. Dec. 1843 in Stokes Cty., NC, died Jan. 9, 1918 in Forsyth Cty., NC. Buried Pfafftown Cem., Forsyth Cty., NC.[329]

Lavina Melvina Henning is the illegitimate daughter of **Elizabeth Henning** and **George Waldraven**.[330]

Lavina Melvina was never married but had three illegitimate children: William, Annie & Carrie.

Lavina Melvina Henning burned to death from an open flame which caught her dress on fire. She was living at Rt. 1, Tobaccoville when she died.[331]

Children of Lavina Melvina Henning are:

176   i.   **William M.[5] Henning** born March 20, 1868 in
Forsyth Cty., NC, died May 10, 1952. Buried
Elm Grove Methodist Church, Forsyth Cty.,
NC. Married **Sarah R. Ball** on May 8, 1892 in
Forsyth Cty., NC. Sarah was born May 26,
1869, died Dec. 13, 1932 and is buried at Elm
Grove Methodist Church, Forsyth Cty., NC.[332]

177   ii.   **Annie Elizabeth Henning** born Nov. 29, 1871
in NC, died May 25, 1924. She married **James
Houston Tucker** on Dec. 9, 1898 in Forsyth
Cty., NC. He was born Dec. 17, 1877.[333]

178   iii.   **Carrie Mae Henning** born March 17, 1883 in
Pfafftown, Forsyth Cty., NC, died May 9, 1976

in Rowan Cty., NC. Buried Woodland Cem., Forsyth Cty., NC.[334]

93. Rosa[4] Henning (Pearlina M.[3], Christian C.[2], John Adam[1]) was born Aug. 10, 1857 in Yadkin Cty., NC, died April 11, 1889. Buried Forbush Baptist Church, Yadkin Cty., NC.[335]

A Bastardy Bond was issued in Yadkin County, NC on May 24, 1878 to Rosa Henning. She refused to name the father of her child. Bondsmen were J. E. Hutchens and J. L. Williams. According to the 1880 Yadkin Cty., NC Census, this child would have been Anna L. Henning.

The 1880 Yadkin County, NC Census shows Rosa doing millinery work at home.

Children of Rosa Henning are:

	179	i.	**Bub[5] Henning** born Abt. 1871.[336] A son of Rosa's is buried at Forbush Baptist Church Cemetery in Yadkin Cty., NC. He is not named and there are no dates given. Carl Hoots only refers to the grave as "Infant - son of Rosa" Henning.[337]
+	180.	ii.	**Joseph E. Henning(s)** born Abt. 1874 in Yadkin Cty., NC, died (?), buried Mt. Sinai Cemetery, Yadkin Cty., NC.[338]
	181	iii.	**Jones F. Henning** born March 8, 1876 in Yadkin Cty., NC, died Feb. 2, 1924. Buried Forbush Baptist Church Cemetery, Yadkin Cty., NC.[339]
	182	iv.	**Anna L. Henning** born Abt. 1878.[340]

98. Henry T.[4] Henning (Amanda Sarah[3], Christian C.[2], John Adam[1]) born Abt. 1856. Married **Fannie L.** born Abt. 1875.[341]

Henry was the illegitimate child of **Amanda Sarah Henning** and **Thomas Norman**. See Bastardy Bond issued in Yadkin County, NC on Sept. 10, 1856.

Children of Henry Henning and Fannie L. are:

183	i.	Virgie A.[5] Henning. His age was not recorded in the census.[342]
184	ii.	Thomas S. Henning. His age was not recorded in the census.[343]
185	iii.	Carl E. Henning born Abt. 1894.[344]
186	iv.	Hobart M. Henning born Abt. 1896.[345]
187	v.	William H. Henning born Abt. 1898.[346] In the 1920 Census we find William living with his uncle Columbus Williams, and aunt, Sarah E. Williams, farming.[347]
188	vi.	Johnny G. Henning born Abt. 1900.[348]
189	vii.	Fannie May Henning born Abt. 1900.[349]
190	viii.	Katy L. Henning born Abt. 1902.[350]
191	ix.	Luther O. Henning born Abt. 1904.[351]
192	x.	Laura M. Henning born Abt. 1904.[352]

99. John Kenyon[4] Henning (Amanda Sarah[3], Christian C.[2], John Adam[1]) was born July 6, 1858 in Yadkin Cty., NC, died Dec. 25, 1924. Buried Salem Cemetery, Forsyth Cty., NC.[353] John died of diabetes.[354] Married **Emma Lee Austin** on Oct. 25, 1893. She was born Feb. 12, 1875 in Stoneville, NC,[355] died Sept. 15, 1930 and is buried in Salem Cemetery, Forsyth Cty., NC.[356]

In the 1900 Forsyth County, NC Census, John and Emma Henning were living on Popular St., Winston, NC. John was a saloon keeper, possibly working with his uncle, Paul Jackson Henning at Halbrook and Henning Saloon in Winston.

The 1910 Forsyth County, NC Census shows John and Emma operating a boarding house. There were seventeen non-related people living with them.

Children of John Henning and Emma Austin are:

+ 193 i. **Ruby Lucille[5] Henning** born Nov. 20, 1896 in Winston, NC, died Feb. 20, 1983. Buried Forsyth Memorial Park, Winston-Salem, NC.[357]

194 ii. **John Kenyon Henning, Jr.** born Dec. 19, 1897 in Winston, NC, died Sept. 1978.[358]

195 iii. **Paul Morris Henning** born July 12, 1900 in NC, died March 28, 1955 and buried in Salem, Cemetery, Forsyth Cty., NC.[359] He married **Elizabeth Mock** on June 17, 1925 in Forsyth Cty., NC.[360] Elizabeth was born Sept. 29, 1907, died March, 1984 in Winston-Salem, NC.[361]

+ 196 iv. **Robert Edward Lee Henning** born Feb. 7, 1907 in Winston, NC, died Jan. 6, 1996 in Winston-Salem, NC.[362]

103. William Turner[4] Hennings (Josiah Tyson[3] Henning, Christian C.[2], John Adam[1]) was born Aug. 4, 1857 in Yadkin Cty., NC, died Aug. 13, 1938. Buried Stony Knoll Methodist church, East Bend, NC.[363] He married **Rosa Anna Augusta Gough** on Sept. 11, 1881.[364] She was the daughter of **James Gough** and **Harriett Burchette**. "Gus" as she was called, was born Nov. 22, 1862 in Yadkin Cty., NC, and died Dec. 23, 1943. She is buried at Stony Knoll Meth., East Bend, NC.[365]

Irene Choplin's work sheet tells us "Willie" as he was known, was a shoemaker at the age of 23. The 1920 census indicates Willie was a farmer and carpenter.[366]

The Henning Family

The following story was among Irene Choplin's family group sheets. The author is **John Howard Adams**.

The last time I saw my grandfather, Willie T. Hennings, was at the gathering of the families for his 81st birthday on the first Sunday in August, 1938. His birthday being the 4th of August the birthday and reunion dinner was always on the first Sunday of that month.

On that day, while we were eating dinner under the shade trees, I heard him say to Uncle Jim Flynn, "Everyone has a row to hoe, and I believe I have mine about hoed out."

The next Saturday night, after a chicken stew at a tobacco barn near the edge of the yard, he and Grandma, Aunt Mirt and Uncle Julius Mikles and some other people, had gone to the front porch of Grandad's house. He and Uncle Julius were sitting on the edge of the porch while the others were in chairs on the porch.

A grandson, Lat Hennings, who grew up in Grandad's home, had positioned his car with the headlights toward the tobacco barn to provide light to eat by.

While they were sitting on the edge of the porch Lat went to move his car. He had to crank it, as the starter failed to start the engine. When it started it somehow slipped into reverse and shot backward right into Uncle Julius and Grandad. Grandad saw it coming and got up from his sitting position, putting his arm up as if to ward off the blow, but of course it was useless. The car hit him and broke his neck, killing him instantly. Uncle Julius' collar bone was broken. There was a big dent in the back of the car, made by Grandad's arm and head.

My brother, Vance, brought my young sister and brother to my house that night. When they came I knew something was the matter and asked Vance what was wrong. He said, "Grandad has been hurt." I asked what had happened and how bad was he hurt. He said, "He is dead."

Grandad had "stepped off this stage of action" and was "now in the presence of the Lord." He always used these phrases in closing his prayers in church where he was Superintendent of Sunday School for many years. Two of the songs sung at his funeral were, *On Jordan's Stormy Banks I Stand*, and *Life's Railway to Heaven*, his favorites.

Grandad had four grandsons named for him: Willie Henning, Willie Smitherman, Willie Adams and Turner Hauser.

Children of William "Willie" Hennings and Rose "Gus" Gough are:

+	197	i.	**Arthur Benbow⁵ Henning** born July 27, 1882 in Yadkin Cty., NC, died April 19, 1966. Buried Mt. Tabor Methodist Church, Forsyth Cty., NC.[367]
+	198	ii.	**Mirtie Lee Henning** born July, 1885 in Yadkin Cty., NC, died Sept. 19, 1974. Buried Stony Knoll Methodist Church, East Bend, NC.[368]
+	199	iii.	**Nellie Mae Henning** born Sept. 22, 1888 in Yadkin Cty., NC, died June 16, 1967. Buried Stony Knoll Methodist Church, East Bend, NC.[369]
+	200	iv.	**Lela Greene Henning** born Dec. 3, 1891 in Yadkin Cty., NC, died Jan. 15, 1963. Buried Enon Baptist Church, Yadkin Cty., NC.[370]
+	201	v.	**Bessie Anna Henning** born Jan. 26, 1895 in Yadkin Cty., NC, died Aug. 21, 1982. Buried Stony Knoll Methodist Church, East Bend, NC.[371]
+	202	vi.	**Ila Ladrone Henning** born July 31, 1898 in Yadkin Cty., NC, died Feb. 28, 1974. Buried Stony Knoll Methodist Church, East Bend, NC.[372]
+	203	vii.	**William Joseph Henning(s)** born March 4, 1901 in Yadkin Cty., NC, died April 15, 1983.[373]

+   204   viii.   **Emily Blanche Henning(s)** born Nov. 7, 1904 in East Bend, Yadkin Cty., NC, died Sept. 12, 1997.[374]

104. Lewis Hiram[4] **Hennings** (Josiah Tyson[3] Henning, Christian C.[2], John Adam[1]) was born May 30, 1859 in NC, died Dec. 15, 1945. Buried Baltimore M.E. Church, Yadkin Cty., NC.[375] Married on Aug. 12, 1883 to **Martha Jane Speer**.[376] She was born Oct. 11, 1860 in NC, died Sept. 7, 1947 and is buried at Baltimore M.E. Church, Yadkin Cty., NC.[377]

In 1887 some of the citizens of Flint Hill decided, following a brush arbor meeting, that they needed a church in their community. That year they bought 2.19 acres of land from **L. H. Hennings** for $20.00. The deed was made to **H. I. Bean, J. M. Hennings** and **W. H. Bean**, trustees.[378]

Children of Lewis Hennings and Martha Speer are:

+   205   i.   **Willie Gray**[5] **Henning** born April 12, 1885 in NC, died July 27, 1955.[379]
+   206   ii.   **John Franklin Henning** born April 4, 1887 in Yadkin Cty., NC, died Aug. 20, 1964. Buried Baltimore M.E. Church, Yadkin Cty., NC.[380]
+   207   iii.   **David Evan Henning** born May 16, 1889, died in Maxwell, Iowa.[381]
+   208   iv.   **Fannie May Henning** born Dec. 11, 1890, died Dec., 1980.[382]
+   209   v.   **Tennie Henning** born Nov. 2, 1892 in NC, died Dec. 12, 1979.[383]
+   210   vi.   **James Wesley Henning** born Oct. 26, 1894 in NC, died Oct. 12, 1961. Buried Baltimore M.E. Church, Yadkin Cty., NC.[384]
+   211   vii.   **Emma Henning(s)** born March 13, 1897, died March 1980 in Rural Hall, NC.[385]
+   212   viii.   **Mattie White Henning(s)** born Feb. 27, 1899

in Yadkin Cty., NC, died April 9, 1983.Buried
Forsyth Memorial Park, Forsyth County, NC.[386]

+   213   ix.   Eliza Henning born Jan. 5, 1901.[387]

105. Joseph Manasseh[4] Hennings (Josiah Tyson[3] Henning,
Christian C.[2], John Adam[1]) was born April 10, 1862 in NC, died Oct.
5, 1926. Buried Stony Knoll Methodist Church, East Bend, NC.[388]
Joseph died of Apoplexy and hypertension.[389] He was married August,
1883 to **Fannie Elizabeth Speer**, daughter of **John Speer** and **Julia
Joyner**. Fannie was born Sept. 30, 1867 in NC, died Dec. 11, 1956.
She is buried at Stony Knoll Methodist Church, East Bend, NC.[390]

The 1920 Yadkin County, NC Census shows Joseph as a farmer.[391]

Children of Joseph Hennings and Fannie Speer are:

	214	i.	**Eugene Walter[5] Hennings** born Feb. 28, 1886; died Oct. 14, 1975 in IL.[392]
+	215	ii.	**Early Harrison Hennings** born Sept. 25, 1888, died June 15, 1973 in IA.[393]
+	216	iii.	**Marvin Hennings** born Nov. 1, 1890 in NC, died Nov. 29, 1890. Buried Stony Knoll Methodist Church, East Bend, NC.[394]
+	217	iv.	**Henry Thomas Hennings** born Jan. 5, 1894 in NC, died March 16, 1963. Buried Stony Knoll Methodist Church, East Bend, NC.[395]
+	218	v.	**Rober Ernest Hennings** born Feb. 24, 1896 in Yadkin Cty., NC, died Nov. 7, 1959. Buried Stony Knoll Methodist Church, East Bend, NC.[396]
+	219.	vi.	**Julia Anna Hennings** born Feb. 26, 1900 in NC, died June 1, 1967.[397]
	220	vii.	**Grace Hennings** born Abt. 1902.[398]
+	221	viii.	**Crawley Mozelle Hennings** born Aug. 5, 1902 in NC, died Nov. 14, 1922.[399]
+	222	ix.	**Lena Hazel Hennings** born Oct. 23, 1908 in

NC, died Dec. 13, 1996. Buried Stony Knoll
Methodist Church, East Bend, NC.[400]

108. Sarah Ann[4] Phillips (Martha A. E.[3] Henning, Adam[2], John
Adam[1]) was born 1857.[401] Her date of death is unknown. She married
George Elisa Hester, son of **Basil Hester** and **Elizabeth
McHenney**.[402] George was born 1860 in TN, and died 1926.[403]

George and Sarah moved to Washington State in 1899.[404]

Children of Sarah Phillips and George Hester are:

	223	i.	Baby[5] Hester.[405]
+	224	ii.	William Hornsby Hester born 1881 in TN, died 1963 in Spokane, WA.[406]
+	225	iii.	Dora Hester born 1883 in TN.[407]
+	226.	iv.	Zeffia Hester born 1883 in TN, died 1966 in Thornton, WA.[408]
	227	v.	Tom Basil Hester born 1889, died 1949 in Thornton, WA.[409]

Tom joined the Army in World War I, was in
the 364th Infantry, 91st Division and served
under General Pershing. He never married.[410]

	228	vi.	Sam Hester born April 20, 1891, died August, 1967 in Thornton, WA.[411]
	229	vii.	Browder Hester born 1893, died 1937 in Thornton, WA.[412]
	230	viii.	Nettie Hester born 1895, died 1921 in Thornton, WA. Married Fred Rohrback.[413]
+	231	ix.	Grace Hester born April 25, 1898, died Sept., 1979 in Spokane, WA.[414]
+	232	x.	Ruth Hester born Jan. 7, 1901, died May 21, 1993 in Seattle, WA.[415]

109. Bettie Jean[4] Phillips (Martha A. E.[3] Henning, Adam[2], John Adam[1]) was born in 1859, died 1916 in Thornton, WA.[416] She married **John Massengale** in 1889 in TN. John was born in 1867, and died 1942 in Thornton, WA.[417]

Children of Bettie Phillips and John Massengale are:

+	233	i.	Lee[5] Massengale born 1894 in Lupton, TN, died 1935 in Spokane, WA.[418]
	234	ii.	Abe Massengale born 1897.[419]
+	235	iii.	George Massengale born Dec. 30, 1897 in Marlo, TN, died Feb., 1986 in Spokane, WA.[420]

111. Iris[4] Henning (Archibald G.[3], Adam[2], John Adam[1]) born 1868, died in 1936 in Thornton, WA.[421] She married **Samuel H. Roberts** who was born in TN, and died 1947 in Thornton, WA.[422]

Sam and Iris moved to Washington state in 1889.[423]

Children of Iris Henning and Samuel Roberts are:

	236	i.	William[5] Roberts born in TN, died 1904 and is buried in Thornton, WA. Died of Small Pox.[424]
+	237	ii.	Anna Roberts born 1891 in WA, died Aug., 1982 in WA.[425]

112. Cordelia[4] Henning (Archibald G.[3], Adam[2], John Adam[1]) was born 1870 in TN, and died 1958 in WA.[426] She married **McCampbell Roberts** in 1890.[427] He died in 1937 in WA.[428]

Children of Cordelia Hennning and McCampbell Roberts are:

+	238	i.	Edgar[5] Roberts born 1891, died 1949.[429]
+	239	ii.	Minnie Roberts born 1893 in Oakesdale, WA.[430]

+   240   iii.   Clive Roberts born 1895 in Oakesdale, WA,
                         died Aug., 1977 in Idaho.[431]

113. Arvel[4] Henning 9Archibald G.[3], Adam[2], John Adam[1]) was
born May 25, 1872 in Robertsville, TN, died Jan., 1971 in Thornton,
Whitman Cty., WA.[432] Arvel married **Frances Louise Lula Geasland**
in 1901 in Emory, TN.[433] Frances died in 1970.[434]

Children of Arvel Henning and Frances Geasland are:

       241   i.   Roy[5] Henning born 1905. Died as a child.[435]
+   242   ii.   **Ralph Stephen Henning** born March 28, 1909
                         in Thornton, Whitman Cty., WA, died July 18,
                         1974 and is buried in Thornton, WA.[436]
+   243   iii.   **Gladys Henning** born 1910, died Aug. 31,
                         1990 in Colfax, Whitman Cty., WA.[437]

120. William Lafayette[4] Henning (Santford Ivan[3], Adam[2], John
Adam[1]) born Feb. 9, 1876 in Clinton, Anderson Cty., TN,[438] died Feb.
22, 1956 in Clinton, TN. He married **Edith Vincent**.[439]

Children of William Henning and Edith Vincent are:

       244   i.   Mary[5] Henning. Died as a child.[440]
       245   ii.   **Everett Henning** born Feb. 26, 1907 in
                         Spokane, WA,[441] died July, 1980 in San
                         Francisco, CA.[442]

123. Julius Adam[4] Henning (Santford Ivan[3], Adam[2], John Adam[1])
was born Sept. 26, 1881 in Clinton, Anderson Cty., TN, died Aug. 16,
1962 in Rosalia, Whitman Cty., WA.[443] He married **Mamie Ellis Fox**
on Jan. 1, 1903 in Oakesdale, Whitman Cty., WA. She was the
daughter of **William Fox** and **Violette Propst**. Mamie was born May
10, 1884, and died Feb., 1967 in Spokane, WA.[444]

Children of Julius Henning and Mamie Fox are:

	246	i.	Nola Jane[5] Henning born Aug. 20, 1904 in Oakesdale, Whitman Cty., WA, died Feb. 19, 1950 in WA.[445]
+	247	ii.	Vena Ann Henning born July 11, 1907 in Thornton, Whitman Cty., WA, died Dec. 3, 1979 in Fairfield, WA.[446]
+	248	iii.	Clarence Eugene Henning born May 26, 1912 in Thornton, Whitman Cty., WA, died 1997 in Sun City, AR.[447]
	249	iv.	Lela Adele Henning born Oct. 24, 1915 in Thornton, Whitman Cty., WA, died Sept. 19, 1921.[448]
+	250	v.	Oren Lloyd Henning born Nov. 7, 1919 in Thornton, Whitman Cty., WA, died Oct. 22, 1995. Buried Pine City Cemetery, Spokane, WA.[449]

124. John Thomas[4] Henning (Santford Ivan[3], Adam[2], John Adam[1]) was born Oct. 23, 1884 in Clinton, Anderson Cty., TN, died Jan. 6, 1952 in St. John, WA. He married **Jessie Wilson**.[450] She died 1953 in St. John, WA.[451]

| | 251 | i. | Lula Mae[5] Henning, born 1908 in Cottonwood Creek, WA, died Oct. 1986 in Clarkston, WA.[452] |
| + | 252. | ii. | James T. Henning born Dec. 15, 1923 in Sunset, WA, died Sept. 17, 1995 and is buried in St. John Cemetery, St. John, WA.[453] |

125. Fred Henry[4] Henning (Santford Ivan[3], Adam[2], John Adam[1]) born Jan. 31, 1889 in Clinton, TN, died Feb. 3, 1969. He married **Hazel Rotan**.[454] Hazel was born March 31, 1892, died Feb., 1975 in Rosalia, WA.[455]

Children of Fred Henning and Hazel Rotan are:

+   253   i.   **Roy[5] Henning** born Oct. 12, 1912 in WA, died July 11, 1989 in WA.[456]

+   254   ii.   **Winifred Henning** born 1914.[457]

       255   iii.   **Max Gerald Henning** born Oct. 25, 1915 in Thornton, WA, died May 17, 1997 in Oakesdale Cem., Oakesdale, WA.[458]

+   256   iv.   **Geraldine Henning** born 1917 in Thornton, WA.[459]

+   257   v.   **Boyd Henning** born 1921 near Oakdale, WA.[460]

+   258   vi.   **Duane Henning** born 1932, died 1982 in WA.[461]

126. Daniel Webster[4] Henning (Santford Ivan[3], Adam[2], John Adam[1]) was born May 20, 1890 in Clinton, TN, died Aug. 25, 1959 in Pine City, WA.[462] He married **Honor Margaret Mortimer** on Dec. 23, 1919 in Spokane, WA. She is the daughter of **Andrew Mortimer** and **Matilda Sparks**. She was born Sept. 25, 1895 in Pine City, WA, died Oct. 12, 1989 in Malden, WA.[463]

Children of Daniel Henning and Honor Mortimer are:

+   259   i.   **Ruth Anna[5] Henning** born Sept. 18, 1920 in Sunset, WA.[464]

+   260   ii.   **Gene Santford Henning** born June 1, 1927 in Malden, WA.[465]

+   261   iii.   **Lawrence Daniel Henning** born May 5, 1930 in Malden, WA.[466]

127. George Washington[4] Henning (Santford Ivan[3], Adam[2], John Adam[1]) was born Oct. 12, 1892 in TN, died 1952 in Colfax, WA. He married **Gladys Hake**.[467]

Children of George Henning and Gladys Hake are:

+   262   i.   **Vernon Dale[5] Henning** born 1934 in Charlo, Montana.[468]
+   263   ii.   **Gail Edward Henning** born 1939 in Colfax, WA.[469]

129. Dora[4] Henning (Santford Ivan[3], Adam[2], John Adam[1]) was born Nov. 21, 1900 in WA, died April, 1979 in WA.[470] She married **Lee Hereford**, son of C. M. Hereford.[471] Lee was born Nov. 6. 1903, died July 1985.[472]

Children of Dora Henning and Lee Hereford are:

+   264   i.   **Robert Charles[5] Hereford** born 1926 in Steptoe, WA, died May 14, 1991 in WA.[473]
+   265   ii.   **Anna Lee Hereford** born 1928 in Thornton, WA.[474]
     266   iii.   **Donald LeRoy Hereford** born 1930, died Jan., 1936 in Thornton, WA.[475]
     267   iv.   **David Verne Hereford** born 1934, died March, 1948 and buried in Mt. Vernon, WA.[476]
     268   v.   **William John Hereford** born 1935, died May, 1945 in Thornton, WA.[477]
     269   vi.   **Michael Gail Hereford** born 1944 in Mt. Vernon, WA.[478]

132. Martha Ophelia[4] Styers (Delilah Louise[3] Henning, Gabriel[2], John Adam[1]) was born March 30, 1861 in Forsyth County, NC, and died June 23, 1940. Buried Salem Cemetery, Forsyth Cty., NC.[479] She married **Jonathan Wesley Bullard** on Sept. 5, 1878 in Forsyth Cty., NC by **C. H. Hanson**, Justice of the Peace.[480] Jonathan was the son of **Walter Bullard** and **Sarah Vogler**. He was born June 18, 1853 in Forsyth Cty., NC, and died May 6, 1935. He is buried Salem Cemetery, Forsyth Cty., NC.[481]

Children of Martha Styers and Jonathan Bullard are:

    270   i.   **Minnie[5] Bullard** born June 26, 1879, died Abt.
                1899 in NC. She was the twin sister of
                Margaret D. Bullard listed below.
+   271   ii.   **Margaret Delilah Bullard** born June 26, 1879.
+   272   iii. **Sarah Ethel Bullard** born Nov. 30, 1880 in
                NC, died Dec. 22, 1971. Buried Moravian
                Cem., Forsyth Cty., NC.[482]
+   273   iv.   **Nathaniel Graham Bullard** born May 21,
                1885 in NC, died Jan. 16, 1965 in Forsyth Cty.,
                NC. Buried Salem Moravian, Winston-Salem,
                NC.[483]
+   274   v.   **Treva Ophelia Bullard** born Sept. 20, 1888 in
                NC, died Nov. 3, 1976 in High Point, NC.
                Buried Forsyth Memorial Park, Winston-Salem,
                NC.[484]
+   275   vi.   **Guy Styers Bullard** born Dec. 4, 1891 in
                Forsyth Cty., NC, died Oct. 27, 1983. Buried
                Forsyth Memorial Park, Winston-Salem, NC.[485]
+   276   vii. **Hoke Vogler Bullard** born Feb. 24, 1895 in
                NC, died Dec. 30, 1981. Buried Evergreen
                Cem., Charlotte, NC.[486]
+   277   viii. **Beulah Louise Bullard** born July 20, 1897 in
                NC, died April, 1976 in Oldsmar, FL.[487]

133. Mary Lutency[4] Styers (Delilah Louise[3] Henning, Gabriel[2], John Adam[1]) was born July 24, 1862 in NC, died July 19, 1920. Buried in God's Acre, Bethabara, Forsyth Cty., NC. She died of cancer.[488]She married **John Reuben Smith** on Feb. 23, 1879. He was the son of **John Smith** and **Christene Walke**. John Reuben Smith was born April 24, 1849 in NC, died April 2, 1928. He is buried at God's Acre, Bethabara, Forsyth Cty., NC.[489]

Children of Mary Lutency Styers and John Smith are:

+   278   i   Cora Belle[5] Smith born Aug. 8, 1879,
                        died April 22, 1963 and is buried at Mt.
                        Tabor Meth., Forsyth Cty., NC.[490]

         279   ii.   **Mamie Rosetta Smith** born June 17, 1884, died
                        Jan. 4, 1886.[491]

         280   iii.   **Clarence Leo Smith** born May 21, 1886, died
                        March 3, 1952. Buried Woodland Cemetery,
                        Forsyth Cty., NC. Married **Zelphia Vinson** on
                        April 6, 1915.[492]

         281   iv.   **Orville Sebastian Smith** April 5, 1892,
                        died Feb. 17, 1964. Buried at Mt. Tabor
                        Meth., Forsyth Cty., NC. Married (1)
                        Maebelle Fulk. Married (2) **Dora**
                        Campbell on June 18, 1932.[493]

         282   v.   **Lelia Lutency Smith** born Aug. 28,
                        1981. Buried Forsyth Memorial Park,
                        Forsyth Cty., NC.[494]

         283   vi.   **Albert McHenry Smith** born Sept. 4,
                        1896, died May 21, 1970. Buried Forsyth
                        Memorial Park, Forsyth Cty., NC. Married
                        Bertha Lowdermilk on Nov. 22, 1919.[495]

134. John Irvin[4] Shore, Jr. (Julia May Ann[3] Henning, Gabriel[2], John Adam[1]) was born Nov. 5, 1862, died March 1, 1932. Buried Union Cross Friends, Yadkin Cty., NC. Married on May 12, 1883 to **(1) Melissa Caudle**, daughter of **Sanford Caudle** and **Elisabeth Bates**. She was born Aug. 14, 1865, died July 6, 1911 and is buried at Union Cross Friends, Yadkin Cty., NC.[496] John then married **(2) Nancy Jane Caudle** sister of Melissa. Nancy Jane was born 1859, died 1940 and is buried at Charity Baptist Church, Yadkin Cty., NC. Nancy had formerly been married to a Mr. Brown.[497]

Children of John Irvin Shore, Jr. and Melissa Caudle are:

284   I.   **William Sanford[5] Shore** born Dec. 17, 1887 in Yadkin Cty., NC, died April 13, 1954 in Yadkin Cty., NC.[498] Buried Pilot View Friends, Yadkin Cty., NC. Married **Della Fannie Spillman** on May 12, 1906.[499] She was born March 22, 1898, died May, 1972 in Cooleemee, NC. Buried Pilot View Friends, Yadkin Cty., NC.[500]

285   ii.   **Thomas G. Shore** born April 8, 1891 in Yadkin Cty., NC, died Dec. 20, 1894. He is buried at Union Cross Friends, Yadkin Cty., NC.[501]

+   286   iii.   **John Henry Shore** born July 28, 1893 in Yadkin Cty., NC, died Sept. 26, 1975. Buried Oaklawn Memorial Gardens, Yadkin Cty., NC.[502]

287   iv.   **Barney Clyde Shore** born Feb. 11, 1896 in Yadkin Cty., NC, died May 28, 1966. Buried Old Town Cem., Forsyth Cty., NC.[503] He married **Della Katherine Hine** on Aug. 29, 1931 in Forsyth Cty., NC.[504] Della was born March 5, 1910, died June 24, 1981 and is buried Bethabara Moravian Cem., Forsyth Cty., NC.[505]

+   288   v.   **Clarence Montgomery Shore** born June 13, 1899 in Yadkin Cty., NC, died Oct. 3, 1931 in Forsyth Cty., NC. Buried Forsyth Memorial Park, Forsyth Cty., NC.[506]

289   vi.   **Alfred Fonzo Shore** born Feb. 22, 1902 in Yadkin Cty., NC, died Aug. 18, 1983. Buried Forsyth Memorial Park, Forsyth Cty., NC. Married **May Eloise McLean** born Dec. 12, 1905 in Hiddenite, NC, died March 19, 1984. Buried Forsyth Memorial Park, Forsyth Cty., NC.[507]

290   vii.   **Ida Alma Shore** born Sept. 21, 1905 in Yadkin Cty., NC, died March 15, 1983. She is buried Woodland Cem., Forsyth Cty., NC. She married

Bishop John Franklin Williams, born May 1, 1894 in Yadkin Cty., NC, died March 30, 1984. He is buried Woodland Cem., Forsyth Cty., NC.[508]

135. Edward T.[4] Boose (Rebecca Catherine[3] Henning, Gabriel[2], John Adam[1]) was born Sept. 15, 1858 in NC, died March 23, 1936. He is buried Mt. Tabor Meth., Forsyth Cty., NC.[509] He married Mary Petree born Oct. 12, 1857 in NC, died Nov. 3, 1939. She is buried Mt. Tabor Meth., Forsyth Cty., NC.[510]

Children of Edward Boose and Mary Petree are:

| | 291 | i. | Charlie A.[5] Boose born 1885 in NC, died 1968. Buried Mt. Tabor Meth., Forsyth Cty., NC. Married Minnie L. Petree born 1891 in NC, died 1953 and is buried at Mt. Tabor Meth., Forsyth Cty., NC.[511] |
| + | 292 | ii. | Henry Arthur Boose born Sept. 3, 1889 in NC, died May 2, 1974. Buried Mt. Tabor Meth., Forsyth Cty., NC.[512] |

137. George Gabriel[4] Boose (Rebecca Catherine[3] Henning, Gabriel[2], John Adam[1]) was born Feb. 28, 1863 in NC, and died June 2, 1950. He buried at Mt. Tabor Meth., Forsyth Cty., NC. He married Elmira Virginia Petree daughter of Isaac Petree and _____ Shamel. Elmira was born Oct. 29, 1862 in NC, died Oct. 12, 1937. She is buried at Mt. Tabor Meth., Forsyth Cty., NC.[513]

Children of George Boose and Elmira Petree are:

| + | 293 | i. | Ellis Lee[5] Boose born April 21, 1893 in NC, died June 16, 1974. He is buried at Mt. Tabor Meth., Forsyth Cty., NC.[514] |
| | 294 | ii. | Ola J. Boose born 1896 in NC, died 1960. He is buried at Mt. Tabor Meth., Forsyth Cty., NC. |

Married **Bertha K.**, born 1899 in NC.[515]

295   iii.   **George Nathaniel Boose** born Dec. 10, 1903 in NC, died March 12, 1982 and is buried at Mt. Tabor Meth., Forsyth Cty., NC. Married **Martha Agness Davis** born Nov. 20, 1910, died March 12, 1982. She is buried at Mt. Tabor Meth., Forsyth Cty., NC.[516]

138. Sanford N.[4] Boose (Rebecca Catherine[3] Henning, Gabriel[2], John Adam[1]) was born May 8, 1865 in NC, died Feb. 3, 1954 and is buried at Mt. Tabor Meth., Forsyth Cty., NC. He married **Eliz Dilworth**, daughter of **Robert Dilworth** and **Mary E.** Mary was born Dec. 13, 1869 in NC, and died July 13, 1947. She is buried at Mt. Tabor Meth., Forsyth Cty., NC.[517]

Children of Sanford Boose and Eliza Dilworth are:

296   i.   **Wiley Sanford[5] Boose** born July 15, 1900 in NC, died May 4, 1971. Buried at Mt. Tabor Meth., Forsyth Cty., NC.[518] Married **Viola Livengood** born May 15, 1902, died Jan. 9, 1992 in NC.[519]

297   ii.   **Frankie Boose** born Nov. 10, 1908 in NC, died Dec. 14, 1918 and buried at Mt. Tabor Meth., Forsyth Cty., NC.[520]

142. Lewis Edwin[4] Snipes (Lauretta Elizabeth[3] Henning, Gabriel[2], John Adam[1]) was born June 1, 1866 in Milledgville, Boone Cty., IN, died June 30, 1899 in Tipton County, IN. He married **(1) Mary Letitia Mullins** on Oct. 2, 1889. Married **(2) Lavina Viola McNew** on Nov. 16, 1893, daughter of **Richard McNew** and **Amanda Helms**. She was born in Boone Cty., IN.[521]

Children of Lewis Snipes and Mary Mullins are:

298   i.   **Mary E.[5] Snipes** born March 30, 1891.[522]

+   299   ii.   **Thomas C. Snipes** born Sept. 10, 1893, died March 26, 1967.[523]

Children of Lewis Snipes and Lavina McNew are:

+   300   i.   **Ethel Rosetta**[5] **Snipes** born March 30, 1895 in Lebanon, IN, died Dec., 1983 in Lafayette, IN.[524]

      301   ii.   **Esther Ellen Snipes** born Jan. 22, 1897 in Lebanon, IN.[525] Esther married **Arthur Floyd** on Dec. 1, 1915 in Boone Cty., IN.[526] Arthur was born Sept. 16, 1895, died March, 1971 in Indianapolis, IN.[527]

Generation No. 5

152. Charlie Earnest[5] **Cline** (James Nathan[4], Peter Solomon[3], Mary Anna[2] Henning, John Adam[1]) Married **Eva Wagoner**.[528]

Child of Charlie Cline and Eva Wagoner is:

      302   i.   **Gladys**[6] **Cline**.[529]

158. Mattie Beatrice[5] **Cline** (Charles Christian[4], Peter Solomon[3], Mary Anna[2] Henning, John Adam[1]) was born July 2, 1885 in Pfafftown, NC, died Oct. 4, 1957 in Winston-Salem, NC. She died of Coronary Artery Disease. She married **Charles Russell Fulk** on Dec. 9, 1900 in Pfafftown, NC. He was the son of **Aaron Fulk** and **Sarah Denny**.[530]

Children of Mattie Cline and Charles Fulk are:

+   303   i.   **Ray Rufus Fulk** born June 8, 1904, died March 30, 1967 in Winston-Salem, NC.[531]

+   304   ii.   **Howard Elmer Fulk** born Nov. 27, 1907. He married (1) **Lelia Frances Hepler** on Sept. 27, 1934 in Shoals Township, Pinnacle, Surry Cty.,

NC. Howard married (2) **Mattie Hepler** on
June 1, 1946 in Pilot Mtn., NC.[532]

Howard Elmer Fulk met Lelia Hepler at Cedar Hill Primitive Baptist
Church (near Whitaker Chapel, Pinnacle area) at a foot washing. He
married her but was already married. He served time in prison for
bigamy. Divorced the first wife and married Lelia again. They lived in
the "Butner House" with Lelia's parents when first married. Lelia's
parents were renting the "Butner House." This house still stands and is
occupied (1999). **Henry Wolfe Butner** built the house in 1880 in
honor of a new daughter. Howard later divorced Lelia and married her
sister Mattie.[533]

+	305	iii.	**Mildred Marie Fulp** born April 20, 1909 in Forsyth County, NC, died Oct., 1985 in Winston-Salem, NC.[534]
+	306	iv.	**Oscar Odell Fulk** born Jan. 28, 1911 in Forsyth Cty., NC, NC, died March, 1969 in Winston-Salem, NC.[535]
+	307	v.	**Hazel Cornelia Fulp** born July 19, 1914, died March, 1979 in Yadkinville, NC.[536]
+	308	vi.	**Herman Glenn Fulk** born June 26, 1918 in Tobaccoville, NC, died Dec. 11, 1992 in Graham, NC.[537]
	309	vii.	**Charles Robert Fulk** born Aug. 7, 1921, died Abt. 1924.[538]

160. Howard Olin[5] Cline (Charles Christian[4], Peter Solomon[3],
Mary Anna[2] Henning, John Adam[1]) was born Dec. 14, 1894 in
Pfafftown, NC, died April 15, 1964 in Pfafftown, NC. Howard married
Hessie Magdalin Smith on May 1913 in Vienna Township, Forsyth
Cty., NC. Howard's name is spelled Kline on the marriage license.
Witnesses were: **W.W. Conrad, Mrs. W. W. Conrad** of Winston-
Salem, and **W. C. Medhar** of Pfafftown. Hessie was the daughter of
H. Smith and **Ella**. Hessie was born in Stokes County, NC.[539]

Children of Howard Cline and Hessie Smith are:

+   310   i.   **Irma**[6] **Cline** born March 12, 1914.[540]

         311   ii.   **Ruth Cline** born Jan. 6, 1919.[541]

         312   iii.   **Howard O. Cline** born Oct. 23, 1924. Married **Frieda Marie Grubbs** on Dec. 21, 1944 in Forsyth Cty., NC.[542]

         313.   iv.   **Wilma Dane Cline** born July 26, 1928. She married **Athal Hall Hill** on June 4, 1949 in Forsyth Cty., NC.[543]

         314   v.   **Rex Cline** born June 21, 1932. Married **Vallie Cornelia Shore** on Dec. 21, 1953 in Forsyth Cty., NC.[544]

162. Everett Odell[5] **Cline** (Peter S.[4], Eli[3], Mary Anna[2] Henning, John Adam[1]) was born July, 1899.[545] He married **Minnie Snow** in 1913 in Forsyth Cty., NC. She was the daughter of **S. Snow** and **Aurora Snow**.[546] Minnie was born July 28, 1894, and died May, 1971 in Pfafftown, NC.[547]

Child of Everett Cline and Minnie Snow is:

         315   i.   **Everett Odell**[6] **Cline, Jr.** born 1916, died 1965. He is buried at Sharon Meth. Church, Forsyth Cty., NC.[548] Married **Frankie Yow** born 1922.[549]

168. Raymond Arthur[5] **Cline** (Pleas David[4], Eli[3], Mary Anna[2] Henning, John Adam[1]) was born Oct. 16, 1904 in Forsyth Cty., NC, died July 6, 1969 in Forsyth Cty., NC. He is buried at Woodland Cem., Forsyth Cty., NC. He married **(1) Sallie Queen**. He married **(2) Irene May Phillips** on Dec. 2, 1922 in Forsyth Cty., NC. She was the

daughter of **Charles Phillips** and **Nannie Poe**. Irene was born Aug. 5, 1904 in Forsyth Cty., NC.[550]

Children of Raymond Cline and Irene Phillips are:

+   316   i.   **Nellie Larue**[6] **Cline** born Sept. 20, 1924 in Forsyth Cty., NC.[551]
+   317   ii.   **Raymond Arthur Cline, Jr.** born Dec. 11, 1926 in Forsyth Cty., NC.[552]
     319   iv.   **Geraldine Cline** born March 24, 1931 in Forsyth Cty., NC. Married **Robert Abraham Brinegar, Jr.** on March 3, 1950 in Forsyth Cty., NC. Robert "Buddy" was born Nov. 10, 1932 in Forsyth Cty., NC.[553]

178. Carrie Mae[5] **Henning** (Lavina Melvina[4], Elizabeth[3] Cline, Catherine[2] Henning, John Adam[1]) born March 17, 1883 in Pfafftown, Forsyth Cty., NC, died May 9, 1976. She is buried at Woodland Cem., Forsyth Cty., NC. Married **Pleas David Cline** on Feb. 11, 1903 in Forsyth Cty., NC. He is the son of **Eli Cline** and **Jane Elizabeth Davenport**. Pleas David was born May 13, 1883 in Lewisville, NC, and died July 17, 1948. He is buried at Woodland Cem., Forsyth Cty., NC.[554] He was a carpenter.

Pleas David Cline's children are listed above under #83.

180. Joseph E.[5] **Hennings** (Rosa[4] Henning, Pearlina M.[3], Christian C.[2], John Adam[1]) was born April 5, 1884 in Yadkin Cty., NC, died Oct. 26, 1964. Buried Mt. Zion Bapt. Church Cem., Yadkin Cty., NC. Married **Lennie Alice North** born March 16, 1886, died March 16, 1969. Buried at Mt. Zion Bapt. Church Cem., Yadkin Cty., NC.[555].

Children of Joseph Hennings and Linnie North are:

     320   i.   **Ena N.**[6] **Hennings** born Sept. 15, 1904, died July 16, 1962.[556]
+   321   ii.   **Sattie Mae Hennings** born March 31, 1915, died March 14, 1987 in Winston-Salem, NC.[557]

322 iii. **Paul J. Hennings** born July 7, 1917, died Jan. 1981 in Yadkinville, NC.[558]

323 iv. **Buford Edison Hennings** born 1920.[559]

324 v. **William Grady Hennings** born Jan. 7, 1923, died Aug. 5, 1959.[560]

193. Ruby Lucille[5] Henning (John Kenyon[4], Amanda Sarah[3], Christian C.[2], John Adam[1]) was born Nov. 20, 1896 in Winston-Salem, NC, died Feb. 20, 1983. Buried Forsyth Memorial Park, Winston-Salem, NC. She married **Ira William Baity** on Oct. 12, 1921.[561] Ira was born Dec. 13, 1893, and died Oct, 1975.[562]

Child of Ruby Henning and Ira Baity is:

325 i. **Ira William[6] Baity, Jr.** born Feb. 19, 1923 in Winston-Salem, NC, died March 14, 1993 in Winston-Salem, NC.[563]

196. Robert Edward Lee[5] Henning (John Kenyon[4], Amanda Sarah[3], Christian C.[2], John Adam[1]) born Feb. 7, 1907 in Winston-Salem, NC, died Jan. 6, 1996 in Winston-Salem, NC.[564] He married **(1) Gladys Louise Davis** on April 7, 1928 in Winston-Salem, NC. She was the daughter of **James Davis** and **Mattie Wilson**. Gladys Louise was born Sept. 12, 1911 in Winston-Salem, NC, died Aug. 23, 1991 in Winston-Salem, NC.[565] He married **(2) Zerah Mae Roberson Holder** on July 18, 1939. She was born may 1, 1907, died Aug. 23, 1991 in Winston-Salem, NC.[566]

Child of Robert Henning and Gladys Davis is:

+ 326 i. **Robert Edward Lee[6] Henning, Jr.** born March 7, 1931 in Winston-Salem, NC.[567]

197. Arthur Benbow[5] Henning (William Turner[4] Hennings, Josiah Tyson[3] Henning, Christian C.[2], John Adam[1]) was born July 27, 1882 in Yadkin Cty., NC, died April 19, 1996. He is buried at Mt. Tabor

Meth., Forsyth Cty., NC.[568] He married Cora Lee Lakey on Dec. 18, 1903. She is the daughter of Franklin Lakey and Elizabeth Murphy. She was born June 6, 1884 in NC, died Oct. 6, 1969 and is buried at Mt. Tabor Meth., Forsyth Cty., NC.[569]

Children of Arthur Henning and Cora Lakey are:

> 327   i.   **Child[6] Henning** born Oct. 24, 1905 in Yadkin Cty., NC, died Oct. 24, 1905 and is buried at Stony Knoll Meth., East Bend, NC.[570]
>
> 328   ii.   **David Oseo Henning** born Nov. 4, 1906 in NC, died 1976. He married **Henrietta Clark** on Dec. 22, 1934 in Forsyth Cty., NC.[571] Henrietta was born Feb. 6, 1902, died Aug. 20, 1995 in Greensboro, NC.[572]
>
> 329   iii.   **James L. Henning** born Nov. 4, 1906, died May, 1976 in Winston-Salem, NC.[573] James died of emphysema. Married **Harley Clark**.[574]

David Oseo Henning and James L. Henning were twins. Their wives, Henrietta and Harley were sisters.

> 330   iv.   **Mamie May Henning** born Aug. 21, 1908 in NC, died April 18, 1924. Buried at Mt. Tabor Meth., Forsyth Cty., NC.[575] Mamie May Henning died of acute nephritis and scarlet fever.[576]
>
> 331   v.   **Roy L. Henning** born Dec. 27, 1909 in NC, died Oct. 10, 1951. Buried Mt. Tabor Meth., Forsyth Cty., NC.[577] Roy died of a heart attack. Never married.[578]
>
> \+   332   vi.   **Grace Gladys Henning** born Aug. 12, 1912.[579]
>
> \+   333   vii.   **Vena Hope Henning** born July 4, 1914, died May 29, 1974 in Winston-Salem, NC.[580]

334 viii. **Irma I. Henning** born Feb. 25, 1916 in NC, died Feb. 7, 1919. Buried Mt. Tabor Meth., Forsyth Cty., NC.[581] Irma was burned to death with hot lard.[582]

+ 335 ix. **William "Willie" Arthur Henning** born May 25, 1919 in Forsyth Cty., NC, died Jan. 27, 1988.[583] Buried Concord United Meth., Lewisville, NC.

+ 336 x. **Dorothy Virginia Henning** born Jan. 1, 1921, died Dec., 1991 in Winston-Salem, NC.[584]

+ 337 xi. **Myrtle Louise Henning** born Feb. 2, 1923.[585]

198. Mirtie Lee[5] Henning (William Turner[4] Hennings, Josiah Tyson[3] Henning, Christian C.[2], John Adam[1]) was born July, 1885 in Yadkin Cty., NC, died Sept. 19, 1974. She is buried at Stony Knoll Methodist Church, East Bend, NC.[586] Married **Julius W. Mikles**. Julius was born 1881 in NC, died 1949 and is buried at Stony Knoll Meth., East Bend, NC.[587]

Child of Mirtie Lee Henning:

+ 338 i. **Grady Laster Hennings** born May 6, 1905 in Yadkin Cty., NC, died April 1, 1999 in East Bend, NC. Buried Stony Knoll Meth., East Bend, NC.[588]

199. Nellie Mae[5] Henning (William Turner[4] Hennings, Josiah Tyson[3] Henning, Christian C.[2], John Adam[1]) was born Sept. 22, 1888 in Yadkin Cty., NC, died June 16, 1967. Nellie is buried at Stony Knoll Meth., East Bend, NC.[589] She married **(1) John Wesley Hauser**. He was born Oct. 1, 1888, died June, 1973 in Yadkin Cty., NC.[590] Nellie married **(2) John Thomas Ridings** son of **John Ridings** and **Rachel Stepberger**. John was born June 11, 1863, died Nov. 6, 1941 in Stony Knoll Meth., East Bend, NC.[591] Nellie married **(3) Floyd Martin**. He was born July 8, 1890 and died Oct. 1978 in Yadkin Cty., NC.[592]

Children of Nellie Henning and John Hauser are:

+   339   i.   **Lois Marie[6] Henning** born Nov. 17, 1912,
              died Jan. 29, 1997.[593]
+   340   ii. **Turner Wesley Hauser** born March 6, 1917,
              died March 7, 1999.[594]
+   341   iii. **Nelle Augusta Hauser** born June 4, 1919.[595]

200. Lela Greene[5] Henning (William Turner[4] Hennings, Josiah
Tyson[3] Henning, Christian C.[2], John Adam[1]) born Dec. 3, 1891 in
Yadkin Cty., NC, died Jan. 15, 1963. She buried at Enon Baptist
Church, Yadkin Cty., NC. Lela died of peritonitis. Married **Eugene
Wade Adams** on Sept. 9, 1916. He was the son of **Zimri Adams** and
Matilda Hutchens. Eugene was born Sept. 1, 1878 in Yadkin Cty.,
NC, died April 5, 1963 and is buried at Enon Bapt. Ch., Yadkin Cty.,
NC. He was a farmer.[596]

Children of Lela Henning and Eugene Adams are:

+   342   i.   **John Howard[6] Adams** born Jan. 20, 1913,
              died Feb. 15, 1972. Buried Military Cem.,
              Culpepper, VA.[597]
+   343   ii. **Irene Hope Adams** born June 28, 1917.[598]
    344   iii. **Vance Eugene Adams** born Dec. 20, 1919 in
              Yadkin Cty., NC, died April 19, 1944 in Army
              Hospital in Atlantic City, NJ. Buried Enon
              Bapt., Yadkin Cty., NC. Died of colon cancer.
              Never married.[599]
+   345   iv. **Hazel Augusta Adams** born June 3, 1922.[600]
+   346   v.   **Jessie Pearl Adams** born May 16, 1924 in
              Booneville, Yadkin Cty., NC.[601]
    347   vi. **Willie Jones Adams** born Sept. 15, 1926 in
              Booneville, Yadkin Cty., NC. Died Nov. 11,
              1970 and is buried at Enon Bapt., Yadkin Cty.,
              NC. He died of kidney failure. Married **Patsy
              Louise Smitherman** on June 3, 1950 in

Centenary Methodist Church, Winston-Salem, NC. Patsy was born Aug. 1, 1930, and died May, 1979. Willie and Patsy later divorced.[602]

201. Bessie Anna[5] Henning (William Turner[4] Hennings, Josiah Tyson[3] Henning, Christian C.[2], John Adam[1]) born Jan. 26, 1895 in Yadkin Cty., NC, died Aug. 21, 1982 and is buried at Stony Knoll Meth., East Bend, NC.[603] She married **(1) Colin T. Kirkman**. He was born July 1, 1906, died Nov., 1981 in Winston-Salem, NC.[604] Next she married **(2) Arzy Fletcher**, son of **Bob Fletcher**. Arzy died in Kent, Ohio. Arzy and Bessie later divorced.[605]

Child of Bessie Henning and Arzy Fletcher is:

+   348   i.   **Jessie Mae[6] Fletcher** born Nov., 1912, died Dec., 1973 in Ohio.[606]

202. Ila Ladrone[5] Henning (William Turner[4] Hennings, Josiah Tyson[3] Henning, Christian C.[2], John Adam[1]) was born July 31, 1898 in Yadkin Cty., NC, died Feb. 28, 1974. Buried Stony Knoll Meth., East Bend, NC.[607] Married **Robert Sampson Smitherman** on Aug. 7, 1916.[608] Robert was born May 28, 1895, died Dec. 21, 1981 and is buried at Stony Knoll Meth., East Bend, NC.[609]

Children of Ila Henning and Robert Smitherman are:

+   349   i.   **Robert Benbow[6] Smitherman** born May 5, 1917.[610]
+   350   ii.   **Willie Jennings Smitherman** born Dec. 4, 1919, died Dec., 1975 in East Bend, NC.[611]
      351   iii.   **Leak Hennings Smitherman**, known as "Jack." born Aug. 10, 1922, died June 1, 1944. Died in Italy of wounds suffered during World War II. Buried Stony Knoll Meth., East Bend, NC.[612]

+	352	iv.	Edgar Martin Smitherman born Nov. 16, 1924.[613]
	353	v.	John Lindbergh Smitherman born June 26, 1927. Married Patty Sue Matthews on July 2, 1949. Patty was born June 10, 1930.[614]
	354	vi.	Howard Gray Smitherman born Aug. 12, 1931.[615]
+	355	vii.	Betty Rose Smitherman born June 30, 1934.[616]

203. William Joseph[5] Hennings (William Turner[4], Josiah Tyson[3] Henning, Christian C.[2], John Adam[1]) born March 4, 1901 in Yadkin Cty., NC, died April 15, 1983.[617] Married **Ina Norman**.[618] Ina was born 1904, died 1987.[619]

Children of William Hennings and Ina Norman are:

+	356	i.	Clarence Norman[6] Hennings born Aug. 8, 1921.[620]
+	357	ii.	Margie Hennings born March 7, 1925.[621]
+	358	iii.	Herbert Hoover Hennings born Nov. 4, 1928.[622]

204. Emily Blanche[5] Hennings (William Turner[4], Josiah Tyson[3] Henning, Christian C.[2], John Adam[1]) was born Nov. 7, 1904 in East Bend, NC, died Sept. 12, 1997.[623] She married **Luther Weldon Cornelius** on Dec. 24, 1933. He was the son of **William Cornelius** and **Mary Phillips**. Luther was born Nov. 11, 1903 in the Baltimore community, Yadkin County, NC.[624]

Children of Blanche Hennings and Luther Cornelius are:

+	359	i.	Richard Gray[6] Cornelius.[625]
	360.	ii.	Ralph Weldon Cornelius. Married Judith Phillips. Later divorced, no children.[626]
+	361	iii.	James Tyson Hennings born Nov. 30, 1929 in

Yadkin Cty., NC. James was born before
Blanche and Luther were married. He is listed in
this particular order because the first two
children did not have a date of birth.[627]

362   iv.   **Robert Joe Cornelius** born Sept. 17, 1934 in
East Bend, NC. He married **Carolyn Cook** on
June 26, 1955. Carolyn was born May 22, 1931
in Advance, Davie Cty., NC. Robert served in
the U.S. Army as an MP in 1956-58. He retired
from R. J. Reynolds Tobacco Co., Winston-
Salem, NC. They had no children. Carolyn
retired from the Sara Lee Corp.[628]

+   363   v.   **Ruby Gail Cornelius** born March 20, 1937.[629]

+   364   vi.   **William Earl Cornelius** born July 1, 1942 in
East Bend, NC.[630]

205. Willie Gray[5] Henning (Lewis Hiram[4] Hennings, Josiah
Tyson[3] Henning, Christian C.[2], John Adam[1]) was born April 12, 1885
in NC, died July 27, 1955. He married **Bessie Livingood on Aug. 20,
1910.** She was the daughter of **W. Livengood and Martha**.[631] Bessie
was born June 29, 1885, died June, 1972. She is buried Forsyth
Memorial Park, Winston-Salem, NC.[632]

Child of Willie Henning and Bessie Livingood is:

365   i.   **Willie Gray[6] Henning, Jr.** Never married.[633]

206. John Franklin[5] Henning (Lewis Hiram[4] Hennings, Josiah
Tyson[3] Henning, Christian C.[2], John Adam[1]) was born April 4, 1887 in
Yadkin Cty., NC, died Aug. 20, 1964. Buried Baltimore M.E. Church,
Yadkin Cty., NC.[634] He married **(1) Lela Belle Pilcher** on Nov. 2,
1912, daughter of **William A. Pilcher and Mary Newsome**. Lela was
born Oct. 16, 1884 in NC, died Feb. 2, 1933. She is buried at
Baltimore M. E. Church, Yadkin Cty., NC.[635]

John married (2) **Pearl O. Harrell** on Jan. 7, 1937. She was the daughter of **William C. Harrell** and **Luretta Laine**.[636] She was born Nov. 12, 1912 in Yadkin Cty., NC.[637]

Children of John Henning and Lela Pilcher are:

366	i.	**Gladys**[6] **Hennings** born May 31, 1913, died March 10, 1973. Buried Forsyth Memorial Park, Forsyth Cty., NC.[638] She married **Clifton Harrell**.[639]
+ 367	ii.	**John Thomas Hennings** born March 4, 1920.[640]
368	iii.	**Edward Henry Hennings** born 1928, died 1969. Had Downs Syndrome.[641]

Children of John Henning and Pearl Harrell are:

+ 369	i.	**Ruth Marlene**[6] **Henning** born July 6, 1939, died May 15, 1991 in Winston-Salem.[642]
+ 370	ii.	**Joan Elizabeth Henning** born June 14, 1943 in Forsyth Cty., NC.[643]

207. David Evan[5] **Henning** (Lewis Hiram[4] Hennings, Josiah Tyson[3] Henning, Christian C.[2], John Adam[1]) born May 16, 1889, died in Maxwell, Iowa.[644] Married **Ida Mae Binkley** on Jan. 8, 1914.[645] She was born Sept. 18, 1891, died Sept. 25, 1956.[646]

Children of David Henning and Ida Binkley are:

371	i.	**Dean**[6] **Henning**.[647]
372	ii.	**Vivian Henning**. Married **Leland Battles**.[648]

208. Fannie May[5] **Henning** (Lewis Hiram[4] Hennings, Josiah Tyson[3] Henning, Christian C.[2], John Adam[1]) born Dec. 11, 1890, died Dec. 1980.[649] Married **Gorrell Smitherman** on April 28, 1918, son of **Dock Smitherman** and **Emma Binkley**.[650]

Children of Fannie Henning and Gorrell Smitherman are:

373	i.	Bryce B.[6] Smitherman.[651]
374	ii.	Edward Smitherman.[652]
375	iii.	Roy Smitherman.[653]
376	iv.	Edith Smitherman.[654]

209. Tennie[5] Henning (Lewis Hiram[4] Hennings, Josiah Tyson[3], Christian C.[2], John Adam[1]) born Nov. 2, 1892 in NC, died Dec. 12, 1979. Married **Lewis Windfield Hutchens** on Aug. 7, 1913.[655] Lewis was born Aug. 13, 1890, died April 12, 1965.[656]

Children of Tennie Henning and Lewis Hutchens are:

	377	i.	**Edna Mae[6] Hutchens** born Sept. 27, 1914.[657]
	378	ii.	**Rube Reen Hutchens** born June 22, 1920.[658]
+	379	iii.	**Guy Edward Hutchens** born May 24, 1924.[659]
	380	iv.	**Dallas Cleaborn Hutchens** born May 12, 1925.[660]

210. James Wesley[5] Henning (Lewis Hiram[4] Hennings, Josiah Tyson[3] Henning, Christian C.[2], John Adam[1]) was born Oct. 26, 1894 in NC, died Oct. 12, 1961. Buried Baltimore M. E. Church, Yadkin Cty., NC.[661] James married **Millie Cordalia Wooten** on Jan. 2, 1918. Millie was the daughter of **Ellis H. Wooten** and **Mahala Lakey**.[662] Millie was born Jan. 14, 1898 in NC, died March 25, 1945. Buried Baltimore M. E. Church, Yadkin Cty., NC.[663]

Children of James Henning and Millie Wooten are:

381	i.	**Weldon[6] Henning.**[664]
382	ii.	**Irene Henning.**[665]
383	iii.	**Annie Bell Henning.**[666]
384	iv.	**Rosa Lee Henning.**[667]
385	v.	**Margaret Henning.**[668]

211. Emma[5] Hennings (Lewis Hiram[4], Josiah Tyson[3] Henning, Christian C.[2], John Adam[1]) born March 13, 1897, died March, 1980 in Rural Hall, NC.[669] Emma married William Ray Pilcher on Dec. 27, 1914. He was the son of **William A. Pilcher** and Mary Newsome. William was born Sept. 19, 1896, died Sept. 13, 1973. He is buried Baltimore M. E. Church, Yadkin Cty., NC.[670]

212. Mattie White[5] Hennings (Lewis Hiram[4], Josiah Tyson[3] Henning, Christian C.[2], John Adam[1]) born Feb. 27, 1899 in Yadkin Cty., NC, died April 9, 1983 and is buried at Forsyth Memorial Park, Forsyth Cty., NC.[671] Mattie married **George Dewey Binkley** in 1915.[672] George was born March 21, 1897 in Yadkin Cty., NC, died March 12, 1965.[673] Buried Forsyth Memorial Park.[674]

Children of Mattie Hennings and George Binkley are:

	392	i.	**William Thomas[6] Binkley** born Dec. 9, 1915 in Yadkin Cty., NC, died May 4, 1968. Buried Forsyth Memorial Park, Forsyth Cty., NC. William married **Hazel Howard** in 1942. Hazel was born Feb. 3, 1914, died March 16, 1995. Buried Forsyth Memorial Park.[675]
+	393	ii.	**Dixie LaVon Binkley** born June 5, 1918 in Maxwell, Iowa.[676]
	394	iii.	**Eldon Guy Binkley** born April 22, 1921 in Yadkin Cty., NC. Married **Ruth Hauser** on Oct. 17, 1942. Ruth was born Oct. 1, 1921 in Forsyth Cty., NC.[677]
+	395	iv.	**Thurmond G. Binkley** born May 21, 1923 in Yadkin Cty., NC.[678]
	396	v.	**George Dewey Binkley, Jr.** born March 4, 1926 in Yadkin Cty., NC, died July 2, 1997. George is buried at Forsyth Memorial Park, Forsyth Cty., NC. He married **Betty Holton** on Jan. 31, 1947. Betty was born Feb. 25, 1925 in Forsyth Cty., NC.[679]

397   vi.   James Donald Binkley born May 5, 1933 in
                Forsyth Cty., NC. Married Velma Coe on Nov.
                11, 1955. Velma was born June 7, 1929 in
                Surry Cty., NC.[680]

213. Eliza[5] Henning (Lewis Hiram[4] Hennings, Josiah Tyson[3] Henning, Christian C.[2], John Adam[1]) was born Jan. 5, 1901. She married **Eulius Saunders** on Dec. 1, 1918.[681]

Children of Eliza Henning and Eulius Saunders are:

398   i.   **Willie[6] Saunders.**[682]
399   ii.   **Imogene Saunders.**[683]
400   iii.   **Ethel Saunders.**[684]

214. Eugene Walter[5] Hennings (Joseph Manasseh[4], Josiah Tyson[3] Henning, Christian C.[2], John Adam[1]) was born Feb. 28, 1886, died Oct. 14, 1975 in Illionis.[685] Married **Edna Porter** on Sept. 17, 1910. Edna was born Nov. 25, 1894, died Jan. 15, 1970.[686]

Children of Eugene Hennings and Edna Porter are:

+   401   i.   **Violet Fannie[6] Henning** born Dec. 2, 1912.[687]
+   402   ii.   **Laurence Walter Henning** born July 7, 1914,
                    died Oct. 29, 1992.[688]
+   403   iii.   **Eugene Russell Henning** born Aug. 27,
                    1920.[689]
+   404   iv.   **Glen David Henning** born Oct. 6, 1926.[690]
+   405   v.   **Douglas Bruce Henning** born Dec. 29,
                    1930.[691]

215. Early Harrison[5] Hennings (Joseph Manasseh[4], Josiah Tyson[3] Henning, Christian C.[2], John Adam[1]) born Sept. 25, 1888, died June 15, 1973 in Iowa.[692] Early married **Anna Pagel** in 1921. She was born March, 1897, died Jan. 23, 1999.[693]

Children of Early Hennings and Anna Pagel are:

406	i.	Robert[6] Henning died May, 1998.[694]
407	ii.	Evelyn Henning married (1) Reinert. She married (2) __?__ Reinert.[695]

217. Henry Thomas[5] Hennings (Joseph Manasseh[4], Josiah Tyson[3] Henning, Christian C.[2], John Adam[1]) was born Jan. 5, 1894 in NC, died March 16, 1963. He is buried at Stony Knoll Methodist Church, East Bend, NC. He married **Emma Sophronie Binkley** on Jan. 31, 1915 in Yadkin Cty., NC. She was born March 11, 1895 in NC, and died April 11, 1985. She is buried at Stony Knoll Methodist Church, East Bend, NC.[696]

Henry Thomas "Tom" Henning (1894-1963) was the fourth son of Joseph and he had four brothers and three sisters. Tom spent his entire life in the Flint Hill community of East Bend where he farmed and was a sawyer for Speas Lumber Company for 18 years. He married Emma Sophronia Binkley from the Baltimore community and they had six children: Elwood, who married Edith Hobson, died at age 21; Adelene, who died at age 7; Helen, who married J. Carroll Simmons and lives in Winston-Salem, NC; Earlene, who married Melvin S. Speas and lives in the Flint Hill community; George J., who married Bonnie Jean Smith and lives in the Flint Hill community; and C. Edgar, who married Mary Anna Routh and lives in Greensboro. There are 12 grandchildren scattered from Virginia Beach, VA to Anchorage, Alaska.[697]

Children of Henry Hennings and Emma Binkley are:

+	408	i.	**Thomas Elwood[6] Hennings** born Jan. 21, 1916 in East Bend, Yadkin Cty., NC, died Feb. 8, 1937. He is buried at Stony Knoll Methodist, East Bend, NC.[698]
	409	ii.	**Adelene Hope Hennings** born Dec. 26, 1917, died Nov. 6, 1924. Died of diphtheria.[699]

+	410	iii.	Helen Elizabeth Hennings born Feb. 5, 1922 in East Bend, NC.[700]
+	411	iv.	Ruth Earlene Hennings born Nov. 19, 1929 in East Bend, NC.[701]
+	412	v.	George Joseph Hennings born Feb. 29, 1932.[702]
+	413	vi.	Charles Edgar Hennings born May 29, 1934 in East Bend, NC.[703]

218. Rober Ernest[5] Hennings (Joseph Manasseh[4], Josiah Tyson[3] Henning, Christian C.[2], John Adam[1]) born Feb. 24, 1896 in Yadkin Cty., NC, died Nov. 7, 1959. Rober is buried at Stony Knoll Meth., East Bend, NC.[704] Rober was a veteran of World War II. He married **Nannie Virginia Norman** on May 29, 1920 in Yadkin Cty., NC. She was the daughter of **James Norman** and **Julia Vestal**. Nannie was born May 12, 1898 in Yadkin Cty., NC, died Dec. 20, 1984 and is buried at Stony Knoll Meth., East Bend, NC.[705]

Children of Rober Hennings and Nannie Norman are:

+	414	i.	Frank Harding[6] Hennings born Dec. 6, 1920 in Yadkin Cty., NC.[706]
+	415	ii.	Fannie Mildred Hennings born Feb. 16, 1922, died Oct. 13, 1985.[707]
+	416	iii.	Crawlie Ann Hennings born June 27, 1931.[708]

219. Julia Anna[5] Hennings (Joseph Manasseh[4], Josiah Tyson[3] Henning, Christian C.[2], John Adam[1]) was born Feb. 26, 1900 in NC, died June 1, 1967.[709] Married **Coleman Hoots**, son of **Winfield Hoots** and **Rachel Cranfield**. Coleman was born July 4, 1898 in NC, died Sept., 1978 in Winston-Salem, NC.[710]

Child of Julia Hennings and Coleman Hoots is:

| + | 417 | i. | Vivian Geraldine[6] Hoots born Dec. 11, 1920.[711] |

221. Crawley Mozelle[5] Hennings (Joseph Manasseh[4], Josiah Tyson[3] Henning, Christian C.[2], John Adam[1]) was born Aug. 5, 1902 in NC, died Nov. 14, 1922. She married **Francis "Frank" Lakey Wooten** on Sept. 11, 1921. He was the son of **Ellis Wooten** and **Mahala J. Lakey**. Francis was born May 16, 1896, died Sept. 11, 1921.[712]

Child of Crawley Hennings and Francis Wooten is:

> 418   i.   **Francis Lakey[6] Wooten, Jr.** born May 16, 1896, died April 12, 1965. Called "Junior." Lives in Savannah, GA (1999).[713]

222. Lena Hazel[5] Hennings (Joseph Manasseh[4], Josiah Tyson[3] Henning, Christian C.[2], John Adam[1]) was born Oct. 23, 1908 in NC, died Dec. 13, 1996. Lena married **Joe Franklin Marler** on Jan. 21, 1928. He was born Sept. 9, 1907, and died Sept., 1969. He is buried at Stony Knoll Meth., East Bend, NC.[714]

Children of Lena Hennings and Joe Marler are:

> 419   i.   **Robert Floyd Marler.**[715]
> 420   ii.   **Carolyn Geraldine Marler.** Married **Max Williams.**[716]
> 421   iii.   **Hazel Marler.** Married **Bennie Cave.**[717]
> 422   iv.   **Charles Elwood Marler.**[718]
> 423   v.   **Richard Harper Marler** born 1931, died 1984. Buried Stony Knoll Meth., East Bend, NC.[719]
> 424   vi.   **Betty Ann Marler** born 1934. Married **Junior Arthur Adams.**[720]
> 425   vii.   **Joe Franklin Marler, Jr.** born Dec. 21, 1947. He married **Sallie Ruth Smitherman.**[721]

224. William Hornsby Hester (Sarah Ann[4] Phillips, Martha A. E.[3] Henning, Adam[2], John Adam[1]) was born in 1881 in TN, died 1963 in Spokane, WA.

William married **Mildred McKinley**. Mildred was born in St. John, WA. She was a pianist.[722]

Children of William Hester and Mildred McKinley are:

+ 426 i. **Florence⁶ Hester**.[723]
+ 427 ii. **George Hester**[724]
+ 428 iii. **Millard Hester** born March 11, 1913 in Washington, died July 18, 1994 in Seattle, WA.[725]

225. Dora⁵ Hester (Sarah Ann⁴ Phillips, Martha A. E.³ Henning, Adam², John Adam¹) was born 1883 in TN. Dora and Zeffia were twins. She married **Mark Tollett**.[726]

Children of Dora Hester and Mark Tollett are:

+ 429 i. **Helen⁶ Tollett**.[727]
+ 430 ii. **Clifford Tollett** born Dec. 14, 1908 in WA, died July 19, 1991.[728]

227. Zeffia⁵ Hester (Sarah Ann⁴ Phillips, Martha A. E.³ Henning, Adam², John Adam¹) was born 1883 in TN, died 1966 in Thornton, WA. She married **Henry Tollett**.[729] Zeffia and Dora were twins.

Children of Zeffia Hester and Henry Tollett are:

431 i. **Roy⁶ Tollett** died in Fairmont Cem., Spokane, WA.[730]
432 ii. **Clair Tollett**.[731]
433 iii. **Alvin Tollett**.[732]

228. Sam⁵ Hester (Sarah Ann⁴ Phillips, Martha A. E.³ Henning, Adam², John Adam¹) was born April 20, 1891, died Aug., 1967 in Thornton, WA.[733] Sam joined the Navy during World War I. He played the violin and drew.

Sam Hester married **Sally Williams**. She died 1944 in Thornton, WA.[734]

Children of Sam Hester and Sally Williams are:

+   434   i.   **John**[6] **Hester** died 1987 in WA.[735]

        435   ii.   **Betty Hester.**[736]

+   436   iii.   **Jack Hester** born 1925.[737]

+   437   iv.   **Mary Jane Hester** born 1926.[738]

231. Grace[5] **Hester** (Sarah Ann[4] Phillips, Martha A. E.[3] Henning, Adam[2], John Adam[1]) born April 25, 1898, died Sept., 1979 in Spokane, WA.[739] She married **Lester Kile, Sr.** He died in 1961.

Child of Grace Hester and Lester Kile is:

+   438   i.   **Lester**[6] **Kile, Jr.**[740]

232. Ruth[5] **Hester** (Sarah Ann[4] Phillips, Martha A. E.[3] Henning, Adam[2], John Adam[1]) born Jan. 7, 1901, died May 21, 1993 in Seattle, WA.[741] Married **George Hyde.**[742] George was born May 3, 1900, died Aug., 1984 in Seattle, WA.[743]

Child of Ruth Hester and George Hyde is:

        439   i.   **Georgene**[6] **Hyde.**[744]

233. Lee[5] **Massengale** (Bettie Jean[4] Phillips, Martha A. E.[3] Henning, Adam[2], John Adam[1]) was born 1894 in Lupton, TN, died 1935 in Spokane, WA.[745] He married **Bertha Squires** in 1921.[746] (See Addendum II at the end of this information).

235. George[5] **Massengale** (Bettie Jean[4] Phillips, Martha A. E.[3] Henning, Adam[2], John Adam[1]) was born Dec. 30, 1897 in Marlo, TN, and died Feb., 1986 in Spokane, WA. He married **Doris Pickett** in 1919. Doris died in 1970 in Colfax, WA.[747]

Children of George Massengale and Doris Pickett are:

+   444.   i.   **Betty Elmira**[6] Massengale born 1924 in WA.[748]
+   445   ii.   **Delores Jeanette Massengale** born 1927 in Rosalia, WA.[749]

237. Anna[5] **Roberts** (Iris[4] Henning, Archibald G.[3], Adam[2], John Adam[1]) was born 1891 in WA, died Aug., 1982 in WA.[750] She married **John A. Franz** in CA.[751]

Children of Anna Roberts and John Franz are:

+   446.   i.   **Mary Iris**[6] **Franz** born 1924.[752]
+   447   ii.   **Robert Leroy Franz** born 1925, died Oct., 1980.[753]

238. Edgar[5] **Roberts** (Cordelia[4] Henning, Archibald G.[3], Adam[2], John Adam[1]) was born 1891, died 1949. He married **Margaret Stenroth**.[754]

Child of Edgar Roberts and Margaret Stenroth is:

+   448   i.   **Wendell**[6] **Roberts**.[755]

239. Minnie[5] **Roberts** (Cordelia[4] Henning, Archibald G.[3], Adam[2], John Adam[1]) was born 1893 in Oakesdale, WA. She married **Harvey Thomas**.[756] Harvey died in 1950 in WA.[757]

Children of Minnie Roberts and Harvey Thomas are:

+   449   i.   **Max**[6] **Thomas** born 1922.[758]
      450   ii.   **Dale Thomas** born 1924. Married **June Black**.[759]
+   451   iii.   **Boyd Thomas** born 1925.[760]
+   452   iv.   **Floyd Thomas** born 1925.[761]

240. Clive[5] Roberts (Cordelia[4] Henning, Archibald G.[3], Adam[2], John Adam[1]) was born 1895 in Oakesdale, WA, died Aug., 1977 in Idaho.[762]

Child of Clive Roberts and Flossie Miller is:

+   453   i.   **Jaina[6] Roberts.**[763]

242. Ralph Stephen[5] Henning (Arvel[4], Archibald G.[3], Adam[2], John Adam[1]) born March 28, 1909 in Thornton, Whitman Cty., WA, died July 18, 1974. Ralph is buried in Thornton, WA. He married **Josephine Lorraine Terrell** on Nov. 16, 1935 in Kentucky. She was the daughter of **Leland Terrell** and **Martha Stinson**.[764]

Children of Ralph Henning and Josephine Terrell are:

         454   i.   **Joanne Louise[6] Henning** born Nov. 11, 1938 in Colfax, Whitman Cty., WA. She married **Frank Tedesco** in NV.[765]
+   455   ii.   **Roger Steven Henning** born March 11, 1942 in Colfax, Whitman Cty., WA.[766]
+   456   iii.   **Wayne Leroy Henning** born Aug. 15, 1943 in Colfax, Whitman Cty., WA.[767]

243. Gladys[5] Henning (Arvel[4], Archibald G.[3], Adam[2], John Adam[1]) born Dec. 23, 1910, died Aug. 31, 1900 in Colfax, Whitman Cty., WA.[768] Married **Eugene Eastep**. He was born June 14, 1909, died Dec. 15, 1989 in Colfax, Whitman Cty., WA.[769]

Children of Gladys Henning and Eugene Eastep are:

+   457   i.   **Larry[6] Eastep.**[770]
         458   ii.   **Garry Eastep** born 1940. Married **Patricia Meyer**. Garry and Patricia have to children (7/1999).[771]

247. Vena Ann[5] Henning (Julius Adam[4], Santford Ivan[3], Adam[2], John Adam[1]) born July 11, 1907 in Thornton, Whitman Cty., WA, died Dec. 3, 1979. She is buried in Fairfield, WA. She married **Edward George Pittman** on Oct. 20, 1936 in Rosalia, Whitman Cty., WA. He was the son of **George Pittman** and **Anna Gregor**.[772]

Children of Vena Henning and Edward Pittman are:

+   459   i.   **Charles Edward[6] Pittman** born Dec. 29, 1937 in Spokane, WA.[773]

        460   ii.   **Stephen Roger Pittman** born June 4, 1940 in Spokane, WA. Married **Janice Valene Darling** on Nov. 24, 1973 in United Meth., Rosalia, Whitman Cty., WA.[774]

        461   iii.   **Carol Ann Pittman** born Dec. 8, 1945 in Spokane, WA.

248. Clarence Eugene[5] Henning (Julius Adam[4], Santford Ivan[3], Adam[2], John Adam[1]) born May 26, 1912 in Thornton, Whitman Cty., WA, died 1997 in Sun City, AR. Married **Marian Elizabeth Betty Barnes** in 1939 in Wrangell, Alaska.[775]

Children of Clarence Henning and Marian Barnes are:

+   462   i.   **Mirene Jean[6] Henning** born 1941 in Ketchikan, Alaska.[776]

+   463   ii.   **Robert Scott Henning** born 1944 in Seattle, WA.[777]

250. Oren Lloyd[5] Henning (Julius Adam[4], Santford Ivan[3], Adam[2], John Adam[1]) was born Nov. 7, 1919 in Thornton, Whitman Cty., WA, died Oct. 22, 1995. He is buried at Pine City Cem., Pine City, WA. He married **Thelma Irene Dahlbert** in 1942. She was born May 12, 1922 in Auburn, WA, died Oct. 9, 1994. She is buried Pine City Cem., Pine City, WA.[778]

The Henning Family

Children of Oren Henning and Thelma Dahlbert are:

+   464   i.   Sharon Ann[6] Henning born 1950.[779]
     465   ii.   Kathleen Mary Henning born 1953. Married
                  Michael --?-- in 1996.[780]
+   466   iii. Michael Garth Henning born 1955.[781]

251. Lula Mae[5] Henning (John Thomas[4], Santford Ivan[3], Adam[2], John Adam[1]) born 1908 in Cottonwood Creek, WA, died Oct. 1986 in Clarkston, WA.[782] Married **Burdett Herron Prince**.[783] He was born June 18, 1905, died May 28, 1994 in Pomeroy, WA.[784]

Children of Lula Henning and Burdett Prince are:

+   467   i.   **Eugene Augustus[6] Prince** born 1930.[785]
+   468   ii.   **Hubert Thomas Prince** born 1934.[786]
+   469   iii. **Arlene Virginia Prince** born 1936.[787]

252. James T.[5] Henning (John Thomas[4], Santford Ivan[3], Adam[2], John Adam[1]) was born Dec. 15, 1923 in Sunset, WA, died Sept. 17, 1995.[788] He was buried St. John Cem., St. John, WA. Married **Florence Hayes**.[789]

Children of James Henning and Florence Hayes are:

+   470   i.   **Nicholas[6] Henning**.[790]
     471   ii.   **Victoria Henning**. She married **Jim Forgey**.[791]

253. Roy[5] Henning (Fred Henry[4], Santford Ivan[3], Adam[2], John Adam[1]) born Oct. 12, 1912 in WA, died July 11, 1989 in WA.[792] Married **(1) Jessie Peters**. Married **(2) Carlie Edwards**.[793]

Children of Roy Henning and Carlie Edwards are:

     472   i.   **Maxine[6] Henning**.[794]
     473   ii.   **Heidi Lee Henning**.[795]

474   iii.   **Robbie Henning.**[796]
475   iv.   **Winadine Henning.**[797]

254. Winifred[5] Henning (Fred Henry[4], Santford Ivan[3], Adam[2], John Adam[1]) was born 1914. She married **Harry Appel**, son of **George Appel.**[798]

Children of Winifred Henning and Harry Appel are:

+   476   i.   **Jerene[6] Appel** born 1940.[799]
      477   ii.   **Larry Appel** born 1945.[800]

256. Geraldine[5] Henning (Fred Henry[4], Santford Ivan[3], Adam[2], John Adam[1]) born 1917 in Thornton, WA. She married **Howard J. McGinnis.**[801]

Children of Geraldine Henning and Howard McGinnis are:

+   478   i.   **George[6] McGinnis** born 1942.[802]
+   479   ii.   **Fred McGinnis** born 1947.[803]
      480   iii.   **Jenene McGinnis** born 1960.[804]

257. Boyd[5] Henning (Fred Henry[4], Santford Ivan[3], Adam[2], John Adam[1]) born 1921 near Oakesdale, WA.[805] Married **Evelyn Westerman.**[806]

Child of Boyd Henning and Evelyn Westerman is:

+   481   i.   **Jerry[6] Henning.**[807]

258. Duane[5] Henning (Fred Henry[4], Santford Ivan[3], Adam[2], John Adam[1]) was born 1932, died 1982 in WA. He married **Neva Gibbons.**[808] Dora Hereford's book, The Henning Family, p. 23, indicates Duane was killed by a man renting his house. No further explanation was given.

Children of Duane Henning and Neva Gibbons are:

+   482   i.   Sandee[6] Henning.[809]
     483   ii.   Raeline Henning.[810]
     484   iii.   Glenna Jo Henning.[811]

259. Ruth Anna[5] Henning (Daniel Webster[4], Santford Ivan[3], Adam[2], John Adam[1]) was born Sept. 18, 1920 in Sunset, WA. She married **Marvin E. Berg** on Oct. 30, 1943 in Spokane, WA.[812]

Children of Ruth Henning and Marvin Berg are:

+   485   i.   **Sharon Lea[6] Berg** born Oct. 19, 1946 in
                   Spokane, WA.[813]
+   486   ii.   **Rilla Jean Berg** born July 30, 1953 in
                   Spokane, WA.[814]

260. Gene Santford[5] Henning (Daniel Webster[4], Santford Ivan[3], Adam[2], John Adam[1]) born June 1, 1927 in Malden, WA. He married **Gwelda McDermid** on March 6, 1953 in Rosalia, WA.[815]

Children of Gene Henning and Gwelda McDermid are:

+   487   i.   **Nancy J.[6] Henning** born April 8, 1954.[816]
+   488   ii.   **Thomas S. Henning** born Sept. 27, 1956.[817]
+   489   iii.   **Sally Ann Henning** born Sept. 26, 1963.[818]
     490   iv.   **Mark C. Henning** born Dec. 26, 1963. He
                   married **Dawn D. Bloxham** on April 8, 1997 in
                   St. Thomas, Virgin Island on a cruise ship.[819]

261. Lawrence Daniel[5] Henning (Daniel Webster[4], Santford Ivan[3], Adam[2], John Adam[1]) was born May 5, 1930 in Malden, WA. He married **Bonnie Marie Hoffman** on Oct. 14, 1972 in Rosalia, WA. She is the daughter of **Elmer Hoffman** and **Marilyn Feldman**.[820]

Children of Lawrence Henning and Bonnie Hoffman are:

    491   i.   **Bruce[6] Henning** born Dec. 5, 1973 in Spokane, WA.[821]

    492   ii.   **Lora Lee Henning** born Sept. 30, 1976 in Spokane, WA.[822]

262. Vernon Dale[5] Henning (George Washington[4], Santford Ivan[3], Adam[2], John Adam[1]) was born 1934 in Charlo, Montana. He married **Carol Ratliff**.[823]

Children of Vernon Henning and Carol Ratliff are:

    493   i.   **Russel Damon Henning** born 1962.[824]

    494   ii.   **Rebecca Lynn Henning** born 1966.[825]

263. Gail Edward[5] Henning (George Washington[4], Santford Ivan[3], Adam[2], John Adam[1]) was born 1939 in Colfax, WA. He married **Karen Scholz**.[826]

Children of Gail Henning and Karen Scholz are:

    495   i.   **Pamela[6] Henning** born 1964.[827]

    496   ii.   **Trudi Henning** born 1965.[828]

    497   iii.   **Gregory James Henning** born 1970.[829]

    498   iv.   **Scott Gregory Henning** born 1971.[830]

264. Robert Charles[5] Hereford (Dora[4] Henning, Santford Ivan[3], Adam[2], John Adam[1]) born 1926 in Steptoe, WA, died May 14, 1991 in WA.[831] He married **Joyce E. Hanson** in 1950.[832]

Children of Robert Hereford and Joyce Hanson are:

    499   i.   **Jeffrey Lee[6] Hereford** born 1951.[833]

    500   ii.   **Robin Ann Hereford** born 1956.[834]

265. Anna Lee[5] Hereford (Dora[4] Henning, Santford Ivan[3], Adam[2], John Adam[1]) was born 1928 in Thornton, WA. She married **Gordon E. Lund** in 1947.[835] Gordon was born July 30, 1927 in WA, died April, 1990.[836]

Children of Anna Hereford and Gordon Lund are:

+	501	i.	**Pamela[6] Lund** born 1951.[837]
	502	ii.	**Barry Lund** born 1956.[838]
	503	iii.	**Garry Lund** born 1960.[839]

271. Margaret Delilah[5] Bullard (Martha Ophelia[4] Styers, Delilah Louise[3] Henning, Gabriel[2], John Adam[1]) was born June 26, 1879 in Forsyth Cty., NC.[840] She married **(1) James Franklin Pearce** on Nov. 1, 1899. She was the son of **J. Pearce** and **R. D.** They were married at Grace Methodist Episcopal Church by J. A. B. Fry.. James was born in 1877.[841] She married **(2) Frank Smith** who died Jan. 12, 1938.[842]

Children of Margaret Bullard and James Pearce are:

	504	i.	**Thelma Margaret[6] Pearce** born July 4, 1900.[843]
	505	ii.	**Pauline Calysta Pearce** born April 5, 1902.[844]
+	506	iii.	**Ruth Bullard Pearce** born Sept. 8, 1905, died Feb. 19, 1940.[845]
+	507	iv.	**Treva James Franklin Pearce** born Nov. 12, 1909, died Abt. 1987.[846]
+	508	v.	**Gladys Pearce.**[847]

272. Sarah Ethel[5] Bullard (Martha Ophelia[4] Styers, Delilah Louise[3] Henning, Gabriel[2], John Adam[1]) born Nov. 30, 1880 in Forsyth Cty., NC, died Dec. 22, 1971. She is buried at the Salem Moravian Cem., Winston-Salem, NC. Ethel married **Walter W. Conrad** on Nov. 11, 1903. Walter was born April 8, 1878 in NC, died June 30, 1973. He is buried at Salem Moravian Cem., Winston-Salem, NC.[848]

Children of Ethel Bullard and Walter Conrad are:

+   509   i.   **Laura Ophelia[6] Conrad** born May 20, 1905 in
                                 NC, died July 22, 1990. Buried Calvary
                                 Moravian Church., Forsyth Cty., NC.[849]

        510   ii.   **Ethel Conrad** born March 8, 1917, died Jan.
                                   17, 1979.[850]

273. Nathaniel Graham[5] Bullard (Martha Ophelia[4] Styers, Delilah
Louise[3] Henning, Gabriel[2], John Adam[1]) born May 21, 1885 in Forsyth
Cty., NC, died Jan. 16, 1965 in Forsyth Cty., NC. Buried Salem
Moravian Church, Winston-Salem, NC.[851] He married **Lillian G.
Fritzgerald** on April 26, 1910. She was the daughter of **A. H.
Fritzgerald** and **Elizabeth**. Lillian's parents were from Wilkie, VA.[852]
Lillian was born April 24, 1887, died May, 1984 in Winston-Salem,
NC.[853]

Nathaniel was a machinist for Bolton Mills in Winston-Salem, in
1910.

Children of Nathaniel Bullard and Lillian Fritzgerald are:

        511   i.   **Nathaniel Graham[6] Bullard, Jr.** born May 16,
                                 1924, died Dec. 14, 1990.[854] According to John
                                 Robert Bullard, Sr., Nathaniel was living in
                                 Georgia in 1985 and had two daughters. This
                                 has not been confirmed.

+   512   ii.   **Martha Louise Bullard** born Oct. 16, 1926,
                                 died May 26, 1996 in Winston-Salem, NC.[855]

274. Treva Ophelia[5] Bullard (Martha Ophelia[4] Styers, Delilah
Louise[3] Henning, Gabriel[2], John Adam[1]) was born Sept. 20, 1888 in
Forsyth Cty., NC, died Nov. 3, 1976 in High Point, NC. Buried at
Forsyth Memorial Park, Forsyth Cty., NC.[856] She married **Charles
Milton Miller** in 1920 in Forsyth Cty., NC. He was the son of **Daniel
Miller** and **Mary Elizabeth**.[857] Charles was born Nov. 24, 1890, died

Oct. 6, 1975. He is buried at Forsyth Memorial Park, Forsyth Cty., NC.[858]

Child of Treva Bullard and Charles Miller is:

+   513   i.   **Treva Bullard[6] Miller** born April 9, 1923 in Forsyth Cty., NC, died Aug. 4, 1996 in High Point, NC.[859]

275. Guy Styers[5] Bullard (Martha Ophelia[4] Styers, Delilah Louise[3] Henning, Gabriel[2], John Adam[1]) was born Dec. 4, 1891 in Forsyth Cty., NC, died Oct. 27, 1983. He is buried at Forsyth Memorial Park, Forsyth Cty., NC. He married **Ruby Estelle Shields** on June 2, 1914 in Rock Hill, SC. She was the daughter of **Joseph L. Shields** and **Marcianna Whitehead**. She was born Oct. 21, 1891 in Scotland Neck, Halifax Cty., NC, died Feb. 5, 1961. She is buried at Forsyth Memorial Park, Forsyth Cty., NC. She suffered from diabetes and heart trouble.[860]

Children of Guy Bullard and Ruby Shields are:

+   514   i.   **Guy Styers[6] Bullard, Jr.** born Jan. 23, 1916.[861]
+   515   ii.   **John Robert Bullard** born Jan. 29, 1918 in Petersburg, VA, died April 3, 1998 in Winston-Salem, NC. He was cremated.[862]
+   516   iii.   **Rebecca Estelle Bullard** born April 16, 1924 in Forsyth Cty., NC, died Feb. 13, 1976. She is buried at Floral Garden Cem., High Point, NC.[863]

276. Hoke Vogler[5] Bullard (Martha Ophelia[4] Styers, Delilah Louise[3] Henning, Gabriel[2], John Adam[1]) was born Feb. 24, 1895 in NC, died Dec. 30, 1981. He is buried at Evergreen Cem., Charlotte, NC.[864] He married **May Evangeline Moore**. She was born May 28, 1900 in NC, died Feb. 13, 1995 in Columbia, SC.[865]

Children of Hoke Bullard and May Moore are:

+ 517 i. **Hoke Vogler[6] Bullard, Jr.**[866]
   518 ii. **Betty M. Bullard.** Lives in Columbia, SC (2000). Never married.[867]
   519 iii. **John Moore Bullard** born May 6, 1932. Lives in Spartanburg, SC. Clergyman, educator. Teaches at Wofford College. Never married.[868]

277. Beulah Louise[5] Bullard (Martha Ophelia[4] Styers, Delilah Louise[3] Henning, Gabriel[2], John Adam[1]) born July 20, 1897 in Forsyth Cty., NC, died April, 1976 in Oldsmar, FL.[869] Beulah married **Carl Marquette Cashion** on Jan. 31, 1918 in Forsyth Cty., NC. He was the son of **J. B. Cashion** and **Sarah**.[870] Carl was born Oct. 12, 1894 in NC, died Oct. 1966. He is buried at Forsyth Memorial Park, Forsyth Cty., NC.[871]

Children of Beulah Bullard and Carl Cashion are:

   520 i. **Wesley[6] Cashion.**[872]
   521. ii. **Louise Cashion.**[873]
   522 iii. **Karl M. Cashion** born Oct. 18, 1918, died Feb. 17, 1990.[874]

278. Cora Belle[5] Smith (Mary Lutency[4] Styers, Delilah Louise[3] Henning, Gabriel[2], John Adam[1]) was born Aug. 8, 1879 in NC, died April 22, 1963. She is buried at Mt. Tabor Meth., Forsyth Cty., NC. She married **William McKindry Coltrane** on Feb. 12, 1896 in the home of Cora Belle's parents in Forsyth Cty., NC. William was born June 26, 1857, died July 20, 1931. William was the son of **Jeffrey H. Coltrane** and **Nancy Jane Alspaugh**. He is buried at Mt. Tabor Meth., Forsyth Cty., NC.[875]

Children of Cora Belle Smith and William Coltrane are:

>523   i.   **Pearl Lutency[6] Coltrane** born Oct. 29, 1896 in NC, died April 24, 1986 in Orlando, FL. Buried May 9, 1986 at Mt. Tabor Meth., Forsyth Cty., NC. Pearl was a deaf mute. She married **Robert L. Floyd** on Nov. 19, 1966 in Washington, DC.[876]

+   524   ii.   **Jeffrey Smith Coltrane** born Oct. 2, 1897 in NC, died June 4, 1960. He is buried at Mt. Tabor Meth., Forsyth Cty., NC.[877]

>523   iii.   **Hugh William Coltrane** born Sept. 12, 1898, died April 13, 1981. He is buried at Forsyth Memorial Park, Forsyth County, NC. He married **Anna Lynn Grubbs** on June 20, 1926.[878]

>526   iv.   **Ruby Belle Coltrane** born June 13, 1902 in Mt. Tabor Community, Forsyth Cty., NC, died June 24, 1999. She is buried at Baltimore Meth., Yadkin Cty., NC. She married **Dewey Hall Johnson** on Oct. 1, 1938, died July 5, 1990.[879]

>527   v.   **Clara Augusta Coltrane** born April 4, 1905, died Dec. 12, 1979. She is buried at Forsyth Memorial Park, Forsyth Cty., NC. She married **William Franklin Hutchins** on Nov. 24, 1927. William was born Aug. 10, 1897 in Davie Cty., NC, died April 7, 1945 and is buried in Forsyth Memorial Park, Forsyth Cty., NC. William died of cancer.[880]

>528   vi.   **Son Coltrane** born 1908, died 1908 and buried at Mt. Tabor Meth., Forsyth Cty., NC.[881]

>529   vii.   **Velna Snow Coltrane** born Jan. 7, 1912, died Feb. 2, 2000.[882] She married **Paul Peter Hadranyi** on Feb. 14, 1953 in Fifth Ave. Presbyterian Church, New York, NY.[883]

530   viii.   **Cora Fannie Coltrane** born Nov. 1, 1913. She
                 married **William F. Phillips** on Dec. 11, 1945
                 in First Church of Christ, Winston-Salem,
                 NC.[884]

531   ix.   **Edith Elena Coltrane** born Jan. 29, 1917. She
                married **Roland L. Bennett** on Feb. 24, 1945 in
                Mt. Tabor Meth., Forsyth Cty., NC.[885]

286. John Henry[5] Shore (John Irvin[4], Julia Mary Ann[3] Henning,
Gabriel[2], John Adam[1]) was born July 28, 1893 in Yadkin Cty., NC,
died Sept. 26, 1975. He is buried Oaklawn Memorial Gardens, Yadkin
Cty., NC. He married **Nora Bovender** on Aug. 18, 1913. She was the
daughter of **William Bovender** and **Permelia Williams**. Nora was
born Feb. 28, 1894, died Jan. 14, 1985. She is buried at Oaklawn
Memorial Gardens, Yadkin Cty., NC.[886]

Child of John Shore and Nora Bovender is:

532   i.   **John Henry[6] Shore, Jr.**[887]

288. Clarence Montgomery[5] Shore (John Irvin[4], Julia Mary Ann[3]
Henning, Gabriel[2], John Adam[1]) born June 13, 1899 in Yadkin Cty.,
NC, did Oct. 3, 1931 in Forsyth Cty., NC. Buried Forsyth Memorial
Park, Forsyth Cty., NC. He married **Stella Mae Whitman** on Jan. 2,
1929 in Forsyth Cty., NC. She was the daughter of **Tobias Whitman**
and **Eliza Kiger**. Stella was born Oct. 1, 1906 in Los Angeles, CA,
died May 11, 1990 in Forsyth Cty., NC. She is buried at Forsyth
Memorial Park, Forsyth Cty., NC.[888]

Child of Clarence Shore and Stella Whitman is:

533   i.   **Clarence Montgomery[6] Shore, Jr.**[889]

292. Henry Arthur[5] Boose (Edward T.[4], Rebecca Catherine[3]
Henning, Gabriel[2], John Adam[1]) born Sept. 3, 1889 in NC, died May
2, 1974. Henry is buried at Mt. Tabor Meth., Forsyth Cty., NC. He

married **Lela Conrad**. She was born Dec. 17, 1895 in NC, died May 13, 1959 and is buried at Mt. Tabor Meth., Forsyth Cty., NC.[890]

Child of Henry Boose and Lela Conrad is:

      534   i.   **Henry Arthur[6] Boose, Jr.** Born Sept. 28, 1919 in NC, died Sept. 1, 1951. He is buried at Mt. Tabor Meth., Forsyth Cty., NC.[891]

293. Ellis Lee[5] Boose (George Gabriel[4], Rebecca Catherine[3] Henning, Gabriel[2], John Adam[1]) born April 21, 1893 in NC, died June 16, 1974 and is buried at Mt. Tabor Meth., Forsyth Cty., NC.[892] He married **Addie Luper**. She was born Sept. 18, 1900 in NC< died Dec., 1986 in Winston-Salem, NC.[893]

Child of Ellis Boose and Addie Luper is:

      535   i.   **Billy E.[6] Boose** born May 5, 1939 in NC, died Jan. 24, 1940. Buried Mt. Tabor Meth., Fosyth Cty., NC.[894]

299. Thomas C.[5] Snipes (Lewis Edwin[4], Lauretta Elizabeth Henning[3], Gabriel[2], John Adam[1]) born Sept. 10, 1893, died March 26, 1967. Married **Cecil M. Herrell**.[895]

Children of Thomas Snipes and Cecil M. Herrell are:

      536   i.   **Flodell A. Snipes[6] Snipes** born Feb. 8, 1916, died Nov. 12, 1991. She married **Max Hasket**.[896]

      537   ii.   **Thomas W. Snipes** born July 15, 1917, died Dec. 4, 1994 in Lakeland, FL.[897]

+   538   iii.   **Mary Fern Snipes** born Jan. 2, 1919.[898]

      539   iv.   **Juanita Marie Snipes** born Oct. 21, 1920. She married **Joseph Anderson**.[899]

+ 541 vi. **Lewis Franklin Snipes** born Dec. 21, 1923 in Tipton Cty., IN, died May 26, 1977 in Kokomo, IN.[900]

542 vii. **Frances Marjean Snipes** born April 23, 1925, died Oct. 21, 1925.[901]

543 viii. **Rudy Eugene Snipes** born June 23, 1926. Married **Wilma**.[902]

544 ix. **Calvin F. Snipes** born April 16, 1928.[903]

545 x. **Phyllis L. Snipes** born Oct. 13, 1930. She married **Marion MacFarland**.[904]

546 xi. **Nancy Carol Snipes** Sept. 7, 1932. She married **Weldon Riley**.[905]

300. Ethel Rosetta[5] Snipes (Lewis Edwin[4], Lauretta Elizabeth[3] Henning, Gabriel[2], John Adam[1]) was born March 30, 1895 in Lebanon, IN, died Dec., 1983 in Lafayette, IN.[906] Ethel married **Isaac Benjamin Hill** on June 7, 1909 in Boone Cty., IN. Later divorced, son of **Isaac Hill** and **Juliette Groover**.[907]

Children of Ethel Snipes and Isaac Hill are:

+ 547 i. **Ebon Lewis[6] Hill** born Sept. 2, 1909 in Boone Cty., IN, died Feb. 12, 1963.[908]

548 ii. **Leona Clara Hill** born Jan. 13, 1912 in Boone, Cty., IN, died April, 1912 in Boone Cty., IN.[909]

+ 549 iii. **Winston Keith Hill** born Oct. 19, 1913 in Boone Cty., IN, died Oct. 9, 1989 in Noblesville, IN.[910]

+ 550 iv. **Wilfred Sellers Hill** born Feb. 19, 1918, died Feb., 1969.[911]

551 v. **Melvin Howard Hill** born July 7, 1920 in Marion Cty., IN, died June 1, 1976 in Lafayette, Tippecanoe Cty., IN. He married **Esther L. Rankin** on Sept. 10, 1948.[912]

+ 552 vi. **Leolin Benjamin Hill** born July 30, 1922 in IN, died March 16, 1995 in FL.[913]

+   553   vii.   Mescal L. Hill born Aug. 25, 1924 in Elwood, Madison Cty., IN, died April 28, 1985 in Lafayette, Tippecanoe Cty., IN.[914]

      554   viii.   **Alpha Theodore Hill** born Jan. 23, 1935 in IN, died Nov., 1992 in Lafayettte, IN. He married **Delores Prather**.[915]

Generation No. 6

303. Ray Rufus[6] **Fulk** (Mattie Beatrice[5] Cline, Charles Christian[4], Peter Solomon[3], Mary Anna[2], John Adam[1]) was born June 8, 1904, died March 30, 1967 in Winston-Salem, NC. He married **(1) Ruth Simmons**, daughter of **John Simmons** and **Mahala Jessup**. He married **(2) Mary Elizabeth Dull** on March 1, 1924. He married **(3) Ola Swanson** on March 4, 1955.[916]

Children of Ray Fulk and Mary Dull is:

      555   i.   (?) **Fulk**[7] born April 7, 1927. Child was stillborn.

305. Mildred Marie[6] **Fulp** (Mattie Beatrice[5] Cline, Charles Christian[4], Peter Solomon[3], Mary Anna[2] Henning, John Adam[1]) was born April 20, 1909 in Forsyth Cty., NC, died Oct., 1985 in Winston-Salem, NC. She married **(1) George Conrad**. She married **(2) William Spencer Reich** on April 5, 1924 in Forsyth Cty., NC. See note about name change under notes on Herman Glenn Fulk, Sr.[917]

Child of Mildred Fulp and George Conrad is:

+   556   i.   **Georgia Marie**[7] **Conrad** born Oct. 30, 1946.

306. Oscar Odell[6] **Fulk** (Mattie Beatrice[5] Cline, Charles Christian[4], Peter Solomon[3], Mary Ann[2] Henning, John Adam[1]) was born Jan. 28,

1911 in Forsyth Cty., NC, died March, 1969 in Winston-Salem, NC.
He married **(1) Ruth Grace Settle**. He married **(2) Mary Francis March** on March 22, 1947 in Forsyth Cty., NC.[918]

Child of Oscar Fulk and Ruth Settle is:

> 557   i.   Curtis Glenn[7] Fulk born Oct. 30, 1936 in
> Forsyth Cty., NC. He married **(1) Jane
> Katherine Lowder** on Aug. 20, 1956 in
> Forsyth Cty., NC. He married **(2) Janie Irene
> York Rabon** on Jan. 24, 1972 in Forsyth Cty.,
> NC.[919]

Child of Oscar Fulk and Mary March is:

> 558   i.   Larry[7] Fulk.[920]

307. Hazel Cornelia[6] Fulp (Mattie Beatrice[5] Cline, Charles
Christian[4], Peter Solomon[3], Mary Anna[2] Henning, John Adam[1]) was
born July 19, 1914, died March, 1979 in Yadkinville, NC. She married
William Isaac Baity. See notes about name change under notes on
Herman Glenn Fulk, Sr.[921]

Children of Hazel Fulp and William Baity are:

> 559   i.   **Sharon[7] Baity** born Aug,. 17, 1940 in Winston-
> Salem, NC.[922]
> 560   ii.   Anne Baity born Abt. 1942.[923]

308. Herman Glenn[6] Fulk (Mattie Beatrice[5] Cline, Charles
Christian[4], Peter Solomon[3], Mary Anna[2] Henning, John Adam[1]) was
born June 26, 1918 in Tobaccoville, NC, died Dec. 11, 1992 in
Graham, NC. He married **Viola Florence Gibson** on Nov. 5, 1937 in
Danville, VA. She was the daughter of **Willie Gibson** and **Betsy
Fulton**.[924]

Herman Glenn Fulk's last name was later changed to "Fulp." Only his birth certificate shows Fulk. Everything else, Marriage License, Social Security and military records show "Fulp." Even his children's last names are "Fulp." This is the way I am listing his children. His two sisters, Hazel and Mildred also use "Fulp."

Herman Glenn Fulk (Fulp), "joined the National Guard in Winston-Salem, NC on April 1, 1938. He was a member of Co. G, 120th Infantry. He was drafted in 1944 and served in the Army of the United States during and after World War II. Entered service on May 23, 1944 and came out of service on February 14, 1946. He served four months as a Private and was promoted to a T/5. He drove a 2 ½ ton truck hauling personnel, engineering supplies and equipment. He saw some action before the war ended in 1945 although he readily admitted it was small in comparison to others. He told about getting shot at and bombs dropped on a bridge they were attempting to blow up. His Army Serial Number was 34 864 045 (dog tags). After the war ended, he served the rest of his term in Naples, Italy running the PX."[925]

Herman died of Pulmonary Edema, secondary to Ischemic Heart Disease. Viola died of Pancreatic Cancer. She suffered from chronic ulcers, severe migraine headaches, phorferia, and Bells Palsy.[926]

Children of Herman Fulk and Viola Gibson are:

+   561   i.   **Martha Kay**[7] **Fulp** born Jan. 7, 1938 in Winston-Salem, NC.[927]
+   562   ii.   **Herman Glenn Fulp, Jr.** born July 27, 1941 in Winston-Salem, NC.[928]

310. Irma[6] **Cline** (Howard Olin[5], Charles Christian[4], Peter Solomon[3], Mary Anna[2] Henning, John Adam[1]) was born March 12, 1914. She married **Charlie Cline**.[929]

Children of Irma Cline and Charlie Cline are:

     563   i.   Norris[7] Cline.[930]
     564   ii.   Karen Cline.[931]

316. Nellie Larue[6] Cline (Raymond Arthur[5], Pleas David[4], Eli[3], Mary Anna[2] Henning, John Adam[1]) was born Sept. 20, 1924 in Forsyth Cty., NC. She married **Louis Russell Arton** on Jan. 30, 1942 in York, SC. Louis & Nellie were later divorced.[932]

Children of Nellie Cline and Louis Arton are:

+   565   i.   **Linda Gayle[7] Arton** born Sept. 24, 1942.[933]
+   566   ii.   **Olivia DeAnn Arton** born Aug. 22, 1945.[934]
+   567   iii.   **Marion Sue Arton** born Aug. 30, 1946.[935]
+   568   iv.   **Louis Michael Arton** born July 31, 1948.[936]

317. Raymond Arthur[6] Cline, Jr. (Raymond Arthur[5], Pleas David[4], Eli[3], Mary Anna[2] Henning, John Adam[1]) was born Dec. 11, 1926 in Forsyth Cty., NC. He married **Flossie Mae Chappell** on March 30, 1943 in York, SC. She was the daughter of **James Chappel** and **Arnita Weddle**.[937] Raymond and Flossie were later divorced.[938]

Children of Raymond Cline and Flossie Chappel are:

     569   i.   **James Raymond[7] Cline** born Sept. 21, 1943. He married **(1) Sandra Amen**. Married **(2) Debra Hobson**.[939]
     570   ii.   **Fredrick Garson Cline** born April 5, 1948.[940]
+   571   iii.   **Susan Irene Cline** born Nov. 24, 1949.[941]
     572   iv.   **Margaret Jean Cline** born May 28, 1951.[942]

318. Phyllis Kathleen[6] Cline (Raymond Arthur[5], Pleas David[4], Eli[3], Mary Anna[2] Henning, John Adam[1]) was born Sept. 10, 1929 in Forsyth Cty., NC, died March 16, 1995 in Kenosha., WI. She married

Felix Thomas Aulozzi on Feb. 23, 1946 in Kenosha, WI.. He was the son of **Louis Aulozzi** and **Teresa Cornelli**.[943] Felix Thomas was born June 17, 1923 in Kenosha, WI, died Dec., 1978 in Kenosha, WI.[944] Flex Thomas was a veteran of World War II. He was a guard after the war at Belcenberger, Germany.[945]

Children of Phyllis Cline and Felix Thomas Aulozzi are:

+	573	i.	**Phyllis Ann**[7] **Aulozzi** born Feb. 5, 1947 in Kenosha, WI.[946]
+	574	ii.	**James Thomas Aulozzi** born Feb. 6, 1949.[947]
+	575	iii.	**Renee Marie Aulozzi** born Sept. 2, 1952.[948]
+	576	iv.	**David Louis Aulozzi** born April 12, 1955.[949]
+	577	v.	**Theresa Lynn Aulozzi** born March 10, 1957.[950]
+	578	vi.	**Kathy Diane Aulozzi** born July 23, 1960.[951]

319. Geraldine[6] **"Jerry"Cline** (Raymond Arthur[5], Pleas David[4], Eli[3], Mary Anna[2] Henning, John Adam[1]) was born March 24, 1931 in Forsyth Cty., NC. Married **Robert Abraham Brinegar, Jr.** on March 3, 1950 in Forsyth Cty., NC. Robert "Buddy" was born Nov. 10, 1932 in Forsyth Cty., NC.[952] (See Addendum I at the end of this information).

321. Sattie Mae[6] **Hennings** (Joseph E.[5], Rosa[4] Henning, Pearlina M.[3], Christian C.[2], John Adam[1]) was born March 31, 1915, died March 14, 1987 in Winston-Salem, NC.[953] She married **Thad Wilson Martin**.[954]

Child of Sattie Hennings and Thad Martin is:

579	i.	**Mary Alice**[7] **Martin**. She married **Jeffrey L. Ferguson**.[955]

326. Robert Edward Lee[6] **Henning, Jr.** (Robert Edward Lee[5], John Kenyon[4], Amanda Sarah[3], Christian C.[2], John Adam[1]) was born

March 7, 1931 in Winston-Salem, NC. He married **Joem Rivers Davis** on Aug. 1, 1952 in Winston-Salem, NC. She is the daughter of **John Davis** and **Annie King**. She was born April 17, 1934 in Washington, DC.[956]

Children of Robert Henning and Joem Davis are:

+   580   i.   **Steven Robert**[7] **Henning** born Sept. 10, 1954 in Winston-Salem, NC.[957]
+   581   ii.   **Bruce Davis Henning** born Feb. 11, 1958 in Richmond, VA.[958]
      582   iii.   **Joanna Denise Henning** born Aug. 24, 1959 in Richmond, VA. She married **Thomas Edward Dow** on March 18 in Winston-Salem, NC. Edward was born June, 1956.[959]

332. Grace Gladys[6] **Henning** (Arthur Benbow[5], William Turner[4] Hennings, Josiah Tyson[3] Henning, Christian C.[2], John Adam[1]) born Aug. 12, 1912.[960] She married **Elmer Calloway** on April 12, 1941. Elmer was born April 30, 1910, died June 8, 1985 in Winston-Salem, NC.[961]

Child of Grace Henning and Elmer Calloway is:

+   583   i.   **Nancy Lee**[7] **Calloway** born Dec. 7, 1943.[962]

333. Vena Hope[6] **Henning** (Arthur Benbow[5], William Turner[4] Hennings, Josiah Tyson[3] Henning, Christian C.[2], John Adam[1]) was born July 4, 1914, died May 29, 1974 in Winston-Salem, NC.[963] Vena died of cancer. She married **Phillip Conrad**.[964]

Children of Vena Henning and Phillip Conrad are:

      584   i.   **Robert Arthur**[7] **Conrad**.[965]
      585   ii.   **Victor Conrad**.[966]

335. William Arthur[6] Henning (Arthur Benbow[5], William Turner[4] Hennings, Josiah Tyson[3] Henning, Christian C.[2], John Adam[1]) was born May 25, 1919 in Forsyth Cty., NC, died Jan. 27, 1988.[967] Bill is buried at Concord Methodist Church, Lewisville, NC. He married **Sadie Pearl Hunt** on June 3, 1939 in Forsyth Cty., NC. She is the daughter of **J. E. Hunt** and **Cora E.** Sadie was born March 21, 1920 in NC.[968]

Bill Henning was employed at R.J. Reynolds Tobacco Co. for forty four years. He was a veteran of World War II in the European Theater, where he received the Purple Heart and other medals for his combat duties.[969]

+	586	i.	Linda[7] Henning.[970]
+	587	ii.	Phyllis Henning.[971]
+	588	iii.	William Richard Henning.[972]

336. Dorothy Virginia[6] Henning (Arthur Benbow[5], William Turner[4] Hennings, Josiah Tyson[3] Henning, Christian C.[2], John Adam[1]) was born Jan. 1, 1921, died Dec., 1991 in Winston-Salem, NC.[973] Dorothy married **Jesse Oliver** born Feb. 4, 1917, died Feb., 1986 in Winston-Salem, NC.[974]

Children of Dorothy Henning and Jessie Oliver are:

+	589	i.	Eddie[7] Oliver.[975]
	590	ii.	Barbara Anne Oliver. Married ____ Uskup.[976]

337. Myrtle Louise[6] Henning (Arthur Benbow[5], William Turner[4] Hennings, Josiah Tyson[3] Henning, Christian C.[2], John Adam[1]) was born Feb. 2, 1923.[977] She married **(1) Theron Armstrong** born June 14, 1921, died March, 1975.[978] Married **(2) Benbow Lakey**.[979] Benbow died July 16, 2000 re Mark & Andrea Armstrong.

Children of Myrtle Henning and Theron Armstrong are:

> 591   i.   **Mary Louise[7] Armstrong**. She married ___ Morrow.[980]
>
> +   592   ii.   **Mark Armstrong**.[981]
>
> 593   iii.   **Theron Otis Armstrong, Jr.**[982]

338. Grady Laster[6] Hennings (Mirtie Lee[5] Henning, William Turner[4] Hennings, Josiah Tyson[3] Henning, Christian C.[2], John Adam[1]) was born May 6, 1906 in Yadkin Cty., NC, died April 1, 1999 in East Bend, NC. He is buried at Stony Knoll United Methodist, East Bend, NC.[983] He married **Lesta Wilmouth Cornelius** on May 22, 1926. She was the daughter of **Leon Cornelius** and **Sophronie Elliott Lakey**. Lesta was born Jan. 21,1 1901 in Yadkin Cty., NC, died June 28, 1993. He was a carpenter.[984]

Children of Lat Hennings and Lesta Cornelius are:

> +   594   i.   **Emily Ruth[7] Hennings** born Dec. 13, 1926 in East Bend, NC.[985]
>
> +   595   ii.   **Paul Eugene Hennings** born Dec. 3, 1930 in East Bend, NC.[986]
>
> +   596   iii.   **Grady Lee Hennings** born Jan. 1, 1933 in East Bend, NC.[987]
>
> +   597   iv.   **Alvis Ray Hennings** born April 14, 1935 in East Bend, NC.[988]
>
> +   598   v.   **Joe Bennett Hennings** born July 29, 1937 in East Bend, NC.[989]
>
> +   599   vi.   **Ruby Carol Hennings** born Jan. 6, 1941 in East Bend, NC.[990]

339. Lois Marie[6] Henning (Nellie Mae[5,] William Turner[4] Hennings, Josiah Tyson[3] Henning, Christian C.[2], John Adam[1]) born Nov. 17, 1912, died Jan. 29, 1997.[991] She married **William Floyd Batten** born Jan. 25, 1913, died Nov. 30, 1987. Lois and William were married Aug. 18, 1932.[992]

Children of Lois Henning and William Batton are:

600	i.	Billy Batten.[993]
601	ii.	Mary Batten.[994]
602	iii.	Freeman Batten.[995]
603	iv.	Wesley Batten.[996]

340. Turner Wesley[6] Hauser (Nellie Mae[5,] William Turner[4] Hennings, Josiah Tyson[3] Henning, Christian C.[2], John Adam[1]) was born March 6, 1917, died March 7, 1999.[997] He married **Edith Pauline Hobson Hennings**. She was born Nov. 30, 1918, died July 13, 1976. Edith was also the widow of Elwood Hennings..[998]

Children of Turner Hauser and Edith Hennings are:

604	i.	**Steve[7] Hauser**. He married ___ **Apperson**.[999]
605.	ii.	**John Anderson Hauser**. He married ___ **Norman**.[1000]
606	iii.	**Debbie Hauser**. She married ___ **Grun**.[1001]
607	iv.	**Greta Hauser**. she married ___ **Dudley**.[1002]
608	v.	**Patricia Elwood Henning** born July 28, 1937. She married **Bobby Gray Davis**.[1003] Patricia was the daughter of Elwood Hennings. She was born six months after he died. Edith then married Turner Hauser. Patricia never changed her last name.[1004]

341. Nelle Augusta[6] Hauser (Nellie Mae[5], William Turner[4] Hennings, Josiah Tyson[3] Henning, Christian C.[2], John Adam[1]) born June 4, 1919. She married **Gerald Blackburn**.They were later divorced.[1005]

Child of Nelle Hauser and Gerald Blackburn is:

609	i.	**Gerald Blackburn, Jr.**[1006]

342. John Howard⁶ Adams (Lela Greene⁵ Henning, William
Turner⁴ Hennings, Josiah Tyson³ Henning, Christian C.², John Adam¹)
was born Jan. 20, 1913, died Feb. 15, 1972 of a heart attack. He is
buried at the Military Cemetery in Culpepper, VA. He married **(1)**
Athelena Joyner. Married **Margaret** ___. He then married **(3)**
Genova Snyder. She was born in Clarksburg, West Virginia. She died
July, 1971 and is also buried at the Military Cemetery in Culpepper,
VA.[1007]

Children of John Adams and Genova Snyder are:

610	i.	**John Howard Adams, Jr.** John married **Sandy** ___ . She was born July, 1946.
+ 611	ii.	**Marilea Adams** born January 22, ___.

343. Irene Hope⁶ Adams (Lela Greene⁵ Henning, William Turner⁴
Hennings, Josiah Tyson³ Henning, Christian C.², John Adam¹) born
June 28, 1917. She married **Wesley Clark Choplin** on Oct. 19, 1935
in Galax, Grayson Cty., VA. He was the son of **Joseph Choplin** and
Sarah Wall. Irene and Wesley were divorced in 1962.[1008] Wesley was
born May 14, 1917, died June 20, 1992 in East Bend, NC.[1009]

Irene Adams Choplin wrote the following on June 30, 1982 as a
tribute to Adam and Elisabeth Henning:

Lest We Forget

On the slope of a little woodsy knoll
Treat, great, great grandfather sleeps,
Grandmother lies peacefully by his side.
Tall Trees their lonely vigil keep.

Over the grave-stones at their heads,
Over the creeping myrtle vines.
He has been there since `twenty-four
And she since eighteen fifty-nine.

Leaves cover the sunken places where
Their forms were laid so long ago,
They make a cozy blanket there
As seasons come and seasons go.

Sleep on, sleep on, as we pass by,
You are not forgotten - though it's been
Over a hundred and fifty years
Since you said, "Auf wiedersehen."

Children of Irene Adams and Wesley Choplin are:

+   612   i.   **Joe Wesley[7] Choplin** born April 7, 1937 in East Bend, Yadkin Cty., NC.[1010]
+   613   ii.   **Carol Jean Choplin** born Feb. 15, 1939 in East Bend, Yadkin Cty., NC.[1011]
+   614   iii.   **Dennis Wade Choplin** born Sept. 21, 1940 in East Bend, Yadkin Cty., NC.[1012]
+   615   iv.   **Charles Edward Choplin** born Sept. 20, 1942 in Winston-Salem, NC.[1013]

345. Hazel Augusta[6] Adams (Lela Greene[5] Henning, William Turner[4] Hennings, Josiah Tyson[3] Henning, Christian C.[2], John Adam[1]) was born June 3, 1922. She married **Eugene Speas Smith** on Dec. 21, 1941. He is the son of **William C. Smith** and **Hattie C.** He was born Sept. 26, 1918.[1014]

Child of Hazel Adams and Eugene Smith is:

      616   i.   **Larry Eugene[7] Smith** born June 8, 1945.[1015]

346. Jessie Pearl[6] Adams (Lela Greene[5] Henning, William Turner[4] Hennings, Josiah Tyson[3] Henning, Christian C.[2], John Adam[1]) was born May 16, 1924 in Booneville, Yadkin Cty., NC. She married

James Luke Taylor on January 5, 1946. James is the son of **Elisha Taylor** and **Victoria Blakely**. He was born May 14, 1923 in Guilford Cty., NC.[1016]

Children of Jessie Adams and James Taylor are:

+   617   i.   **James Monroe**[7] **Taylor** born June 22, 1947.[1017]
      618   ii.   **Jeffrey Kyle Taylor** born Jan. 29, 1961. He married **Leslie Anne Meekins** on June 25, 1983.[1018]

348. Jessie Mae[6] **Fletcher** (Bessie Anna[5] Henning, William Turner[4] Hennings, Josiah Tyson[3] Henning, Christian C.[2], John Adam[1]) was born Nov., 1912, died Dec., 1973 in Ohio.[1019] Jessie married **Everette Dula**. He was born Sept. 22, 1917, died Nov. 14, 1981 in Kent, Ohio.[1020]

Child of Jessie Fletcher and Everette Dula is:

      619   i.   **Jimmie Mack**[7] **Dula** was born in 1931. He married **Irene Day**.[1021]

349. Robert Benbow[6] **Smitherman** (Ila Ladrone[5] Henning, William Turner[4] Hennings, Josiah Tyson[3] Henning, Christian C.[2], John Adam[1]) was born May 5, 1917. Robert was a carpenter.[1022] Robert married **Bertha Pearl Hunt** on Nov. 11, 1937. She was born Aug. 13, 1916, died March 13, 1994.[1023]

Children of Robert Smitherman and Bertha Hunt are:

+   620   i.   **Polly Ann**[7] **Smitherman**.[1024]
+   621   ii.   **Allen Benbow Smitherman**.[1025]
      622   iii.   **Marlene Smitherman**. She married **Jeff Crotts**.[1026]
+   623   iv.   **Howard Thomas Smitherman**.[1027]

350. Willie Jennings[6] Smitherman (Ila Ladrone[5] Henning, William Turner[4] Hennings, Josiah Tyson[3] Henning, Christian C.[2], John Adam[1]) was born Dec. 4, 1919, died Dec., 1975 in East Bend, NC. Served in U.S. Army, World War II. He was a carpenter.[1028] He married **Novella Hunt** on Nov. 4, 1939. She was born Feb. 28, 1919.[1029]

Children of Willie Smitherman and Novella Hunt are:

	624	i.	Hilda Janet[7] Smitherman.[1030]
+	625	ii.	Robert Burgess Smitherman.[1031]
+	626	iii.	Kirby Jennings Smitherman.[1032]

352. Edgar Martin[6] Smitherman (Ila Ladrone[5] Henning, William Turner[4] Hennings, Josiah Tyson[3] Henning, Christian C.[2], John Adam[1]) was born Nov. 16, 1924. Ed served in World War II.[1033] He married **Aggie Mae Speer** on Sept. 30, 1945. She was the daughter of **Tom Speer** and **Minerva Mikles**. She was born Jan. 15, 1927.[1034]

Child of Ed Smitherman and Aggie Speer is:

	627	i.	Teresa Jean[7] Smitherman.[1035]

355. Betty Rose[6] Smitherman (Ila Ladrone[5] Henning, William Turner[4] Hennings, Josiah Tyson[3] Henning, Christian C.[2], John Adam[1]) was born June 30, 1934.[1036] She married **Edward Lee Collins** on Aug. 29, 1954.[1037] He was born on Aug. 25, 1935.[1038]

Children of Betty Smitherman and Edward Collins are:

	628	i.	Edward Lee[7] Collins, Jr.[1039]
+	629	ii.	Mitchell Van Collins.[1040]

356. Clarence Norman[6] Hennings (William Joseph[5], William Turner[4] Hennings, Josiah Tyson[3] Henning, Christian C.[2], John Adam[1]) born Aug. 8, 1921.

Clarence married **Pauline Redding** on May 16, 1942. She was the daughter of **Paul Redding** and **Mette Roop**. Pauline was born Sept. 21, 1922.[1041]

Children of Clarence Hennings and Pauline Redding are:

+	630	i.	**Janice**[7] **Hennings**.[1042]
+	631	ii.	**Connie Hennings**.[1043]

357. Margie[6] **Hennings** (William Joseph[5], William Turner[4] Hennings, Josiah Tyson[3] Henning, Christian C.[2], John Adam[1]) was born March 7, 1925. She married **John Sandford Green** on March 9, 1946. John was the son of **James Green** and **Stella Seaford**. He was born March 7, 1925.[1044]
l
Children of Margie Hennings and John Green are:

+	632	i.	**Tony**[7] **Green** born Feb. 25, 1947.[1045]
+	633	ii.	**Michael Green** born April 7, 1951.[1046]

358. Herbert Hoover[6] **Hennings** (William Joseph[5], William Turner[4] Hennings, Josiah Tyson[3] Henning, Christian C.[2], John Adam[1]) was born Nov. 4, 1928.[1047] He married **Helen Ann Long**. She was the daughter of **John Long** and **Ethel Doub**. Helen was born July 17, 1930.[1048]

Children of Herbert Hennings and Helen Long are:

634	i.	**Sarah Elizabeth**[7] **Hennings** born April 2, 1948. She married **George Terry Davis**.[1049]
635	ii.	**Shirley Ann Hennings** born Sept. 10, 1950. She married **Charles Leon Brown**.[1050]
636	iii.	**Gary Lee Hennings** born Feb. 5, 1956.[1051]
637	iv.	**Larry Joseph Hennings** born May 9, 1957.[1052]

359. Richard Gray[6] Cornelius (Emily Blanche[5] Hennings,William Turner[4] Hennings, Josiah Tyson[3] Henning, Christian C.[2], John Adam[1]) He married **Frances Medlin**.[1053]

Children of Richard Cornelius and Frances Medlin are:

638	i.	**Denise[7]Cornelius**.[1054]
639	ii.	**Ricky Cornelius**.[1055]
640	iii.	**Christy Cornelius**.[1056]

361. James Tyson[6] Hennings (Emily Blanche[5] Hennings,William Turner[4] Hennings, Josiah Tyson[3] Henning, Christian C.[2], John Adam[1]) was born Nov. 30, 1929 in Yadkin Cty., NC.[1057] He married **Celia Elliott** on July 12, 1952 in Winston-Salem, NC. She was born Sept. 18, 1932 in Wilkes Cty., NC. James was listed under the children of Luther and Emily Hennings Cornelius. James was born prior to Emily's marriage to Luther.[1058]

Children of James Hennings and Celia Elliott are:

+	641	i.	**Lisa Ann[7] Hennings** born April 30, 1959.[1059]
	642	ii.	**Karen Sue Hennings** born March 3, 1962. She married **Paul O. Flotz** on April 26, 1987.They were later divorced.[1060]

363. Ruby Gail[6] Cornelius (Emily Blanche[5] Hennings,William Turner[4] Hennings, Josiah Tyson[3] Henning, Christian C.[2], John Adam[1]) was born March 20, 1937. She married **William Ray Bray** on July 13, 1956. He was born Dec. 16, 1933.[1061]

Children of Ruby Cornelius and William Bray are:

	643	i.	**Robin Elizabeth[7] Bray**.[1062]
	644	ii.	**Rose Marie Bray**.[1063]
+	645	iii.	**Martha Gail Bray** born March 20, 1957.[1064]
+	646	iv.	**Ashley Forrest Bray** born June 28, 1958.[1065]

364. William Earl[6] Cornelius (Emily Blanche[5] Hennings,William Turner[4] Hennings, Josiah Tyson[3] Henning, Christian C.[2], John Adam[1]) was born July 1, 1942 in East Bend, Yadkin Cty., NC.[1066] He married **Eleanor Jeanette Matthews** on June 24, 1961. She is the daughter of **R. Matthews** and **Martha Davis**. Eleanor was born in 1943. William and Jeanette were later divorced.[1067]

Children of William Cornelius and Eleanor Matthews are:

647	i.	**Sharon R.[7] Cornelius**. She married **Eric Allen Fisher** on May 26, 1984 in East Bend Methodist Church, East Bend, NC.[1068]
648	ii.	**Marsha R. Cornelius**.[1069]

367. John Thomas[6] Hennings (John Franklin[5] Henning, Lewis Hiram[4] Hennings, Josiah Tyson[3] Henning, Christian C.[2], John Adam[1]) was born March 4, 1920. John married **Bertha Forbis** on Dec. 22, 1944. Bertha was born Dec. 10, 1919.[1070]

Child of John Hennings and Bertha Forbis is:

+	649	i.	**Thomas Wayne[7] Hennings** born May 6, 1946.[1071]

369. Ruth Marlene[6] Henning (John Franklin[5] Henning, Lewis Hiram[4] Hennings, Josiah Tyson[3] Henning, Christian C.[2], John Adam[1]) born July 6, 1939, died May 15, 1991 in Winston-Salem, NC. She married **Donald Ray Vogler, Sr.**[1072]

Children of Ruth Henning and Donald Vogler are:

650	i.	**Donald Ray[7] Vogler, Jr.** born Feb. 28, 1960 in Forsyth Cty., NC.[1073]
651	ii.	**John Christopher Vogler** born June 10, 1965.[1074]

370. Joan Elizabeth[6] Henning (John Franklin[5] Henning, Lewis Hiram[4] Hennings, Josiah Tyson[3] Henning, Christian C.[2], John Adam[1]) was born June 14, 1943 in Forsyth Cty., NC. She married **Richard Gary Myers**.[1075]

> 652   i.   **Gary[7] Myers**.[1076]
> 653   ii.   **Richard Sherman Myers** born Dec. 13, 1963 in Forsyth Cty., NC.[1077]

379. Guy Edward[6] Hutchens (Tennie[5] Hennings, Lewis Hiram[4] Hennings, Josiah Tyson[3] Henning, Christian C.[2], John Adam[1]) was born May 24, 1924.[1078]

Children of Guy Edward Hutchens are:

> 654   i.   **Guy Edward[7] Hutchens, Jr.**[1079]
> 655   ii.   **Rhonda Hutchens**. She married Gossett.[1080]

386. William Ralph[6] Pilcher (Emma[5] Hennings, Lewis Hiram[4] Hennings, Josiah Tyson[3] Henning, Christian C.[2], John Adam[1]) was born March 2, 1920,[1081] died Nov. 27, 1991.[1082] William married **Brownie Lee Spears** on May 4, 1940.[1083] Brownie was born Feb. 7, 1923.[1084]

Children of William Pilcher and Brownie Spears are:

> +   656   i.   **Shelby[7] Pilcher** born Sept. 25, 1944.[1085]
> +   657   ii.   **Allen Wayne Pilcher** born July 9, 1948.[1086]

388. Lewis David[6] Pilcher (Emma[5] Hennings, Lewis Hiram[4] Hennings, Josiah Tyson[3] Henning, Christian C.[2], John Adam[1]) was born Aug. 23, 1923.[1087] He married **Lucy Speer**, daughter of **Hubert Speer** and **Parris Wooten**. Lucy was born March 18, 1928.[1088]

Children of Lewis Pilcher and Lucy Speer are:

658	i.	David Lee[7] Pilcher born March 21, 1948.[1089]
659	ii.	Grady James Pilcher born Jan. 11, 1950. He married Wanda Hawks on May 16, 1976.[1090]
660	iii.	Arnold Gray Pilcher born Sept. 15, 1951. He married Nancy Groce on June 10, 1972.[1091]
661	iv.	Larry Ray Pilcher born Sept. 7, 1953.[1092]
662	v.	Sarah Joanna Pilcher born Aug. 12, 1961.[1093]

389. William Ray[6] Pilcher, Jr. (Emma[5] Hennings, Lewis Hiram[4] Hennings, Josiah Tyson[3] Henning, Christian C.[2], John Adam[1]) was born 1938, died April 6, 1987.[1094] He married **Elizabeth Hobson** in 1958. They later divorced. She is the daughter of **Oscar Hobson** and **Vernie Mae**. Elizabeth died March 10, 1987.[1095]

Children of William Pilcher and Elizabeth Hobson are:

663	i.	Denny Lee[7] Pilcher born 1961.[1096]
664	ii.	Donald Gray Pilcher born 1963.[1097]
665	iii.	Jeffrey Dale Pilcher born 1965.[1098]
666	iv.	Michael Dean Pilcher born 1968.[1099]

391. Martha Inez[6] Pilcher (Emma[5] Hennings, Lewis Hiram[4] Hennings, Josiah Tyson[3] Henning, Christian C.[2], John Adam[1]) was born May 6, 1942[1100] She married **(1) Johnny Hampton** on Nov. 25, 1959.[1101] Johnny died on Nov. 10, 1979.[1102] Martha married **(2) Bobby Ray Johnson**.[1103]

Children of Martha Pilcher and Johnny Hampton are:

667	i.	Jerry Wayne[7] Hampton born Aug. 11, 1958. He married **Jill Lanham** on Aug. 22, 1998. Jill was born Oct. 29 ___.[1104]
+ 668	ii.	Charles Ray Hampton born Feb. 23, 1964.[1105]

Children of Martha Pilcher and Bobby Johnson are:

+   669   i.   **James Vernon**[7] **Johnson** born May 8, 1960.[1106]
+   670   ii.   **Lartha Lynn Johnson** born April 3, 1964.[1107]
+   671   iii.   **Randy Lee Johnson** born Oct. 3, 1965.[1108]
+   672   iv.   **Donna Jean Johnson** born April 6, 1968.[1109]

393. Dixie LaVon[6] **Binkley** (Mattie White[5] Hennings, Lewis Hiram[4] Hennings, Josiah Tyson[3] Henning, Christian C.[2], John Adam[1]) was born June 5, 1918 in Maxwell, Iowa. She married **(1) Roy Dwight Welborn** in 1935. They divorced in 1947. He was born Sept. 3, 1914, died May 31, 1976. She married **(2) Chester S. Horton** on July 4, 1953. Chester was born April 12, 1920, died Oct. 22, 1968.[1110]

Child of Dixie Binkley and Roy Welborn is:

+   673   i.   **Judith Ann**[7] **Welborn** born Jan. 22, 1941.[1111]

395. Thurmond G.[6] **Binkley** (Mattie White[5] Hennings, Lewis Hiram[4] Hennings, Josiah Tyson[3] Henning, Christian C.[2], John Adam[1]) was born May 21, 1923 in Yadkin Cty., NC. He married **Mary Hege** on Oct. 9, 1942. She was born April 30, 1925 in Forsyth Cty., NC.[1112]

Child of Thurmond Binkley and Mary Hege is:

     674   i.   **Thurmond G.**[7] **Binkley, Jr.**[1113]

401. Violet Fannie[6] **Henning** (Eugene Walter[5] Hennings, Joseph Manasseh[4], Josiah Tyson[3] Henning, Christian C.[2], John Adam[1]) was born Dec. 2, 1912.[1114] She married **William John Weaver** on Dec. 2, 1930.[1115] He was June 29, 1906.[1116]

Children of Violet Henning and William Weaver are:

+   675   i.   **William Wesley**[7] **Weaver** born July 8, 1932.[1117]
+   676   ii.   **Nancy Elloise Weaver** born Aug. 10, 1937.[1118]

402. Laurence Walter[6] Henning (Eugene Walter[5] Hennings, Joseph Manasseh[4], Josiah Tyson[3] Henning, Christian C.[2], John Adam[1]) was born July 7, 1914, died Oct. 29, 1992. He married **Mildred Nordmeyer**. She was born in 1918.[1119]

Children of Laurence Henning and Mildred Nordmeyer are:

+	677	i.	**Constance Gae[7] Henning** born Aug. 26, 1942[1120].
+	678	ii.	**David Laurence Henning** born May 30, 1944.[1121]
	679	iii.	**Steven Michael Henning** born July 18, 1948. He married **(1) Jane**. He married **(2) Joyce Piggush** in Aug., 1970. He married **(3) Sherry Nelson** in May, 1984.[1122]
+	680	iv.	**Paula Jean Henning** born Jan. 15, 1955.[1123]

403. Eugene Russell[6] Henning (Eugene Walter[5] Hennings, Joseph Manasseh[4], Josiah Tyson[3] Henning, Christian C.[2], John Adam[1]) was born Aug. 27, 1920. He married **(1) Dorothy Donough**. She was born March, 1920. He married **(2) Claudia** in April, 1977. She was born May 20, 1934.[1124]

Children of Eugene Henning and Dorothy Donough are:

+	681	i.	**Eugene Russell[7] Henning, Jr.** born July 5, 1943.[1125]
+	682	ii.	**Donna Jean Henning** born Sept, 1946.[1126]
+	683	iii.	**Sally Ann Henning** born July 21, 1948.[1127]
+	684	iv.	**Bruce Lee Henning** born Nov. 9, 1950.[1128]
+	685	v.	**George Walter Henning** born Feb. 22, 1955.[1129]
	686	vi.	**James Allen Henning** born March 25, 1962.[1130]

404. Glen David[6] Henning (Eugene Walter[5] Hennings, Joseph Manasseh[4], Josiah Tyson[3] Henning, Christian C.[2], John Adam[1]) was born Oct. 6, 1926. He married **Virlin Dittus** on March 24, 1945. She was born Aug. 13, 1925.[1131]

	687	i.	**Jerry Glen[7] Henning** born Sept. 8, 1949, died Nov. 27, 1972.[1132]
	688	ii.	**Danny Ray Henning** born Feb. 27, 1952, died March 4, 1952.[1133]
+	689	iii.	**Jack Duane Henning** born Sept. 18, 1953.[1134]

405. Douglas Bruce[6] Henning (Eugene Walter[5] Hennings, Joseph Manasseh[4], Josiah Tyson[3] Henning, Christian C.[2], John Adam[1]) was born Dec. 29, 1930.[1135] He married **Magdalena Flocchini** on July 4, 1955. She was born May 24, ___.[1136]

Children of Douglas Henning and Magdalena Flocchini are:

	690	i.	**Brian Douglas[7] Henning** born March 7, ___.[1137]
+	691	ii.	**Susan Marie Henning** born July 29, 1963.[1138]

408. Thomas Elwood[6] Hennings (Henry Thomas[5], Joseph Manasseh[4], Josiah Tyson[3] Henning, Christian C.[2], John Adam[1]) was born Jan. 21, 1916 in East Bend, NC, died Feb. 8, 1937. Elwood died of pneumonia. He is buried at Stony Knoll Meth. Church, East Bend, NC.[1139] He married **Edith Pauline Hobson** on Oct. 13, 1935. Edith was born Nov. 30, 1918, died July 13, 1976.[1140] See **Turner Wesley Hauser** family.

Child of Elwood Hennings and Edith Hobson is:

	692	i.	**Patricia Elwood[7] Hennings** born July 28, 1937.[1141]

410. Helen Elizabeth[6] Hennings (Henry Thomas[5], Joseph Manasseh[4], Josiah Tyson[3] Henning, Christian C.[2], John Adam[1]) was born Feb. 5, 1922 in East Bend, NC. She married **James Carroll Simmons** on April 4, 1942. James served in the U. S. Air Force in World War II.[1142]

Children of Helen Hennings and James Simmons are:

+   693   i.   **Judith Marie[7] Simmons** born April 23, 1943.[1143]

        694   ii.   **Betty Jean Simmons** born Nov. 18, 1948, died March 3, 1949.[1144]

        695   iii.   **David Carroll Simmons** born July 18, 1954. He married **(1) Patricia Lee Smith** in 1983. Patricia was born Nov. 18, 1956. They divorced in 1993. David married **(2) Camille Billings Martin** on July 23, 1994. Camille was born Feb. 10, 1943.[1145]

411. Ruth Earlene[6] Hennings (Henry Thomas[5], Joseph Manasseh[4], Josiah Tyson[3] Henning, Christian C.[2], John Adam[1]) born Nov. 19, 1929 in East Bend, NC. She married **Melvin Sprinkle Speas** on April 8, 1950. He was born Jan. 9, 1930.[1146]

Children of Ruth Hennings and Melvin Speas are:

+   696   i.   **Julia Hope[7] Speas** born July 10, 1955.[1147]

        697   ii.   **Melissa Ruth Speas** born July 17, 1961. She married **Charles Allen Beck** who was born July 10, 1964.[1148]

412. George Joseph[6] Hennings (Henry Thomas[5], Joseph Manasseh[4], Josiah Tyson[3] Henning, Christian C.[2], John Adam[1]) was born Feb. 29, 1932. He married **Bonnie Jean Smith** on Oct. 8, 1955. Bonnie was born Sept. 30, 1937. George served in the U. S. Army during the Korean Conflict.[1149]

Children of George Hennings and Bonnie Smith are:

698   i.   **Eddy Eugene**[7] **Hennings** born Oct. 14, 1956. He married **Vicki Lynn Foster** on April 24, 1982. Vicky was born June 22, 1953.[1150]

\+   699   ii.   **Andy Joseph Hennings** born March 22, 1958.[1151]

\+   700   iii.   **Cindy Jean**[7] **Hennings** born Sept. 13, 1959.[1152]

413. Charles Edgar[6] **Hennings** (Henry Thomas[5], Joseph Manasseh[4], Josiah Tyson[3] Henning, Christian C.[2], John Adam[1]) born May 29, 1934 in East Bend, NC. He married **Mary Anna Routh** on Sept. 5, 1954. She was born Oct. 22, 1934. Ed served in the U. S. Army from 1957 to 1958.[1153]

Children of Charles Hennings and Ann Routh are:

\+   701   i.   **Edgar Thomas**[7] **Hennings** born Sept. 23, 1958.[1154]

\+   702   ii.   **Ellen Ann Hennings** born Aug. 22, 1961.[1155]

703   iii.   **Steven Kenneth Hennings** born July 5, 1965.[1156]

414. Frank Harding[6] **Hennings** (Rober Ernest[5], Joseph Manasseh[4], Josiah Tyson[3] Henning, Christian C.[2], John Adam[1]) was born Dec. 6, 1920 in Yadkin Cty., NC. He married **Mozelle Izella Hobson** on Jan. 15, 1945. She was born Oct. 24, 1922.[1157]

Child of Frank Hennings and Mozelle Hobson is:

\+   704   i.   **Frankie Gail**[7] **Hennings** born April 13, 1946.[1158]

415. Fannie Mildred[6] **Hennings** (Rober Ernest[5], Joseph Manasseh[4], Josiah Tyson[3] Henning, Christian C.[2], John Adam[1]) born Feb. 16, 1922, died Oct. 13, 1985. She married (1) **Clarence Thomas**

The Henning Family

Lawson. He was born April 30, 1920, died March 9, 1979. She married (2) **Kenneth Ray Cook** on Dec. 25, 1938. He was born Sept. 28, 1920, died Abt. 1940.[1159]

Child of Fannie Hennings and Kenneth Cook is:

> 705 i. **Ray Harding**[7] **Cook** born April 3, 1941, died April 4, 1941. He is buried at Stony Knoll Meth., East Bend, NC.[1160]

416. Crawlie Ann[6] **Hennings** (Rober Ernest[5], Joseph Manasseh[4], Josiah Tyson[3] Henning, Christian C.[2], John Adam[1]) was born June 27, 1931. She married **Willard Aldean Matthews** on June 20, 1953. He was born April, 1928.[1161]

Children of Crawlie Hennings and Willard Matthews are:

> + 706 i. **Michael Dean**[7] **Matthews** born June 4, 1954.[1162]
>   707 ii. **Timothy Joel Matthews** born Nov. 30, 1956. He married **Linda Tuttle** on Aug. 30, 1980.[1163]

417. Vivian Geraldine[6] **Hoots** (Julia Anna[5] Hennings, Joseph Manasseh[4], Josiah Tyson[3] Henning, Christian C.[2], John Adam[1]) born Dec. 11, 1920. She married **Arthur Lee Googe** on April 7, 1943. He was born Feb. 19, 1919.[1164]

Children of Vivian Hoots and Arthur Googe are:

> + 708 i. **Stephen Lee**[7] **Googe** born Oct. 26, 1946.[1165]
> + 709 ii. **Ann Victoria Googe** born June 6, 1950.[1166]

426. Florence[6] **Hester** (William Hornsby[5], Sarah Ann[4] Phillips, Martha A. E.[3] Henning, Adam[2], John Adam[1]) She married **Elmer Schaefer**.[1167]

Child of Florence Hester and Elmer Schaefer is:

+   710   i.   Mildred Ann[7] Schaefer.[1168]

427. George[6] Hester (William Hornsby[5], Sarah Ann[4] Phillips, Martha A. E.[3] Henning, Adam[2], John Adam[1]) George married **Nancy Hanson** in 1941 in Las Vegas, Nevada. Nancy was the daughter of **Alfred Hanson** and **Alexina Estrom**.[1169]

Children of George Hester and Nancy Hanson are:

+   711   i.   **Nancy Lee[7] Hester** born 1942 in Glendale, CA.[1170]
       712   ii.   **Robert George Hester** born 1945 in Glendale, CA. He married **Suzanne Lisbee** born 1947 in Detroit, MI.[1171]

428. Millard[6] Hester (William Hornsby[5], Sarah Ann[4] Phillips, Martha A. E.[3] Henning, Adam[2], John Adam[1]) born March 11, 1913 in WA, died July 18, 1994 in Seattle, WA.[1172] He married **Marion Dahlstrom**.[1173]

Children of Millard Hester and Marion Dahlstrom are:

       713   i.   **William F.[7] Hester** born 1943. He married **Charlene Gehring**.[1174]
+   714   ii.   **Linnea Hester** born 1946 in Seattle, WA.[1175]

429. Helen[6] Tollett (Dora[5] Hester, Sarah Ann[4] Phillips, Martha A. E.[3] Henning, Adam[2], John Adam[1]) She married **Milford Crowley**.[1176]

Child of Helen Tollett and Milford Crowley is:

       715   i.   **James Crowley** - physician, who had four children.[1177]

430. Clifford⁶ Tollett (Dora⁵ Hester, Sarah Ann⁴ Phillips, Martha A. E.³ Henning, Adam², John Adam¹) was born Dec. 14, 1908 in WA, died July 19, 1991.[1178] He married **Mary Lee Humphrey** on June 8, 1935.[1179]

Children of Clifford Tollett and Mary Humphrey are:

	716	i.	**Richard Mark⁷ Tollett** born March 22, 1936, died March 22, 1936.[1180]
+	717	ii.	**Patricia Ann Tollett** born Dec. 19, 1938.[1181]
+	718	iii.	**Marcus William Tollett** born May 6, 1941.[1182]
+	719	iv.	**Elizabeth Rebecca Tollett** born Sept. 22, 1949.[1183]

434. John⁶ Hester (Sam⁵, Sarah Ann⁴ Phillips, Martha A. E.³ Henning, Adam², John Adam¹) died 1987 in WA. He married **Rose Anna Birdwell**.[1184]

Children of John Hester and Rose Birdwell are:

| 720 | i. | **Roseanna⁷ Hester** born 1942.[1185] |
| 721 | ii. | **Sarah Jane Hester** born 1944.[1186] |

436. Jack⁶ Hester (Sam⁵, Sarah Ann⁴ Phillips, Martha A. E.³ Henning, Adam², John Adam¹) was born 1925. Married **Ruby Edith Radi**.[1187]

Children of Jack Hester and Ruby Radi are:

722	i.	**Chet Wayne⁷ Hester** born 1954.[1188]
723	ii.	**John Brian Hester** born 1957.[1189]
724	iii.	**Sally Ann Hester** born 1960.[1190]

437. Mary Jane⁶ Hester (Sam⁵, Sarah Ann⁴ Phillips, Martha A. E.³ Henning, Adam², John Adam¹) was born in 1926. She married **(1) Carl Crowe**, son of **James Crowe**.

Mary Jane married (2) Monty Austin after 1951.[1191]

Children of Mary Hester and Monty Austin are:

    725   i.   Ann Marie[7] Austin.[1192]
    726   ii.   David Wayne Austin.[1193]

438. Lester[6] Kile, Jr. (Grace[5] Hester, Sarah Ann[4] Phillips, Martha A. E.[3] Henning, Adam[2], John Adam[1]) He married **Virginia Cook.**[1194]

Children of Lester Kile and Virginia Cook are:
    727   i.   Vicky[7] Kile.[1195]
    728   ii.   Larry Kile.[1196]
    729   iii.   Jeannie Kile.[1197]
    730   iv.   Cindy Kile.[1198]

444. Betty Elmira[6] Massengale (George[5], Bettie Jean[4] Phillips, Martha A. E.[3] Henning, Adam[2], John Adam[1]) born 1924 in WA.[1199] She married **Lester Butterfield** born Aug. 7, 1917, died March 3, 1992.[1200]

Children of Betty Massengale and Lester Butterfield are:

    731   i.   **David Bruce[7] Butterfield** born 1948.[1201]
    732   ii.   **Susan Lee Butterfield** born 1950.[1202]
    733   iii.   **James Douglas Butterfield** born 1954.[1203]
    734   iv.   **Lois Janette Butterfield** born 1958.[1204]

445. Delores Jeanette[6] Massengale (George[5], Bettie Jean[4] Phillips, Martha A. E.[3] Henning, Adam[2], John Adam[1]) born 1927 in Rosalia, WA. She married **Berle Brannon.** He was born in Hay, WA.[1205]

Children of Delores Massengale and Berle Brannon are:

+   735   i.   **Margaret Joan[7] Brannon** born 1946.[1206]
+   736   ii.   **Kathleen Brannon** born 1948.[1207]

737   iii.   **Keith Brannon** born 1953.[1208]

446. Mary Iris[6] Franz (Anna[5] Roberts, Iris[4] Henning, Archibald G.[3], Adam[2], John Adam[1]) was born in 1924. Mary served as a Navy WAVE from 1944 to 1947. She married **(1) Bill Bryant** in 1948. He died in 1950. She married **(2) to David Bevers**.[1209]

738   i.   **Denise[7] Bevers** born 1957.[1210]
739   ii.   **Gregory Bevers** born 1959.[1211]

447. Robert Leroy[6] Franz (Anna[5] Roberts, Iris[4] Henning, Archibald G.[3], Adam[2], John Adam[1]) born 1925, died Oct., 1980.[1212] He married **Mary Ann Leinweber**.[1213]

Children of Robert Franz and Mary Leinweber are:

740   i.   **Brian[7] Franz**.[1214]
741   ii.   **Leroy Franz** born 1959.[1215]
742   iii.   **Randall Franz** born 1963.[1216]

448. Wendell[6] Roberts (Edgar[5], Cordelia[4] Henning, Archibald G.[3], Adam[2], John Adam[1]) No date of birth is available, nor is the name of Wendell's wife available.

" . . . entered World War II as a B17 Bomber pilot. He flew 17 missions over Germany before his plane was shot down. He parachuted safely but was captured upon landing and was a prisoner of war for three years until the end of the war. He continued in the Air Force as a career officer and retired with the rank of Major."[1217]

Children of Wendell Roberts are:

743   i.   **Karen E.[7] Roberts** born in 1947.[1218]
744   ii.   **Gary Wendell Roberts** born 1950.[1219]
745   iii.   **Paula Kay Roberts** born 1953.[1220]

449. Max[6] Thomas (Minnie[5] Roberts, Cordelia[4] Henning, Archibald G.[3], Adam[2], John Adam[1]) was born 1922. He married **Bonnie Smith** in 1944.[1221]

Children of Max Thomas and Bonnie Smith are:

+   746   i.   **Kathleen[7] Thomas.**[1222]
         747   ii.   **Gerry Thomas.**[1223]
         748   iii.   **Rae Ann Thomas.**[1224]
         749   iv.   **Kim Susanne Thomas.**[1225]

451. Boyd[6] Thomas (Minnie[5] Roberts, Cordelia[4] Henning, Archibald G.[3], Adam[2], John Adam[1]) was born 1925. He married **Lois Lind**. Boyd and Floyd Thomas are twins. See Floyd Thomas listed below.[1226]

+   750   i.   **Jana Dee[7] Thomas.**[1227]
         751   II.   **Kristi Lee Thomas.**[1228]

452. Floyd[6] Thomas (Minnie[5] Roberts, Cordelia[4] Henning, Archibald G.[3], Adam[2], John Adam[1]) was born 1925. He married **Patricia Prague**. Floyd and Boyd Thomas are twins. See Boyd Thomas listed above.[1229]

Child of Floyd Thomas and Patricia Prague is:

         752   i.   **Kirk David[7] Thomas.**[1230]

453. Jaina[6] Roberts (Clive[5], Cordelia[4] Henning, Archibald G.[3], Adam[2], John Adam[1]) She married **(1) James E. Deasy** in 1949.[1231] She married **(2) Ronald Springer**.[1232]

Children of Jaina Roberts and James Deasy are:

         753   i.   **James Scott[7] Deasy** born 1950.[1233]
         754   ii.   **Kathryn Campbell Deasy** born 1952.[1234]

755   iii.   **Craig Roberts Deasy** born 1955.[1235]

Children of Jaina Roberts and Ronald Springer are:

756   i.   **Elizabeth Rielly**[7] **Springer**. Elizabeth is the twin of Sara Springer listed below.[1236]

757   ii.   **Sara Miller Springer**. Twin of Elizabeth listed above.[1237]

758   iii.   **Ann Marie Springer**.[1238]

759   iv.   **Clive Matthew Springer**.[1239]

455. Roger Steven[6] **Henning** (Ralph Stephen[5], Arvel[4], Archibald G.[3], Adam[2], John Adam[1]) was born March 11, 1942 in Colfax, Whitman Cty., WA. He married **Carolee Neill**.[1240] Roger and Carolee were divorced and remarried in 1995.[1241]

Children of Roger Henning and Carolee Neill are:

760   i.   **Julie Ann**[7] **Henning** born May 23, 1967 in CA. Married **Adam Munson** on Sept. 20, 1997.[1242]

+   761   ii.   **Heidi Lynn Henning** born Oct. 23, 1973 in Spokane, WA.[1243]

762   iii.   **Paul Stephen Henning** born July 13, 1976 in Spokane, WA.[1244]

456. Wayne Leroy[6] **Henning** (Ralph Stephen[5], Arvel[4], Archibald G.[3], Adam[2], John Adam[1]) was born Aug. 15, 1943 in Colfax, Whitman Cty., WA. He married **Christine Louise Skindlov** on Oct. 28, 1972 in Spokane, WA.[1245]

Children of Wayne Henning and Christine Skindlov are:

763   i.   **Steven Wayne**[7] **Henning** born May 5, 1974 in Spokane, WA. He married **Heidi Sutter** on Oct. 17, 1998 in Spokane, WA.[1246]

764 ii. **Anne Louise Henning** born Feb. 3, 1979 in Spokane, WA.[1247]

457. Larry[6] Eastep (Gladys[5] Henning, Arvel[4], Archibald G.[3], Adam[2], John Adam[1]) He married **Connie Ray Ensley**.[1248]

Children of Larry Eastep and Connie Ensley are:

765 i. **Chad[7] Eastep**.[1249]
766 ii. **Lori Eastep**.[1250]
767 iii. **Loni Eastep**.[1251]

459. Charles Edward[6] Pittman (Vena Ann[5] Henning, Julius Adam[4], Santford Ivan[3], Adam[2], John Adam[1]) was born Dec. 29, 1937 in Spokane, WA. He married **Julie Jeanne Painter** on July 27, 1974 at the United Methodist Church, Rosalia, Whitman Cty., WA. Julie is the daughter of **James Painter and Delores Terrell**.[1252]

Children of Charles Pittman and Julie Painter are:

768 i. **Justin Charles[7] Pittman** born May 28, 1977 in Spokane, WA.[1253]
769 ii. **Jessica Charlene Pittman** born Nov. 24, 1983 in Spokane, WA.[1254]

462. Mirene Jean[6] Henning (Clarence Eugene[5], Julius Adam[4], Santford Ivan[3], Adam[2], John Adam[1]) was born 1941 in Ketchikan, Alaska. She married **(1) Thomas M. Vogel II** in 1963. She married **(2) Carl Culp** on April 7, 1990 in Salt Lake City, Utah.[1255]

Children of Mirene Henning and Thomas Vogel are:

+ 770 i. **Eric Richard[7] Vogel** born 1965 in Seattle, WA.[1256]
 771 ii. **Kent Wesley Vogel** born 1969 in Palo Alto, CA.[1257]

463. Robert Scott[6] **Henning** (Clarence Eugene[5], Julius Adam[4], Santford Ivan[3], Adam[2], John Adam[1]) was born 1944 in Seattle, WA. He married **Mary Ann Robblee** in 1970.[1258]

Children of Robert Henning and May Robblee are:

> 772   i.   **Scott Andrew**[7] **Henning** born 1972 in Seattle, WA.[1259]
>
> 773   ii.   **Ann Marie Henning** born 1975.[1260]

464. Sharon Ann[6] **Henning** (Oren Lloyd[5], Julius Adam[4], Santford Ivan[3], Adam[2], John Adam[1]) was born in 1950. She married **Carl Snyder** in June, 1973 in Spokane, WA.[1261]

Children of Sharon Henning and Carl Snyder are:

> 774   i.   **Jeremy**[7] **Snyder.**[1262]
>
> 775   ii.   **Jennifer Snyder.**[1263]
>
> 776   iii.   **Sarah Snyder.**[1264]

466. Michael Garth[6] **Henning** (Oren Lloyd[5], Julius Adam[4], Santford Ivan[3], Adam[2], John Adam[1]) was born 1955. Michael was married in 1977 in Spokane, WA but the name of his wife is unknown.[1265]

Child of Michael Garth Henning is:

> 777   i.   **Ross**[7] **Henning.**[1266]

467. Eugene Augustus[6] **Prince** (Lula Mae[5] Henning, John Thomas[4], Santford Ivan[3], Adam[2], John Adam[1]) was born 1930. He married **(1) Sherry Knittel.** He married **(2) Sherri Pagliare** in 1990.[1267]

Children of Eugene Prince and Sherry Knittel are:

    778   i.   **Stephen Randall[7] Prince**.[1268]
    779   ii.   **Suzanne Prince**.[1269]

468. Hubert Thomas[6] Prince (Lula Mae[5] Henning, John Thomas[4], Santford Ivan[3], Adam[2], John Adam[1]) was born 1934. He married **Donna Deeds**.[1270]

Children of Hubert Prince and Donna Deeds are:

    780   i.   **Russell Burdett[7] Prince**.[1271]
    781   ii.   **Randy Thomas Prince**. He married **Lorinda Hoffman**..[1272]
    782   iii.   **Robert James Prince**.[1273]

469. Arlene Virginia[6] Prince (Lula Mae[5] Henning, John Thomas[4], Santford Ivan[3], Adam[2], John Adam[1]) was born 1936. She married **Raymond Beale**.[1274]

Children of Arlene Prince and Raymond Beale are:

    783   i.   **Loren[7] Beale**.[1275]
    784   ii.   **Matthew Beale**.[1276]

470. Nicholas[6] Henning (James T.[5], John Thomas[4], Santford Ivan[3], Adam[2], John Adam[1]) He married **Sue Stott**.[1277]

Children of Nicholas Henning and Sue Stott are:

    785   i.   **Lisa Lynn[7] Henning**. She married **Jason R. Williams** on July 16, ___ in Las Vegas, Nevada.[1278]
    786   ii.   **Dana Suzann Henning** born April, 1971.[1279]

476. Jerene[6] Appel (Winifred[5] Henning, Fred Henry[4], Santford Ivan[3], Adam[2], John Adam[1]) was born 1940. She married **Elmer Gibbons**.[1280]

Children of Jerene Appel and Elmer Gibbons are:

787   i.   **Dale[7] Gibbons**.[1281]
788   ii.   **Jeanel Gibbons**.[1282]

478. George[6] McGinnis (Geraldine[5] Henning, Fred Henry[4], Santford Ivan[3], Adam[2], John Adam[1]) was born 1942. Married **Marilyn G. King**.[1283]

Children of George McGinnis and Marilyn King are:
789   i.   **Sean Patrick[7] McGinnis** born 1967.[1284]
790   ii.   **Shani Patrice McGinnis** born 1970.[1285]

479. Fred[6] McGinnis (Geraldine[5] Henning, Fred Henry[4], Santford Ivan[3], Adam[2], John Adam[1]) was born in 1947. He married **Patricia Steele**.[1286]

Children of Fred McGinnis and Patricia Steele are:

791   i.   **Sandra Lee[7] McGinnis** born 1970.[1287]
792   ii.   **Brenda Lee McGinnis** born 1973.[1288]

481. Jerry[6] Henning (Boyd[5], Fred Henry[4], Santford Ivan[3], Adam[2], John Adam[1]) He married **Susan Rothenbukler**.[1289]

Children of Jerry Henning and Susan Rothenbukler are:

793   i.   **Sharon[7] Henning**.[1290]
794   ii.   **Carmen Henning**.[1291]
795   iii. **Gerald Boyd Henning**.[1292]

482. Sandee[6] Henning (Duane[5], Fred Henry[4], Santford Ivan[3], Adam[2], John Adam[1]) She married **Randy Porter**.[1293]

Children of Sandee Henning and Randy Porter are:

796	i.	**Amber[7] Porter**.[1294]
797	ii.	**Infant Porter**.[1295]
798	iii.	**Chase Porter** born 1984.[1296]

485. Sharon Lea[6] Berg (Ruth Anna[5] Henning, Daniel Webster[4], Santford Ivan[3], Adam[2], John Adam[1]) was born Oct. 19, 1946 in Spokane, WA. She married **William Bartel** on Aug. 12, 1969 in Spokane, WA.[1297]

Child of Sharon Berg and William Bartel is:
+   799   i.   **Tabitha[7] Bartel** born June 14, 1971.[1298]

486. Rilla Jean[6] Berg (Ruth Anna[5] Henning, Daniel Webster[4], Santford Ivan[3], Adam[2], John Adam[1]) was born July 30, 1953 in Spokane, WA. She married **George Babits** on Jan. 7, 1978 in Oregon.[1299]

Children of Rilla Berg and George Babits are:

800	i.	**Sadie D.[7] Babits** born April 6, 1979.[1300]
801	ii.	**Elizabeth Babits** born May 5, 1980.[1301]

487. Nancy J.[6] Henning (Gene Santford[5], Daniel Webster[4], Santford Ivan[3], Adam[2], John Adam[1]) was born April 8, 1954. She married **Terry Cochran** on Dec. 24, 1989 in Hawaii.[1302]

Children of Nancy Henning and Terry Cochran are:

802	i.	**Maggie[7] Cochran** born Aug. 20, 1992.[1303]
803	ii.	**Benjamin J. Cochran** born Feb. 7, 1994.[1304]

488. Thomas S.[6] Henning (Gene Santford[5], Daniel Webster[4], Santford Ivan[3], Adam[2], John Adam[1]) was born Sept. 27, 1956. He married **Peggy Hill** on April 15, 1978 in Malden, WA. She was the daughter of **Elton Hill** and **Diane Buergel**.[1305]

Children of Thomas Henning and Peggy Hill are:

> 804   i.   **Sara K.[7] Henning** born Aug. 5, 1983 in WA.[1306]
>
> 805   ii.   **Randall Thomas Henning** born Dec. 19, 1986.[1307]

489. Sally Ann[6] Henning (Gene Santford[5], Daniel Webster[4], Santford Ivan[3], Adam[2], John Adam[1]) born Sept. 26, 1963. She married **Gary Hommell** on May 18, 1991 in Malden, WA.[1308]

Children of Sally Henning and Gary Hommell are:

> 806   i.   **Nathan Allen[7] Hommell** born Oct. 9, 1992.[1309]
>
> 807   ii.   **Matthew Joseph Hommell** born Nov. 7, 1995.[1310]

501. Pamela[6] Lund (Anna Lee[5] Hereford, Dora[4] Henning, Santford Ivan[3], Adam[2], John Adam[1]) was born in 1951. She married **Scott Ovenell** in 1971.[1311]

Child of Pamela Lund and Scott Ovenell is:

> 808   i.   **Heidi Kay[7] Ovenell** born 1972.[1312]

506. Ruth Bullard[6] Pearce (Margaret Delilah[5] Bullard, Martha Ophelia[4] Styers, Delilah Louise[3] Henning, Gabriel[2], John Adam[1]) was born Sept. 8, 1905, died Feb. 19, 1940. She married **Cary Basham**.[1313]

Children of Ruth Pearce and Gary Basham are:

> 809 i. **Joe[7] Basham**.[1314]
> 810 ii. **Ruth Basham** died Abt. 1987.[1315]

507. Treva James Franklin[6] Pearce (Margaret Delilah[5] Bullard, Martha Ophelia[4] Styers, Delilah Louise[3] Henning, Gabriel[2], John Adam[1]) was born Nov. 12, 1909, deceased. She married **Ralph Hobson**.[1316]

Children of Treva Pearce and Ralph Hobson are:

> 811 i. **Richard David[7] Hobson** deceased.[1317]
> 812 ii. **Julia Gray Hobson** married **Kelly Ray Jones**.[1318]
> 813 iii. **Margaret Fay Hobson** married **Benjamin Martin**.[1319]

508. Gladys[6] Pearce (Margaret Delilah[5] Bullard, Martha Ophelia[4] Styers, Delilah Louise[3] Henning, Gabriel[2], John Adam[1]) She married **Thorne Cornelius Hartle**. He was born April 10, 1904, died May 2, 1983.[1320]

Children of Gladys Pearce and Thorne Hartle are:

> 814 i. **Pauline Pearce[7] Hartle** born Oct. 31, 1929. Married **Robert Charles Gray**.[1321]
> 815 ii. **Margaret Lona Hartle** born Jan. 8, 1933.[1322]
> 816 iii. **Thorne Cornelius Hartle** born Sept. 25, 1938. She married **James F. Gay III**.[1323]
> 817 iv. **Ruth Louise Hartle** born Jan. 22, 1941. She married **(1) Albert Greene**. She married **(2) Harvey Ayers**.[1324]

509. Laura Ophelia[6] Conrad (Sarah Ethel[5] Bullard, Martha Ophelia[4] Styers, Delilah Louise[3] Henning, Gabriel[2], John Adam[1]) was born May 20, 1905 in NC, died July 22, 1990. She is buried at Calvary

Moravian Church, Forsyth Cty., NC.[1325] Ophelia graduated from Salem College in 1926. She married **C. Burt Fordham** on Oct. 12, 1929. He was born January 9, 1900 in NC, died Feb. 5, 1964 in NC.[1326]

Child of Laura Conrad and Burt Fordham is:

+   818   i.   **Sarah**[7] **Fordham** born Jan. 29, 1936 in NC.[1327]

512. Martha Louise[6] **Bullard** (Nathaniel Graham[5], Martha Ophelia[4] Styers, Delilah Louise[3] Henning, Gabriel[2], John Adam[1]) was born Oct. 16, 1926, died May 26, 1996 in Winston-Salem, NC.[1328] She married **Tommy Mock**. They were later divorced.[1329] Tommy was born Oct. 29, 1925, died July, 1979 in Winston-Salem, NC.[1330]

Children of Martha Bullard and Tommy Mock are:

    819   i.   **Billy**[7] **Mock**.[1331]
    820   ii.   **Bobby Mock**.[1332]

513. Treva Bullard[6] **Miller** (Treva Ophelia[5] Bullard, Martha Ophelia[4] Styers, Delilah Louise[3] Henning, Gabriel[2], John Adam[1]) was born April 9, 1923 in Forsyth Cty., NC, died Aug. 4, 1996 in High Point, NC.[1333] She married **Royal G. Jennings, Jr.** on Oct. 2, 1948. He was the son of **Royal Jennings** and **Nell Hester**. He was born in 1921.[1334]

Children of Treva Miller and Royal Jennings are:

    821   i.   **Jeanne**[7] **Jennings** born Dec. 1, 1951 in New York, NY. She married **Arthur Farrah Tuciser** on Oct. 18, 1975.[1335]
    822   ii.   **Susan Miller Jennings** born Sept. 30, 1954 in High Point, NC. She married **James Edward Vance** on May 8, 1982.[1336]

514. Guy Styers[6] Bullard, Jr. (Guy Styers[5], Martha Ophelia[4] Styers, Delilah Louise[3] Henning, Gabriel[2], John Adam[1]) born Jan. 23, 1916 in NC.[1337] Suffers from diabetes. Married **Dorothy Frances Early** on May 7, 1949. Married by Ralph A. Herring. Witnesses were: Bertha Long, John R. Bullard, and T. A. Early. She was the daughter of **Thomas Early** and **Adelaide Pardee**.[1338] She was born March 15, 1915.[1339] She has suffered from a hearing loss.

+   823   i.   Dorothy Ann[7] Bullard born Feb. 9, 1950.[1340]

      824   ii.   Elizabeth Kay Bullard born June 27, 1952. She married **(1) Mark Hutcherson** in 1976, divorced in 1979. She married **(2) Edward Joseph McCabe, Jr.** on July 5, 1981. She married **(3) Douglas White** on June 6, 1998. Lives in Worchester, MA (1998). [1341]

515. John Robert[6] Bullard (Guy Styers[5], Martha Ophelia[4] Styers, Delilah Louise[3] Henning, Gabriel[2], John Adam[1]) born Jan. 29, 1918 in Petersburg, VA, died April 3, 1998 in Winston-Salem, NC of lung cancer. Suffered from Multiple Sclerosis for many years. He was cremated. Married **Ruth Joye Tuttle** on Jan. 10, 1943 in Winston-Salem, NC. Witnesses were: Nancy Lee Tuttle, Gray Fletcher, and L. V. Scott.[1342] She was born July 25, 1921.[1343]

Children of John Bullard and Ruth Joye Tuttle are:

      825   i.   John Robert[7] Bullard, Jr. born May 14, 1944 in Winston-Salem, NC.[1344] Bobby lives in Morehead City, NC (1998).

      826   ii.   Kent Lee Bullard born May 14, 1950. He married **(1) Cindy Holcomb**. He married **(2) Ann Clark Rollins** on Nov. 17, 1984 in Rockingham, NC. Ann was born April 23, 1950.[1345] Kent lives in Wrightsville Beach, NC (1998).

+   827   iii.   Faye Bullard born July 19, 1955.[1346]

516. Rebecca Estelle⁶ Bullard (Guy Styers⁵, Martha Ophelia⁴ Styers, Delilah Louise³ Henning, Gabriel², John Adam¹) born April 16, 1924 in Forsyth Cty., NC, died Feb. 13, 1976. Suffered from hypertension. Died from an aneurysm. She is buried at Floral Garden Cem., High Point, NC. She married **William Simpson Griffith** on Sept. 23, 1950 at Centenary Meth. Church, Winston-Salem, NC. He was the son of **William Enoch Griffith** and **Orion Simpson**. Bill was born Feb. 14, 1925 in Forsyth Cty., NC, died June 19, 1996. Died of cancer. He is buried at Foral Garden Cem., High Point, NC.[1347]

Child of Rebecca Bullard and William Griffith is:

828   i.   **Lynn Edna⁷ Griffith** born Aug. 11, 1951 in Burlington, Alamance Cty., NC. Married **Michael Ray Ester** on June 17, 1972 at First Baptist Church, Jamestown, NC. Michael was born April 3, 1952 in Elkin, NC. He is the son of **Elmer Ray Ester** and **Inez P. Gentry**.

517. Hoke Vogler⁶ Bullard, Jr. (Hoke Vogler⁵, Martha Ophelia⁴ Styers, Delilah Louise³ Henning, Gabriel², John Adam¹) He married **Mary Jane Shumacher**.[1348]

Children of Hoke Bullard and Mary Shumacher are:

829   i.   **Graham Wesley⁷ Bullard** born Aug. 13, 1955.[1349]
830   ii.   **Margaret Hayden Bullard** born Jan. 15, 1957.[1350]
831   iii. **Hoke Vogler Bullard III** born Mary 17, 1961.[1351]
832   iv.   **Mary Jane Bullard** born Nov. 1, 1962.[1352]

524. Jeffrey Smith⁶ Coltrane (Cora Belle⁵ Smith, Mary Lutency⁴ Styers, Delilah Louise³ Henning, Gabriel², John Adam¹) was born Oct. 2, 1897 in NC, died June 4, 1960. He is buried at Mt. Tabor

Methodist, Forsyth Cty., NC. He married **Sarah Nettie Hendricks** on April 9, 1925 at Pudding Ridge Farm, Cana, VA. Sarah was the daughter of **Melver Hendricks** and **Emma Eaton**. She was born May 13, 1902, died Aug. 23, 1962. She too is buried at Mt. Tabor Meth., Forsyth Cty., NC.[1353]

Children of Jeffrey Coltrane and Sarah Hendricks are:

833	i.	**Emma Bell[7] Coltrane** born March 11, 1926. She married **Harry W. Philpott**.[1354]
834	ii.	**Jeffrey Smith Coltrane, Jr.** born Sept. 19, 1927.[1355]
835	iii.	**Virginia Hall Coltrane** born May 11, 1929. She married **Linneaus F. Mock** in Mt. Tabor Meth. Church, Forsyth Cty., NC. Suffers from Multiple Sclerosis.[1356]
836	iv.	**Helen Eaton Coltrane** born Feb. 25, 1931.[1357]
837	v.	**Sarah Elizabeth Coltrane** born March 27, 1933.[1358]
838	vi.	**William Jackson Coltrane** born April 10, 1935, died Feb. 19, 1977 in Cana, VA. William is buried at Love's Meth. Church, Walkertown, NC. He married **Jean Diane Jones** on Aug. 14, 1964 at Love's Methodist Church.[1359]
839	vii.	**Robert McKinley Coltrane** born March 23, 1941, died Oct. 13, 1969 in San Antonio, TX. Buried at Mt. Tabor Meth., Forsyth Cty., NC. He married **Patricia A. Summitt** on Feb. 14, 1965 at Salem Lutheran Church, Rowan Cty., NC.[1360]

538. Mary Fern[6] Snipes (Thomas C.[5], Lewis Edwin[4], Lauretta Elizabeth[3] Henning, Gabriel[2], John Adam[1]) was born Jan. 2, 1919. She married **Melvin Clapper**.[1361]

Child of Mary Snipes and Melvin Clapper is:

    840   i.   Marilyn Janeen[7] Clapper. She married _____Wilson.[1362]

541. Lewis Franklin[6] Snipes (Thomas C.[5], Lewis Edwin[4], Lauretta Elizabeth[3] Henning, Gabriel[2], John Adam[1]) was born Dec. 21, 1923 in Tipton County, IN, died May 26, 1977 in Kokomo, IN. He married **June E. Lacy** on Aug. 14, 1943.[1363]

Children of Lewis Snipes and June Lacy are:

    841   i.   Ron[7] Snipes.[1364]
    842   ii.   Randy Snipes.[1365]
    843   iii.   Lynn Ann Snipes. She married Philip Miller.[1366]
    844   iv.   Anita Snipes. She married Bruce Chalk.[1367]
    845   v.   Sandra Snipes. She married Kenneth Totten.[1368]
    846   vi.   Teena Snipes.[1369]

547. Ebon Lewis[6] Hill (Ethel Rosetta[5] Snipes, Lewis Edwin[4], Lauretta Elizabeth[3] Henning, Gabriel[2], John Adam[1]) was born Sept. 2, 1909 in Boone Cty., IN, died Feb. 12, 1963. He married **Margaret K. Mascoe.**[1370]

Children of Ebon Hill and Margaret Mascoe are:

    847   i.   Ebon Lewis[7] Hill, Jr.[1371]
    848   ii.   Robert Earl Hill.[1372]
    849   iii.   Richard Lee Hill.[1373]
    850   iv.   Wanda Lucille Hill born 1936.[1374]

549. Winston Keith[6] Hill (Ethel Rosetta[5] Snipes, Lewis Edwin[4], Lauretta Elizabeth[3] Henning, Gabriel[2], John Adam[1]) was born Oct. 19, 1913 in Boone Cty., IN, died Oct. 9, 1989 in Noblesville, IN.

He married **Lucille M. Mascoe** on Aug. 1, 1936.[1375]

Children of Winston Hill and Lucille Mascoe are:

851   i.   **Gordon K.**[7] **Hill.**[1376]
852   ii.   **Gerald George Hill.** Married **Phronica Patterson.**[1377]
853   iii. **Judith Ann Hill.** She married ____ Smith.[1378]
854   iv. **Karen Sue Hill.** She married ____ Swinford.[1379]

550. Wilfred Sellers[6] **Hill** (Ethel Rosetta[5] Snipes, Lewis Edwin[4], Lauretta Elizabeth[3] Henning, Gabriel[2], John Adam[1]) was born Feb. 19, 1918 in IN, died March, 1969.[1380] He married **Lucille Doyle.**[1381]

Children of Wilfred Hill and Lucille Doyle are:

855   i.   **Harold**[7] **Hill.**[1382]
856   ii.   **Michael Lee Hill.**[1383]
857   iii. **Dennis Hill.**[1384]
858   iv. **Steven Hill.**[1385]
859   v.   **Robert Hill.**[1386]

552. Leolin Benjamin[6] **Hill** (Ethel Rosetta[5] Snipes, Lewis Edwin[4], Lauretta Elizabeth[3] Henning, Gabriel[2], John Adam[1]) was born July 30, 1922 in IN, died March 16, 1995 in FL. He married **Doris Rusk** in Oct., 1949.[1387]

Children of Leolin Hill and Doris Ruck are:

860   i.   **Douglas Lee**[7] **Hill** born May, 1950.[1388]
861   ii.   **Kevin J. Hill** born Jan. 23, 1952.[1389]

553. Mescal L.[6] **Hill** (Ethel Rosetta[5] Snipes, Lewis Edwin[4], Lauretta Elizabeth[3] Henning, Gabriel[2], John Adam[1]) was born Aug. 25, 1924 in Elwood, Madison Cty., IN, died April 28, 1985 in Lafayette,

IN. She married **Wilbur Andrew Pendleton** on July 5, 1947 in Lafayette, IN. He was the son of **George Pendleton** and **Alva Ritchie**. He was born June 11, 1921 in Tippecanoe Cty., IN, died April, 1992 in Tippecanoe Cty., IN. He served in World War II in the 94th Division.[1390]

Children of Mescal Hill and Wilbur Pendleton are:

+   862   i.   **Diane Sue**[7] **Pendleton** born March 19, 1950 in Lafayette, Tippecanoe Cty., IN.[1391]
+   863   ii.   **David Andrew Pendleton** born July 6, 1952 in Lafayette, Tippecanoe Cty., IN.[1392]
+   864   iii.   **Darlene Kay Pendleton** born Sept. 21, 1955 in Lafayette, Tippecanoe Cty., IN.[1393]

Generation No. 7

556. Georgia Marie[7] **Conrad** (Mildred Marie[6] Fulp, Mattie Beatrice[5] Cline, Charles Christian[4], Peter Solomon[3], Mary Anna[2] Henning, John Adam[1]) was born Oct. 30, 1946. She married **Thomas Willard Mahon** on July 11, 1964 in Forsyth Cty., NC.[1394]

Child of Georgia Conrad and Thomas Mahon is:

    865   i.   **Infant**[8] **Mahon** born Feb. 11, 1954.[1395]

561. Martha Kay[7] **Fulp** (Herman Glenn[6] Fulk, Mattie Beatrice[5] Cline, Charles Christian[4], Peter Solomon[3], Mary Anna[2] Henning, John Adam[1]) born Jan. 7, 1938 in Winston-Salem, NC. She married **Cuthbert Toso Hauser, Jr.** on June 15, 1957 in Bethania, NC. He was the son of **Cuthbert Hauser** and **Mattie Ziglar**.[1396] Cuthbert Toso Hauser, Jr. was born Jan. 9, 1937, died Aug., 1969.[1397] See notes about name change (Fulk & Fulp) under Herman Glenn Fulk, Sr.

Children of Martha Fulp and Cuthbert Hauser are :

+   866   i.   **Rodney Toso**[8] **Hauser** born March 18, 1958 in Winston-Salem, NC.[1398]

    867   ii.   **Rhonda Kay Hauser** born March 30, 1962 in Winston-Salem, NC. She married **Timothy Monore Navy** on March 23, 1997 in Kernersville, NC.[1399]

562. Herman Glenn[7] **Fulp, Jr.** (Herman Glenn[6] Fulk, Mattie Beatrice[5] Cline, Charles Christian[4], Peter Solomon[3], Mary Anna[2] Henning, John Adam[1]) was born July 27, 1941 in Winston-Salem, NC. He married (1) **Rebecca Caudle** Abt. 1965. He married (2) **Kathy Meisenheimer** in 1974. He married (3) **Jackie Cheek** on Dec. 31, 1987 in Wake Cty., NC.[1400]

Child of Herman Fulp and Rebecca Caudle are:

    868   i.   **Lisa Fulp** was born Aug. 21, 1967.[1401]

Children of Herman Fulp and Kathy Meisenheimer are:

    869   i.   **David Glenn**[8] **Fulk** born April 20, 1977.[1402]
    870   ii.   **Michael Glenn Fulk** born Oct. 25, 1980.[1403]

Note: Numbers 871 & 872 are being omitted.

565. Linda Gayle[7] **Arton** (Nellie Larue[6] Cline, Raymond Arthur[5], Pleas David[4], Eli[3], Mary Anna[2] Henning, John Adam[1]) was born Sept. 24, 1942. She married **Kent Jones**.[1404]

Children of Linda Arton and Kent Jones are:

    873   i.   **Paige**[8] **Jones**.[1405]
    874   ii.   **April Jones**.[1406]
    875   iii.   **Carter Jones**.[1407]

566. Olivia deAnn[7] Arton (Nellie Larue[6] Cline, Raymond Arthur[5], Pleas David[4], Eli[3], Mary Anna[2] Henning, John Adam[1]) was born Aug. 22, 1945. She married **Frank Smithdeal III**. They were later divorced.[1408]

Child of Olivia Arton and Frank Smithdeal is:

    876   i.   Ashley[8] Smithdeal.[1409]

567. Marion Sue[7] Arton (Nellie Larue[6] Cline, Raymond Arthur[5], Pleas David[4], Eli[3], Mary Anna[2] Henning, John Adam[1]) was born Aug. 30, 1946. She married **(1) Jerry Boyles**. She married **(2) Clay Jones**.[1410]

Children of Marion Arton and Jerry Boyles are:

    877   i.   **Jennifer[8] Boyles.**[1411]
    878   ii.   **Chris Boyles.**[1412]

568. Louis Michael[7] Arton (Nellie Larue[6] Cline, Raymond Arthur[5], Pleas David[4], Eli[3], Mary Anna[2] Henning, John Adam[1]) was born July 31, 1948. He married **(1) Nancy Bruce**. He married **(2) Claudia Busic**.[1413]

    879   i.   **Jamie[8] Arton.**[1414]
    880   ii.   **Andrew Arton.**[1415]

571. Susan Irene[7] Cline (Raymond Arthur[6], Raymond Arthur[5], Pleas David[4], Eli[3], Mary Anna[2] Henning, John Adam[1]) born Nov. 24, 1949. She married **(1) Terry Jolly**. She married **(2) Richard Furches**.[1416]

Children of Susan Cline and Richard Furches are:

    881   i.   **Randall[8] Furches.**[1417]
    882   ii.   **Brian Furches.**[1418]

883   iii.   Derrick Furches.[1419]

573. Phyllis Ann[7] Aulozzi (Phyllis Kathleen[6] Cline, Raymond Arthur[5], Pleas David[4], Eli[3], Mary Anna[2] Henning, John Adam[1]) was born Feb. 5, 1947 in Kenosha Cty., Wisconsin. She married **(1) Robert Leroy Bowker.** She married **(2) Stewart Holcomb.**[1420]

Children of Phyllis Aulozzi and Robert Bowker are:

888   i.   **Tamara[8] Bowker.**[1421]
885   ii.   **Carolyn Bowker.**[1422]

574. James Thomas[7] Aulozzi (Phyllis Kathleen[6] Cline, Raymond Arthur[5], Pleas David[4], Eli[3], Mary Anna[2] Henning, John Adam[1]) was born Feb. 6, 1949. He married **Pam Rosko.**[1423]

Children of James Aulozzi and Pam Rosko are:

886   i.   **Felix[8] Aulozzi.**[1424]
887   ii.   **Jenny Aulozzi.**[1425]

575. Renee Marie[7] Aulozzi (Phyllis Kathleen[6] Cline, Raymond Arthur[5], Pleas David[4], Eli[3], Mary Anna[2] Henning, John Adam[1]) was born Sept. 2, 1952. She married **Daniel Boring.**[1426]

Children of Renee Aulozzi and Daniel Boring are:

888   i.   **Danielle[8] Boring.**[1427]
889   ii.   **Deanna Boring.**[1428]

576. David Louis[7] Aulozzi (Phyllis Kathleen[6] Cline, Raymond Arthur[5], Pleas David[4], Eli[3], Mary Anna[2] Henning, John Adam[1]) born April 12, 1955. He married **Sue Suchorda.**[1429]

Children of David Aulozzi and Sue Suchorda are:

> 890 i. Ginelle[8] Aulozzi.[1430]
> 891 ii. Amber Aulozzi.[1431]

577. Theresa Lynn[7] Aulozzi (Phyllis Kathleen[6] Cline, Raymond Arthur[5], Pleas David[4], Eli[3], Mary Anna[2] Henning, John Adam[1]) was born March 10, 1957. she married **James Tabbert**.[1432]

Children of Theresa Aulozzi and James Tabbert are:

> 892 i. Jami[8] Tabbert.[1433]
> 893 ii. Jeremy Tabbert.[1434]
> 894 iii. Gina Tabbert.[1435]

578. Kathy Diane[7] Aulozzi (Phyllis Kathleen[6] Cline, Raymond Arthur[5], Pleas David[4], Eli[3], Mary Anna[2] Henning, John Adam[1]) was born July 23, 1960. She married **Rick Antes**. They were later divorced.[1436]

Children of Kathy Aulozzi and Rick Antes are:
> 895 i. Moriah[8] Antes.[1437]
> 896 ii. Nicholas Antes.[1438]
> 897 iii. Adam Antes.[1439]

580. Steven Robert[7] Henning (Robert Edward Lee[6], John Kenyon[4], Amanda Sarah[3], Christian C.[2], John Adam[1]) was born Sept. 10, 1954 in Winston-Salem, NC. He married **Deborah Rutter** in St. Thomas, Ontario, Canada. Deborah was born Dec. 5, ____ in Ontario, Canada.[1440]

Child of Steven Henning and Deborah Rutter is:

> 898 i. **Brett Skyler[8] Henning** born Oct. 19, 1983 in Baltimore, MD.[1441]

581. Bruce Davis[7] Henning (Robert Edward Lee[6], John Kenyon[4], Amanda Sarah[3], Christian C.[2], John Adam[1]) was born Feb. 11, 1958 in Richmond, VA. He married **Dianne Virginia Wallace** on Aug. 16, 1986 in Raleigh, NC. She is the daughter of **Charles Wallace** and **Helen McCranie**. She was born July 15, 1960 in Chapel Hill, NC.[1442]

Child of Bruce Henning and Dianne Wallace is:

> 899   i.   **Sarah Stewart[8] Henning** born April 27, 1989 in Charlotte, NC.[1443]

583. Nancy Lee[7] Calloway (Grace Gladys[6] Henning, Arthur Benbow[5], William Turner[4] Hennings, Josiah Tyson[3] Henning, Christian C.[2], John Adam[1]) was born Dec. 7, 1943. She married **(1) Steve Blanchard**. She married **(2) Dr. Rickey L. Snipe**.[1444]

Children of Nancy Calloway and Steven Blanchard are:

> 900   i.   **Steve Michael[8] Blanchard** born July 26, 1966.[1445]
> 901   ii. **Shannon Blanchard** born May 15, 1969.[1446]

586. Linda[7] Henning (William Arthur[6], Arthur Benbow[5], William Turner[4] Hennings, Josiah Tyson[3] Henning, Christian C.[2], John Adam[1]) She married **Billy Moore**.[1447]

Children of Linda Henning and Billy Moore are:

> 902   i.   **James[8] Moore**. He married **Kristie ____**.[1448]
> 903   ii. **Cheri Moore**.[1449]

587. Phyllis[7] Henning (William Arthur[6], Arthur Benbow[5], William Turner[4] Hennings, Josiah Tyson[3] Henning, Christian C.[2], John Adam[1]) She married **Charles R. Loehr**.[1450]

Children of Phyllis Henning and Charles Loehr are:

     904   i.   **Stephanie[8] Loehr.**[1451]
     905   ii.   **Daniel Loehr.**[1452]

588. William Richard[7] Henning (William Arthur[6], Arthur Benbow[5], William Turner[4] Hennings, Josiah Tyson[3] Henning, Christian C.[2], John Adam[1]) He married **Peggy** _____.[1453]

Child of William Henning and Peggy is:

     906   i.   **Taylor[8] Henning.**[1454]

589. Eddie[7] Oliver (Dorothy Virginia[6] Henning, Arthur Benbow[5], William Turner[4] Hennings, Josiah Tyson[3] Henning, Christian C.[2], John Adam[1]) He married **Sylvia** _____.[1455]

Child of Eddie Oliver and Sylvia is:

     907.   i.   **Katie[8] Oliver.**[1456]

592. Mark[7] Armstrong (Myrtle Louise[6] Henning, Arthur Benbow[5], William Turner[4] Hennings, Josiah Tyson[3] Henning, Christian C.[2], John Adam[1]) He married **(1) Denise Davis.** He married **(2) Andrea Burchette** on May 22, 1993.[1457]

Children of Mark Armstrong and Denise Davis are:

     908   i.   **Jonathan David[8] Armstrong** born Jan. 3, 1984.[1458]
     909   ii.   **Jayna Christine Armstrong** born March 1, 1986.[1459]

Child of Mark Armstrong and Andrea Burchette is:

910   i.   **Kayla Michelle**[8] Armstrong born Aug. 21, 1997.[1460]

594. Emily Ruth[7] **Hennings** (Grady Laster[6], Mirtie Lee[5] Henning, William Turner[4] Hennings, Josiah Tyson[3] Henning, Christian C.[2], John Adam[1]) was born Dec. 13, 1926 in East Bend, Yadkin Cty., NC. She married **Glendon Elbert Wooten** on July 4, 1948 in Yadkin Cty., NC. He was born June 22, 1927 in Yadkin Cty., NC.[1461]

Children of Emily Hennings and Glendon Wooten are:

+   911   i.   **Emily Carol**[8] **Wooten** born April 12, 1950 in Winston-Salem, NC.[1462]

      912   ii.   **Anne Wilmoth Wooten** born July 9, 1951 in Winston-Salem, NC. She married **James J. Teeling III** on June 19, 1993 in Christ the King Catholic Church, Dallas, TX. James was born May 5, 1944 in Dallas, TX.[1463]

+   913   iii. **Mark Elbert Wooten** born May 25, 1956 in Winston-Salem, NC.[1464]

+   914   iv. **Sarah Vanna Wooten** born Dec. 12, 1957 in Winston-Salem, NC.[1465]

      915   v.   **Glenda Sue Wooten** born July 31, 1960 in Winston-Salem, NC.[1466]

595. Paul Eugene[7] **Hennings** (Grady Laster[6], Mirtie Lee[5] Henning, William Turner[4] Hennings, Josiah Tyson[3] Henning, Christian C.[2], John Adam[1]) was born Dec. 3, 1930 in East Bend, Yadkin Cty., NC. Retired Air Force Major. He married **Norma Jean Kelley** on Aug. 22, 1953. She was born May 19, 1935.[1467]

Children of Paul Hennings and Norma Kelley are:

> 916   i.   **Stephen Paul**[8] **Hennings** born Feb. 11, 1956.[1468]
>
> \+   917   ii.   **Brian David Hennings** born May 17, 1959 in Okinawa, Japan.[1469]
>
> 918   iii.   **Joel Kelley Hennings** born Jan. 27, 1963.[1470]

596. Grady Lee[7] **Hennings** (Grady Laster[6], Mirtie Lee[5] Henning, William Turner[4] Hennings, Josiah Tyson[3] Henning, Christian C.[2], John Adam[1]) was born Jan. 1, 1933in East Bend, NC. Served in the Korean Conflict. He married **Jan M. Myers** on March 30, 1956. She was the daughter of **Howard Myers** and **Josephine H.** Jan was born Feb. 2, 1935.[1471]

Children of Grady Hennings and Jan Myers are:

> \+   919   i.   **Russell Myers**[8] **Hennings** born June 20, 1958.[1472]
>
> 920   ii.   **Stephanie Leigh Hennings** born April 20, 1968.[1473]

597. Alvis Ray[7] **Hennings** (Grady Laster[6], Mirtie Lee[5] Henning, William Turner[4] Hennings, Josiah Tyson[3] Henning, Christian C.[2], John Adam[1]) was born April 14, 1935in East Bend, NC. He married **Luzana Jane Brown** on July 14, 1956. She was the daughter of **Austin Brown** and **Molly Styers.** She was born April 23, 1937 in Yadkin Cty., NC.[1474]

Children of Alvis Hennings and Luzana Brown are:

> \+   921   i.   **Karen Renee**[8] **Hennings** born July 17, 1958.[1475]
>
> 922   ii.   **Brockton Ray Hennings** born Aug. 27, 1969 in Forsyth Cty., NC. He married **Ginger Diane Evans** on Dec. 3, 1994 in Deep Creek Baptist

Church, Yadkin Cty., NC. Ginger was born
Nov. 18, 1969 in Forsyth Cty., NC.[1476]

598. Joe Bennett[7] Hennings (Grady Laster[6], Mirtie Lee[5] Henning,
William Turner[4] Hennings, Josiah Tyson[3] Henning, Christian C.[2], John
Adam[1]) was born July 29, 1937 in East Bend, NC. He married **Marie
Annette Brown** on April 13, 1957 at Union Cross Friends Church,
Yadkin Cty., NC. She is the daughter of **Austin Brown** and **Molly
Styers**.[1477]

Children of Joe Hennings and Marie Brown are:

+   923   i.   **Kevin Bennett[8] Hennings** born Sept. 10, 1960
                         in Winston-Salem, NC.[1478]
+   924   ii.   **Joe Barrett Hennings** born Jan. 13, 1962 in
                         Winston-Salem, NC.[1479]
+   925   iii.   **Darren Zell Hennings** born March 19, 1965 in
                         Winston-Salem, NC.[1480]
+   926   iv.   **Brittley L. Hennings** born Aug. 26, 1969 in
                         Winston-Salem, NC.[1481]

599. Ruby Carol[7] Hennings (Grady Laster[6], Mirtie Lee[5] Henning,
William Turner[4] Hennings, Josiah Tyson[3] Henning, Christian C.[2], John
Adam[1]) was born Jan. 6, 1941 in East Bend, NC. She married **Richard
Lee Murphy** on Feb. 6, 1960 in East Bend, NC. He was the son of
William Murphy and **Hazel Jane ____**. He was born Dec. 25, 1937
in East Bend, NC.[1482]

Children of Ruby Hennings and Richard Murphy are:

+   927   i.   **Jennifer Carol[8] Murphy** born Nov. 10, 1960
                         in Winston-Salem, NC.[1483]
+   928   ii.   **Heather Leigh Murphy** born Jan. 3, 1973 in
                         Winston-Salem, NC.[1484]

611. Marilea[7] Adams (John Howard[6], Lela Greene[5] Henning, William Turner[4] Hennings, Josiah Tyson[3] Henning, Christian C.[2], John Adam[1]) was born Jan. 22, ____. She married **L. Gordon Heflin**.[1485]

Children of Marilea Adams and L. Gordon Heflin are:

> 929   i.   **Vincent Wayen[8] Heflin**.[1486]
> 930   ii.   **Leanna Heflin**.[1487]
> 931   iii.   **Kelly Heflin**.[1488]

612. Joe Wesley[7] Choplin (Irene Hope[6] Adams, Lela Greene[5] Henning, William Turner[4] Hennings, Josiah Tyson[3] Henning, Christian C.[2], John Adam[1]) was born April 7, 1937 in East Bend, NC. He married **Roxie Olivia Collins** on Dec. 11, 1955 at Lee Memorial Presbyterian Church, Winston-Salem, NC. She was the daughter of **Herman Collins** and **Wilma Masten**. Roxie was born Jan. 14, 1937.[1489]

Children of Joe Choplin and Roxie Collins are:

> 932   i.   **Keith Darwin[8] Choplin** born Jan. 20, 1957 in Winston-Salem, NC. He married **Lou Ann Spell** on Sept. 19, 1976 at Reynolda Presbyterian Church, Winston-Salem, NC. Lou Ann was born July ____.[1490]
> 933   ii.   **William Herman Choplin** born May 14, 1958 in Winston-Salem, NC. He married **Carol Jean Doepper** on Oct. 20, 1979 at Holy Cross Lutheran Church, Commack, NY.[1491]
> + 934   iii.   **Tamala Dawn Choplin** born Dec. 26, 1961 in Winston-Salem, NC.[1492]
> 935   iv.   **Christopher Wayne Choplin** born Nov. 10, 1963 in Winston-Salem, NC.[1493]

613. Carol Jean[7] Choplin (Irene Hope[6] Adams, Lela Greene[5] Henning, William Turner[4] Hennings, Josiah Tyson[3] Henning, Christian

C.[2], John Adam[1]) was born Feb. 15, 1939 in East Bend, NC. She married **David Paul McDuffie, Jr.** on Feb. 28, 1957 at Griffith Baptist Church, Forsyth Cty., NC. He was the son of **David McDuffie** and **Esta Edwards**. David, Jr. was born Aug. 28, 1938 in Red Springs, Robeson Cty., NC.[1494]

Children of Carol Choplin and David McDuffie are:

+ 936   i.   **Kerry David[8] McDuffie** born May 30, 1958 in Lake Charles, LA.[1495]

  937   ii.   **Lynn Carol McDuffie** born July 9, 1962 in Winston-Salem, NC.[1496]

614. Dennis Wade[7] Choplin (Irene Hope[6] Adams, Lela Greene[5] Henning, William Turner[4] Hennings, Josiah Tyson[3] Henning, Christian C.[2], John Adam[1]) was born Sept. 21, 1940 in East Bend, NC. He married **Margaret Louise Weidner** on March 13, 1961 in High Point, NC. She was the daughter of **Orville Weidner** and **Nellie Shears**. Margaret was born Nov. 22, 1941.[1497]

Children of Dennis Choplin and Margaret Weidner are:

  938   i.   **Michael Lynn[8] Choplin** born Oct. 19, 1961.[1498]

  939   ii.   **Denise Jean Choplin** born Oct. 16, 1962. She married **Mark Lee Vogt** on June 23, 1984. Mark was born Oct. 13, 196_.[1499]

  940   iii.   **Mark Allen Choplin** born May 26, 1967.[1500]

615. Charles Edward[7] Choplin (Irene Hope[6] Adams, Lela Greene[5] Henning, William Turner[4] Hennings, Josiah Tyson[3] Henning, Christian C.[2], John Adam[1]) was born Sept. 20, 1942 in Winston-Salem, NC. He married **Barbara Anne Bowen** on Oct. 23, 1964 at First Alliance Church Parsonage, Winston-Salem, NC. She was the daughter of **Fred Bowen** and **Margaret Myers**. Barbara was born Feb. 3, 1947.[1501]

Children of Charles Choplin and Barbara Bowden are:

      941   i.   Scott Allen[8] Choplin born Dec. 3, 1968.[1502]

      942   ii.   Jennifer Paige Choplin born Jan. 5, 1978.[1503]

617. James Monroe[7] Taylor (Jessie Pearl[6] Adams, Lela Greene[5] Henning, William Turner[4] Hennings, Josiah Tyson[3] Henning, Christian C.[2], John Adam[1]) was born June 22, 1947. He married **Debra Joe Atkins** on May 14, 1972. She was the daughter of **Gene Atkins** and **Ruth Burger**. Debra was born Jan. 28, 1952.[1504]

Children of James Taylor and Debra Atkins are:

      943   i.   **James Chad[8] Taylor** born Jan. 5, 1973.[1505]

      944   ii.   **William Luke Taylor** born May 13, 1975.[1506]

620. Polly Ann[7] Smitherman (Robert Benbow[6], Ila Ladrone[5] Henning, William Turner[4] Hennings, Josiah Tyson[3] Henning, Christian C.[2], John Adam[1]) She married **(1) Thomas E. Crews, Sr.** She married **(2) Gene Dudley**.[1507]

Children of Polly Smitherman and Thomas Crews are:

+   945   i.   **Melinda[8] Crews**.[1508]

+   946   ii.   **Jeff Crews**.[1509]

      947   iii.   **Lynn Crews**.[1510]

+   948   iv.   **Bo Crews**.[1511]

+   949   v.   **Thomas E. Crews, Jr.**.[1512]

621. Allen Benbow[7] Smitherman (Robert Benbow[6], Ila Ladrone[5] Henning, William Turner[4] Hennings, Josiah Tyson[3] Henning, Christian C.[2], John Adam[1]) He married **Wanda Flynn**.[1513]

Children of Allen Smitherman and Wanda Flynn are:

      950   i.   **Shawn[8] Smitherman**.[1514]

951   ii.   **Shannon Smitherman.** She married ____
Gentry.[1515]

623. Howard Thomas[7] **Smitherman** (Robert Benbow[6], Ila
Ladrone[5] Henning, William Turner[4] Hennings, Josiah Tyson[3] Henning,
Christian C.[2], John Adam[1]) He married **Jenny Blankenship.**[1516]

Children of Howard Smitherman and Jenny Blankenship are:

952   i.   **Daniel**[8] **Smitherman.**[1517]
953   ii.   **Jessica Smitherman.**[1518]
954   iii.   **Kara Smitherman.**[1519]

625. Robert Burgess[7] **Smitherman** (Willie Jennings[6], Ila Ladrone[5]
Henning, William Turner[4] Hennings, Josiah Tyson[3] Henning, Christian
C.[2], John Adam[1])

Children of Robert Burgess Smitherman are:

+   955   i.   **Marty**[8] **Smitherman.**[1520]
+   956   ii.   **Penny Smitherman.**[1521]

626. Kirby Jennings[7] **Smitherman** (Willie Jennings[6], Ila Ladrone[5]
Henning, William Turner[4] Hennings, Josiah Tyson[3] Henning, Christian
C.[2], John Adam[1])

Children of Kirby Jennings Smitherman are:

957   i.   **Jody**[8] **Smitherman.**[1522]
958   ii.   **Jason Smitherman.**[1523]

629. Mitchell[7] **Van Collins** (Betty Rose[6] Smitherman, Ila Ladrone[5]
Henning, William Turner[4] Hennings, Josiah Tyson[3] Henning, Christian
C.[2], John Adam[1])

Child of Mitchell Van Collins is:

    959   i.   **Katie Rose[8] Collins**.[1524]

630. Janice[7] Hennings (Clarence Norman[6], William Joseph[5], William Turner[4] Hennings, Josiah Tyson[3] Henning, Christian C.[2], John Adam[1]) She married **William Craig**.[1525]

Children of Janice Hennings and William Craig are:

    960   i.   **Amy[8] Craig**.[1526]
    961   ii.   **Christopher Craig**.[1527]
    962   iii.   **Bradley Craig**.[1528]

631. Connie[7] Hennings (Clarence Norman[6], William Joseph[5], William Turner[4] Hennings, Josiah Tyson[3] Henning, Christian C.[2], John Adam[1]) She married **Jerry Runyon**.[1529]

Child of Connie Hennings and Jerry Runyon is:

    963   i.   **Karen[8] Runyon**[1530]

632. Tony[7] Green (Margie[6] Hennings, William Joseph[5], William Turner[4] Hennings, Josiah Tyson[3] Henning, Christian C.[2], John Adam[1]) was born Feb. 25, 1947. He married **Barbara Gough**.[1531]

Children of Tony Green and Barbara Gough are:

    964   i.   **Paula[8] Green** born Dec. 30, 1972.[1532]
    965   ii.   **Jason Green** born Dec. 29, 1975.[1533]

633. Michael[7] Green (Margie[6] Hennings, William Joseph[5], William Turner[4] Hennings, Josiah Tyson[3] Henning, Christian C.[2], John Adam[1]) was born April 7, 1951. He married **Debra Snyder**.[1534]

Children of Michael Green and Debra Snyder are:

    966   i.   April[8] Green born Sept. 15, 1972.[1535]
    967   ii.   Tara Green born June 23, 1976.[1536]

641. Lisa Ann[7] Hennings (James Tyson[6], Emily Blanche[5], William Turner[4] Hennings, Josiah Tyson[3] Henning, Christian C.[2], John Adam[1]) was born April 30, 1959. She married **Raymond J. Spillane** on Aug. 11, 1979.[1537]

Child of Lisa Hennings and Raymond Spillane is:

    968   i.   **Shannon Nicolle[8] Spillane** born Nov. 24, 1992.[1538]

645. Martha Gail[7] Bray (Ruby Gail[6] Cornelius, Emily Blanche[5], William Turner[4] Hennings, Josiah Tyson[3] Henning, Christian C.[2], John Adam[1]) was born March 20, 1957. She married **Daniel Peddycord** on June 24, 1977. Daniel and Martha were divorced in 1993.[1539]

Children of Martha Bray and Daniel Peddycord are:

    969   i.   **Lauren Elizabeth[8] Peddycord** born March 28, 1983.[1540]
    970   ii.   **Travis Carroll Peddycord** born June 15, 1986.[1541]

646. Ashley Forrest[7] Bray (Ruby Gail[6] Cornelius, Emily Blanche[5], William Turner[4] Hennings, Josiah Tyson[3] Henning, Christian C.[2], John Adam[1]) was born June 28, 1958. He married **Linda Bates** on June 1, 1985 in Holland, Michigan.[1542]

Children of Ashley Bray and Linda Bates are:
    971   i.   **William Benjamin[8] Bates** born Aug. 31, 1986.[1543]

972 ii.   Meredith Ashley Bates born Nov. 21, 1990.[1544]

649. Thomas Wayne[7] Hennings (John Thomas[6], John Franklin[5] Henning, Lewis Hiram[4] Hennings, Josiah Tyson[3] Henning, Christian C.[2], John Adam[1]) was born May 6, 1946. He married **Betty Fulk**.[1545]

Children of Thomas Hennings and Betty Fulk are:

973 i.   **Cindy Leann[8] Hennings** born March 20, 1970.[1546]

974 ii.   **Jeffrey Wayne Hennings** born March 23, 1977.[1547]

975 iii.   **Christie Nichole Hennings** born May 19, 1978.[1548]

656. Shelby[7] Pilcher (William Ralph[6], Emma[5] Hennings, Lewis Hiram[4] Hennings, Josiah Tyson[3] Henning, Christian C.[2], John Adam[1]) was born Sept. 25, 1944. She married **Wayne Johnson** in Feb., 1963.[1549]

Child of Shelby Pilcher and Wayne Johnson is:

976 i.   **Adrian Keith[8] Johnson** born July 6, 1972.[1550]

657. Allen Wayne[7] Pilcher (William Ralph[6], Emma[5] Hennings, Lewis Hiram[4] Hennings, Josiah Tyson[3] Henning, Christian C.[2], John Adam[1]) was born July 9, 1948.[1551] He married **Debra Ann Billings** on May 8, 1976. Debra was born July 27, 1954.[1552]

Children of Allen Pilcher and Debra Billings are:

977 i.   **Candace Lee[8] Pilcher** born Nov. 17, 1978.[1553]

978 ii.   **Justin Wayne Pilcher** born Dec. 10, 1981.[1554]

668. Charles Ray[7] Hampton (Martha Inez[6] Pilcher, Emma[5] Hennings, Lewis Hiram[4] Hennings, Josiah Tyson[3] Henning, Christian

C.[2], John Adam[1]) was born Feb. 23, 1964.[1555] Hew married **Heather Bossi** on Oct. 13, 1990. She was born Sept. 24, 1968.[1556]

Children of Charles Hampton and Heather Bossi are:

979 i. **Kevin Ray[8] Hampton** born Sept. 29, 1992.[1557]
980 ii **Charity Faith Hampton** born July 13, 1995.[1558]

669. James Vernon[7] Johnson (Martha Inez[6] Pilcher, Emma[5] Hennings, Lewis Hiram[4] Hennings, Josiah Tyson[3] Henning, Christian C.[2], John Adam[1]) was born May 8, 1960.[1559]

Child of James Vernon Johnson is:

981 i. **Lindsay Nichole[8] Johnson** born July 9, 1989.[1560]

670. Lartha Lynn[7] Johnson (Martha Inez[6] Pilcher, Emma[5] Hennings, Lewis Hiram[4] Hennings, Josiah Tyson[3] Henning, Christian C.[2], John Adam[1]) was born April 3, 1964.[1561] She married **Daniel Ray Butler** on Dec. 15, 1984. He was born Oct. 4, 1963.[1562]

Children of Lartha Johnson and Daniel Butler are:

982 i. **Kimberly Dawn[8] Butler** born July 18, 1985.[1563]
983 ii. **Daniel Joshua Butler** born June 4, 1986.[1564]
984 iii. **Wendy Marie Butler** born Oct. 15, 1991.[1565]

671. Randy Lee[7] Johnson (Martha Inez[6] Pilcher, Emma[5] Hennings, Lewis Hiram[4] Hennings, Josiah Tyson[3] Henning, Christian C.[2], John Adam[1]) was born Oct. 3, 1965. He married **Susan Renee Bowman** on Aug. 23, 1986. She was born June 19, 1967.[1566]

Child of Randy Johnson and Susan Bowman is:

    985   i.   Kendria Michelle[8] Johnson born June 21, 1995.[1567]

672. Donna Jean[7] Johnson (Martha Inez[6] Pilcher, Emma[5] Hennings, Lewis Hiram[4] Hennings, Josiah Tyson[3] Henning, Christian C.[2], John Adam[1]) was born April 6, 1968. She married **David Windfield Matthews** on Feb. 9, 1992.[1568]

Child of Donna Johnson and David Matthews is:

    986   i.   David Grant[8] Matthews born April 25, 1999.[1569]

673. Judith Ann[7] Welborn (Dixie LaVon[6] Binkley, Mattie White[5] Hennings, Lewis Hiram[4] Hennings, Josiah Tyson[3] Henning, Christian C.[2], John Adam[1]) was born Jan. 22, 1941. She married **Peter Frank Conte** on Aug. 3, 1963. He was born Sept. 23, 1930, died April 10, 1988.[1570]

Child of Judith Welborn and Peter Conte is:

+   987   i.   **Cathy Lynn[8] Conte** born April 30, 1964.[1571]

675. William Wesley[7] Weaver (Violet Fannie[6] Henning, Eugene Walter[5] Hennings, Joseph Manasseh[4], Josiah Tyson[3] Henning, Christian C.[2], John Adam[1]) was born July 8, 1932. He married **(1) Patricia Aann Cotton** on June 10, 1956. She was born May 1, 1939. He married **(2) Debra Sue Combs** on Dec. 10, 1983. She was born Feb. 7, ___.[1572]

Children of William Weaver and Patricia Cotton are:

    988   i.   Catherine Lynn[8] Weaver born Jan. 21, 1957.[1573]

+   989   ii.   **William Joe Weaver** born Oct. 24, 1958.[1574]
+   990   iii.   **Scott Wesley Weaver** born May 26, 1962.[1575]

Child of William Weaver and Debra Combs is:

       991   i.   **Sarah Elizabeth**[8] **Weaver** born June 21, 1987.[1576]

676. Nancy Elloise[7] **Weaver** (Violet Fannie[6] Henning, Eugene Walter[5] Hennings, Joseph Manasseh[4], Josiah Tyson[3] Henning, Christian C.[2], John Adam[1]) was born Aug. 10, 1937. She married **Donald Bray** on Dec. 15, 1956. He was born Sept. 16, 1935.[1577]

Children of Nancy Weaver and Donald Bray are:

+   992   i.   **Robyn Annette**[8] **Bray** born Feb. 26, 1958.[1578]
+   993   ii.   **Alycen Elizabeth Bray** born Jan. 1, 1960.[1579]
+   994   iii.   **Josalyn Alane Bray** born Aug. 16, 1961.[1580]
+   995   iv.   **Kristyn Eloise Bray** born Nov. 16, 1967.[1581]
       996   v.   **Jonathan Owen Bray** born Jan. 18, 1970.[1582]

677. Constance Gae[7] **Henning** (Laurence Walter[6], Eugene Walter[5] Hennings, Joseph Manasseh[4], Josiah Tyson[3] Henning, Christian C.[2], John Adam[1]) was born Aug. 26, 1942. she married **(1) Duane Denault** in June, 1960. He was born Oct. 4, 1939. She married **(2) James Bland** in May, 1984. He was born Nov. 13, 1943.[1583]

Children of Constance Henning and Duane Denault are:

+   997   i.   **Gregory Duane**[8] **Denault** born July 3, 1961.[1584]
+   998   ii.   **Douglas Scott Denault** born Feb. 13, 1963.[1585]
+   999   iii.   **Jeffrey Brian Denault** born Jan. 14, 1964.[1586]
+   1000   iv.   **Lance Joseph Denault** born June 22, 1967.[1587]
   1001   v.   **Marc Eugene Denault** born Oct. 15, 1968.[1588]

678. David Laurence[7] Henning (Laurence Walter[6], Eugene Walter[5] Hennings, Joseph Manasseh[4], Josiah Tyson[3] Henning, Christian C.[2], John Adam[1]) was born May 30, 1944. He married **Joann Colehour**.[1589]

Children of David Henning and Joann Colehour are:

1002	i.	**Shawn[8] Henning** born Sept. 22, 1968.[1590]
1003	ii.	**Brian David Henning** born Nov., 1969, died Feb., 1970.[1591]
1004	iii.	**Kelly Gregory Henning** born Feb. 17, 1972.[1592]
1005	iv.	**Michael Joseph Henning** born March 8, 1974.[1593]
1006	v.	**David Laurence Henning, Jr.** born Aug. 30, 1976. He married **Gwen** in 1995.[1594]

680. Paula Jean[7] Henning (Laurence Walter[6], Eugene Walter[5] Hennings, Joseph Manasseh[4], Josiah Tyson[3] Henning, Christian C.[2], John Adam[1]) was born Jan. 15, 1955. She married **Bruce Kreft** on Jan., 1972. He was born March 10, 1952.[1595]

1007	i.	**Daniel Lee[8] Kreft** born July 17, 1972.[1596]
1008	ii.	**Jonathan Bruce Kreft** born Oct. 21, 1986.[1597]
1009	iii.	**David Michael Kreft** born June 5, 1988.[1598]

681. Eugene Russell[7] Henning (Eugene Russell[6], Eugene Walter[5] Hennings, Joseph Manasseh[4], Josiah Tyson[3] Henning, Christian C.[2], John Adam[1]) was born July 5, 1943. He married **(1) Barbara**. He married **(2) Karen** in Sept., 1967.[1599]

Children of Eugene Henning and Barbara are:

+	1010	i.	**Tiffany[8] Henning**.[1600]
+	1011	ii.	**Andrew Henning**.[1601]

Child of Eugene Russell Henning & Karen is:

    1012 i.   **Teresa Henning** born Feb., 1969.[1602]

682. Donna Jean[7] Henning (Eugene Russell[6], Eugene Walter[5] Hennings, Joseph Manasseh[4], Josiah Tyson[3] Henning, Christian C.[2], John Adam[1]) was born Sept., 1946.[1603]

Child of Donna Jean Henning is:
    1013 i.   **Johnny[8] Henning** born Sept., 1970.[1604]

683. Sally Ann[7] Henning (Eugene Russell[6], Eugene Walter[5] Hennings, Joseph Manasseh[4], Josiah Tyson[3] Henning, Christian C.[2], John Adam[1]) was born July 21, 1948. She married **(1) Earl Nutter** in Aug., 1966. She married **(2) Tony Brueggert** in July, 1984.[1605]

Children of Sally Ann Henning and Earl Nutter are:

+	1014	i.	**Mary Ann[8] Nutter** born March 11, 1968.[1606]
+	1015	ii.	**Christine Marie Nutter** born May 11, 1970.[1607]
+	1016	iii.	**Sue Lynn Nutter** born Feb. 6, 1974.[1608]
	1017	iv.	**Gina Dorothy Nutter** born May, 1975.[1609]
	1018	v.	**Toni Lynn Nutter** born March, 1981.[1610]

684. Bruce Lee[7] Henning (Eugene Russell[6], Eugene Walter[5] Hennings, Joseph Manasseh[4], Josiah Tyson[3] Henning, Christian C.[2], John Adam[1]) was born Nov. 9, 1950. He married **(1) Barbara**. He then married **(2) Terry** in 1996.[1611]

Child of Bruce Henning and Barbara is:

    1019 i.   **Brian[8] Henning** born July, 1984.[1612]

685. George Walter[7] Henning (Eugene Russell[6], Eugene Walter[5] Hennings, Joseph Manasseh[4], Josiah Tyson[3] Henning, Christian C.[2],

John Adam[1]) was born Feb. 22, 1955. He married **Dana** in 1974. Children of George Henning and Dana are:

    1020 i.   Victor[8] Henning born Sept., 1974.[1613]
    1021 ii.   Jeremy Henning born June, 1978.[1614]

689. Jack Dune[7] Henning (Glen David[6], Eugene Walter[5] Hennings, Joseph Manasseh[4], Josiah Tyson[3] Henning, Christian C.[2], John Adam[1]) was born Sept. 18, 1953. He married **Ruth Kirk** on Oct. 15, 1971. Ruth was born April 12, 1957.[1615]

Children of Jack Henning and Ruth Kirk are:

    1022 i.   **Monica Sue[8] Henning** born Aug. 5, 1979.[1616]
    1023 ii.   **Kirk David Henning** born Oct. 16, 1980.[1617]
    1024 iii.   **Leah Elizabeth Alexandria Henning** born July 7, 1982.[1618]
    1025 iv.   **Jaclin Ruth Henning** born Dec. 6, 1984.[1619]
    1026 v.   **Seth Edward Thomas Henning** born July 3, 1986.[1620]
    1027 vi.   **Micah Ray Henning** born Sept. 4, 1988.[1621]
    1028 vii.   **Isaac Micah Henning** born Feb. 21, 1990.[1622]

691. Susan Marie[7] Henning (Douglas Bruce[6], Eugene Walter[5] Hennings, Joseph Manasseh[4], Josiah Tyson[3] Henning, Christian C.[2], John Adam[1]) was born July 29, 1963. She married **David Nims**.[1623]

Children of Susan Henning and David Nims are:

    1029 i.   **Colin Douglas[8] Nims**.[1624]
    1030 ii.   **Travis Mark Henning** born May 16, 1981.[1625]

692. Patricia Elwood[7] Hennings (Thomas Elwood[6], Henry Thomas[5], Joseph Manasseh[4], Josiah Tyson[3] Henning, Christian C.[2], John Adam[1]) was born July 28, 1937. she married **Bobby Gray Davis** on Nov. 13, 1952. Bobby was born Jan. 20, 1932.[1626]

Child of Patricia Hennings and Bobby Davis is:

+   1031   i.   Timothy Gray[8] Davis born April 21, 1958.[1627]

693. Judith Marie[7] Simmons (Helen Elizabeth[6] Hennings, Henry Thomas[5], Joseph Manasseh[4], Josiah Tyson[3] Henning, Christian C.[2], John Adam[1]) was born April 23, 1943. She married **John Allen Dorn** on June 30, 1962. He was born Jan. 1, 1940.[1628]

Children of Judith Simmons and John Dorn are:

     1032   i.   **Jay Russell[8] Dorn** born Oct. 1, 1964. He married (1) **Lisa Wilson** in 1988. Jay & Lisa divorced in 1991. He married (2) **Laura Elizabeth Timmons Taylor** on March 15, 1997.[1629]

+   1033   ii.   **Janis Marie Dorn** born June 2, 1970.[1630]

696. Julia Hope[7] Speas (Ruth Earlene[6] Hennings, Henry Thomas[5], Joseph Manasseh[4], Josiah Tyson[3] Henning, Christian C.[2], John Adam[1]) was born July 10, 1955. She married **Charles William Sain, Jr.** on Sept. 16, 1978. He was born Jan. 19, 1954.[1631]

Children of Julia Speas and Charles Sain are:

     1034   i.   **Anna Hope[8] Sain** born May 19, 1982.[1632]
     1035   ii.   **Gregory Charles Sain** born Oct. 31, 1987.[1633]

699. Andy Joseph[7] Hennings (George Joseph[6], Henry Thomas[5], Joseph Manasseh[4], Josiah Tyson[3] Henning, Christian C.[2], John Adam[1]) was born March 22, 1958. He married **Debra Lee Jones** on April 23, 1977. She was born Aug. 15, 1957.[1634]

Child of Andy Hennings and Debra Jones is:

> 1036   i.   **Amanda Elizabeth**[8] **Hennings** born Oct. 4, 1987.[1635]

700. Cindy Jean[7] **Hennings** (George Joseph[6], Henry Thomas[5], Joseph Manasseh[4], Josiah Tyson[3] Henning, Christian C.[2], John Adam[1]) was born Sept. 13, 1959. She married **Arvon Martin Davis** on Nov. 19, 1983. He was born May 4, 1959.[1636]

Child of Cindy Hennings and Arvon Davis is:

> 1037   i.   **Cara Jean**[8] **Davis** born Aug. 9, 1988.[1637]

701. Edgar Thomas[7] **Hennings** (Charles Edgar[6], Henry Thomas[5], Joseph Manasseh[4], Josiah Tyson[3] Henning, Christian C.[2], John Adam[1]) was born Sept. 23, 1958. He married **Deborah Gail Stanley** on Aug. 1, 1981. She was born April 27, 1959.[1638]

Children of Edgar Hennings and Deborah Stanley are:

> 1038   i.   **Ashley Michelle**[8] **Hennings** born June 19, 1985.[1639]
> 1039   ii.   **Bradley Thomas Hennings** born April 24, 1991.[1640]

702. Ellen Ann[7] **Hennings** (Charles Edgar[6], Henry Thomas[5], Joseph Manasseh[4], Josiah Tyson[3] Henning, Christian C.[2], John Adam[1]) was born Aug. 22, 1961. She married **James Stuart Nesbit** on July 16, 1983. He was born Sept. 8, 1959.[1641]

Child of Ellen Hennings and James Nesbit is:

> 1040   i.   **Emma Heartgrave**[8] **Nesbit** born Dec. 19, 1996.[1642]

704. Frankie Gail[7] Hennings (Frank Harding[6], Rober Ernest[5], Joseph Manasseh[4], Josiah Tyson[3] Henning, Christian C.[2], John Adam[1]) was born April 13, 1946. She married **Rex Warren Hinshaw** on Nov. 26, 1966. He was the son of **Oscar Hinshaw** and **Florence Hobson**. Rex was born in 1939.[1643]
Child of Frankie Hennings and Rex Hinshaw is:

  1041 i.   **Jeffrey Warren Hinshaw** born Sept. 13, 1968.[1644] He married **Laura Brown** on May 8, 1999.[1645]

706. Michael Dean[7] Matthews (Crawlie Ann[6], Rober Ernest[5], Joseph Manasseh[4], Josiah Tyson[3] Henning, Christian C.[2], John Adam[1]) was born June 4, 1954. He married **Susan Seal** on May 3, 1984.[1646]

Child of Michael Matthews and Susan Seal is:

  1042 i.   **Amanda Ann[8] Matthews** born Nov. 3, 1984.[1647]

708. Stephen Lee[7] Googe (Vivian Geraldine[6] Hoots, Julia Anna[5] Hennings, Joseph Manasseh[4], Josiah Tyson[3] Henning, Christian C.[2], John Adam[1]) was born Oct. 26, 1946. He married **Susan Lawrence** on July 2, 1977. She was born June 29, 1954.[1648]

Children of Stephen Googe and Susan Lawrence are:

  1043 i.   **Jordan[8] Googe** born May 30, 1980.[1649]
  1044 ii. **William L. Googe** born Nov. 1, 1982.[1650]

709. Ann Victoria[7] Googe (Vivian Geraldine[6] Hoots, Julia Anna[5] Hennings, Joseph Manasseh[4], Josiah Tyson[3] Henning, Christian C.[2], John Adam[1]) was born June 6, 1950. She married **Allen Nusbaum** on Nov. 16, 1975. He was born Nov. 11, 1950.[1651]

Children of Ann Googe and Allen Nusbaum are:

    1045 i.   Andrew[8] Nusbaum born Dec. 18, 1980.[1652]
    1046 ii.   Lindsay Ann Nusbaum born March 11, 1983.[1653]
    1047 iii.   Matthew Nusbaum born Dec. 23, 1987.[1654]

710. Mildred Ann[7] Schaefer (Florence[6] Hester, William Hornsby[5], Sarah Ann[4] Phillips, Martha A. E.[3] Henning, Adam[2], John Adam[1]) She married **(1) Edward A. Perkins** in 1951. She married **(2) Claude Collins** in 1953.[1655]

Child of Mildred Schaefer and Edward Perkins is:

    1048 i.   Michael Edward[8] Perkins born in 1952 in WA.[1656]

Children of Mildred Schaefer and Claude Collins are:

    1049 i.   Claudia Ann[8] Collins born 1955 in WA.[1657]
    1050 ii.   Kenneth Gordon Collins born 1956 in WA.[1658]
    1051 iii.   Ronald David Collins born 1957 in WA.[1659]
    1052 iv.   Kathleen Ruth Collins born 1960 in WA.[1660]
    1053 v.   Candi Lee Collins born 1962 in WA.[1661]

711. Nancy Lee[7] Hester (George[6], William Hornsby[5], Sarah Ann[4] Phillips, Martha A. E.[3] Henning, Adam[2], John Adam[1]) was born 1942 in Glendale, CA. She married **Harold Dean McAlister**.[1662]

Child of Nancy Hester and Harold McAlister is:

    1054 i.   Jennifer Anne[8] McAlister born 1970 in Huntington Beach, CA.[1663]

714. Linnea[7] Hester (Millard[6], William Hornsby[5], Sarah Ann[4] Phillips, Martha A. E.[3] Henning, Adam[2], John Adam[1]) was born 1946 in Seattle, WA. She married **Craig Hale**.[1664]

Children of Linnea Hester and Craig Hale are:

>   1055   i.   **Jenny Sue⁸ Hale** born 1966 in Seattle, WA.[1665]
>   1056   ii.   **Charles Arthur Hale** born 1968 in Seattle,
>   WA.[1666]

717. Patricia Ann⁷ Tollett (Clifford⁶, Dora⁵ Hester, Sarah Ann⁴ Phillips, Martha A. E.³ Henning, Adam², John Adam¹) was born Dec. 19, 1938. She married **(1) Jacob D. Jones** on April 26, 1958. She married **(2) Robert Clyde Mercer** after 1966.[1667]

Children of Patricia Tollett and Jacob Jones are:

>   1057   i.   **Joel Richard⁸ Jones** born Jan. 27, 1959, died
>   July 9, 1965.[1668]
> +   1058   ii.   **Sheila Rene Jones Mercer** born Sept. 9, 1960.
>   Sheila was adopted by Robert Mercer.[1669]
> +   1059   iii.   **Kevin Jacob Jones Mercer** born Jan. 7, 1963,
>   died May 4, 1991. Kevin was adopted by
>   Robert Mercer.[1670]

Children of Patricia Tollett and Robert Mercer are:

>   1060   i.   **Kim Marie⁸ Mercer** born May 26, 1968. She
>   married **Jessie Lijassi** on June 9, 1991.[1671]
> +   1061   ii.   **Julie Annette Mercer** born Dec. 8, 1972.[1672]

718. Marcus William⁷ Tollett (Clifford⁶, Dora⁵ Hester, Sarah Ann⁴ Phillips, Martha A. E.³ Henning, Adam², John Adam¹) was born May 6, 1941. He married **Janice E. Parsons** on Jan. 30, 1071.[1673]

Children of Marcus Tollett and Janice Parsons are:

>   1062   i.   **Michael Darin⁸ Tollett** born July 14, 1971.[1674]

1063 ii. **Matthew Dean Tollett** born July 14, 1971. He married **Amy McComas** on June 28, 1997.[1675]

1064 iii. **Clifford Marcus Tollett** born Sept. 19, 1972. He married **Corrie Jordan** on June 6, 1998.[1676]

719. Elizabeth Rebecca[7] Tollett (Clifford[6], Dora[5] Hester, Sarah Ann[4] Phillips, Martha A. E.[3] Henning, Adam[2], John Adam[1]) was born Sept. 22, 1949. She married **Benjamin Vincent III**.[1677]

Children of Elizabeth Tollett and Benjamin Vincent are:

1065 i. **Brian Benjamin[8] Vincent** born March 13, 1975.[1678]

1066 ii. **Alan Marcus Vincent** born March 9, 1977.[1679]

1067 iii. **Adam Christopher Vincent** born June 1, 1980.[1680]

735. Margaret Joan[7] Brannon (Delores Jeannette[6] Massengale, George[5], Bettie Jean[4] Phillips, Martha A. E.[3] Henning, Adam[2], John Adam[1]) was born in 1946. She married **Tom Lynch**.[1681]

Child of Margaret Brannon and Tom Lynch is:

1068 i. **Michelle Renie[8] Lynch**.[1682]

736. Kathleen[7] Brannon (Delores Jeannette[6] Massengale, George[5], Bettie Jean[4] Phillips, Martha A. E.[3] Henning, Adam[2], John Adam[1]) was born in 1948. She married **John Rivas**.[1683]

Child of Kathleen Brannon and John Rivas is:

1069 i. **John Paul[8] Rivas**.[1684]

746. Kathleen[7] Thomas (Max[6], Minnie[5] Roberts, Cordelia[4] Henning, Archibald G.[3], Adam[2], John Adam[1]) She married **Paul Mitchell**.[1685]

Children of Kathleen Thomas and Paul Mitchell are:

    1070 i.   **Nicole**[8] **Mitchell**.[1686]
    1071 ii.   **Scott Mitchell**.[1687]

750. Jana Dee[7] **Thomas** (Boyd[6], Minnie[5] Roberts, Cordelia[4] Henning, Archibald G.[3], Adam[2], John Adam[1]) She married **Jim Wahl**.[1688]

Child of Jana Thomas and Jim Wahl is:

    1072 i.   **Jeffrey**[8] **Wahl**.[1689]

761. Heidi Lynn[7] **Henning** (Roger Steven[6], Ralph Steven[5], Arvel[4], Archibald G.[3], Adam[2], John Adam[1]) was born Oct. 23, 1973 in Spokane, WA. She married **Justin Abbott**.[1690]

Child of Heidi Henning and Justin Abbott is:

    1073 i.   **Ashley Lynn**[8] **Abbott** born Sept. 15, 1997.[1691]

770. Eric Richard[7] **Vogel** (Mirene Jean[6] Henning, Clarence Eugene[5], Julius Adam[4], Santford Ivan[3], Adam[2], John Adam[1]) was born 1965 in Seattle, WA. He married **Kim ____**.[1692]

Child of Eric Vogel and Kim is:

    1074 i.   **Paige**[8] **Vogel** born April 30, 1996.[1693]

799. Tabitha[7] **Bartel** (Sharon Lea[6] Berg, Ruth Anna[5] Henning, Daniel Webster[4], Santford Ivan[3], Adam[2], John Adam[1]) was born June 14, 1971. She married **Archer Dymoke**.[1694]

The Henning Family

Children of Tabitha Bartel and Archer Dymoke are:

    1075 i.   Jordon[8] Dymoke born July 20, 1996.[1695]
    1076 ii.   Katarina Eve Dymoke born Sept. 14, 1997.[1696]

818. Sarah[7] Fordham (Laura Ophelia[6] Conrad, Sarah Ethel[5] Bullard, Martha Ophelia[4] Styers, Delilah Louise[3] Henning, Gabriel[2], John Adam[1]) was born Jan. 29, 1936 in NC. She married **James S. Harvey**.[1697]

Child of Sarah Fordham and James Harvey is:

    1077 i.   Steven Burt[8] Harvey.[1698]

823. Dorothy Ann[7] Bullard (Guy Styers[6], Guy Styers[5], Martha Ophelia[4] Styers, Delilah Louise[3] Henning, Gabriel[2], John Adam[1]) was born Feb. 9, 1950 in Winston-Salem, NC. She married **Norris Ray Higgins** on Oct. 27, 1973 at First Baptist Church, Winston-Salem, NC. Norris was born March 13, 1950.[1699]

Child of Dorothy Bullard and Norris Higgins is:

+   1078 i.   Melanie[8] Higgins born July 23, 1977 in Morganton, NC.[1700]

827. Faye[7] Bullard (John Robert[6], Guy Styers[5], Martha Ophelia[4] Styers, Delilah Louise[3] Henning, Gabriel[2], John Adam[1]) was born July 19, 1955. She married **Joe Cleveland Hinkle, Jr.** in Winston-Salem, NC. Joe was born May 29, 1952.[1701]

Children of Faye Bullard and Joe Hinkle are:

    1079 i.   Cristalle Marie[8] Hinkle born Sept. 16, 1978.[1702]
    1080 ii.   Joe Cleveland Hinkle III born Feb. 24, 1981.[1703]

862. Diane Sue[7] Pendleton (Mescal L.[6] Hill, Ethel Rosetta[5] Snipes, Lewis Edwin[4], Lauretta Elizabeth[3] Henning, Gabriel[2], John Adam[1]) was born March 19, 1950 in Lafayette, Tippecanoe Cty., IN. She married **Paul J. Riehle** on Oct. 7, 1972 in Lafayette, Tippecanoe Cty., IN.[1704]

Children of Diane Pendleton and Paul Riehle are:

+   1081   i.   **Paul Andrew[8] Riehle** born Oct. 10, 1973 in Lafayette, IN.[1705]

     1082   ii.   **Mark Joseph Riehle** born Feb. 24, 1977 in Lafayette, IN.[1706]

     1083   iii.   **Brian Adam Riehle** born April 26, 1983 in Lafayette, IN.[1707]

863. David Andrew[7] Pendleton (Mescal L.[6] Hill, Ethel Rosetta[5] Snipes, Lewis Edwin[4], Lauretta Elizabeth[3] Henning, Gabriel[2], John Adam[1]) was born July 6, 1952 in Lafayette, Tippecanoe Cty., IN. He married **Pamela Jeanne Horn** on July 9, 1976 in Lafayette, IN. She was the daughter of **Marshall Horn** and **Dorothy Whitman**. She was born Oct. 13, 1952 in Tippecanoe Cty., IN.[1708]

Children of David Pendleton and Pamela Horn are:

     1084   i.   **Jenna Diane[8] Pendleton** born June 21, 1985 in Lafayette, Tippecanoe Cty., IN.[1709]

     1085   ii.   **Troy Andrew Pendleton** born Nov. 12, 1987 in Lafayette, Tippecanoe Cty., IN.[1710]

864. Darlene Kay[7] Pendleton (Mescal L.[6] Hill, Ethel Rosetta[5] Snipes, Lewis Edwin[4], Lauretta Elizabeth[3] Henning, Gabriel[2], John Adam[1]) was born Sept. 21, 1955 in Lafayette, Tippecanoe Cty., IN. She married **(1) Paul Buckles** on July 10, 1982 in Lafayette, IN. She married **(2) Jack Burns** in April, 1997.[1711]

Children of Darlene Pendleton and Paul Buckles are:

> 1086 i. **Justin Matthew[8] Buckles** born Feb. 2, 1983 in Lafayette, IN.[1712]
> 1087 ii. **Derrick Allen Buckles** born Dec. 17, 1985 in Lafayette, IN.[1713]

Generation No. 8

866. Rodney Toso[8] Hauser (Martha Kay[7] Fulp, Glenn[6] Fulk, Mattie Beatrice[5] Cline, Charles Christian[4], Peter Solomon[3], Mary Anna[2] Henning, John Adam[1]) was born March 18, 1958 in Winston-Salem, NC. He married **Wanda Lynn Wilson** on August 22, 1981 in Walkertown, NC at Loves United Methodist Church.[1714]

Child of Rodney Hauser and Wanda Wilson is:

> 1088 i. **Jessica Lynn[9] Hauser** born Feb. 18, 1985.[1715]

883. Derrick[8] Furches (Susan Irene[7] Cline, Raymond Arthur[6], Raymond Arthur[5], Pleas David[4], Eli[3], Mary Anna[2] Henning, John Adam[1])

Child of Derrick Furches is:

> 1089 i. **Scott[9] Furches**.[1716]

911. Emily Carol[8] Wooten (Emily Ruth[7] Hennings, Grady Laster[6], Mirtie Lee[5] Henning, William Turner[4] Hennings, Josiah Tyson[3] Henning, Christian C.[2], John Adam[1]) was born April 12, 1950 in Winston-Salem, NC. She married **John Alvin Duncan, Jr.** on Jan. 18, 1975 in East Bend United Methodist Church, East Bend, NC. John is the son of **John Alvin Duncan, Sr.** He was born April 21, 1949 in Mebane, NC.[1717]

Children of Emily Wooten and John Duncan are:

1090 i.   **Jeffrey Alvin**[9] **Duncan** born March 2, 1976 in Guilford Cty., Greensboro, NC.[1718]

1091 ii.   **Joseph Daniel Duncan** born Oct. 9, 1980 in Guilford Cty., Greensboro, NC.[1719]

1092 iii.   **Carrie Emily Duncan** born Oct. 9, 1980 in Guilford Cty., Greensboro, NC.[1720]

913. Mark Elbert[8] **Wooten** (Emily Ruth[7] Hennings, Grady Laster[6], Mirtie Lee[5] Henning, William Turner[4] Hennings, Josiah Tyson[3] Henning, Christian C.[2], John Adam[1]) was born May 25, 1956 in Winston-Salem, NC. He married **Joan Raye Hoots** on Dec. 30, 1978 at Deep Creek Baptist Church, Yadkin Cty., NC. Joan is the daughter of **Ray Hoots**. She was born Dec. 5, 1955 in Yadkinville, NC.[1721]

Children of Mark Wooten and Joan Hoots are:

1093 i.   **Jenna Raye**[9] **Wooten** born Aug. 30, 1984 in Rutherfordton, NC.[1722]

1094 ii.   **Mark Tyler Wooten** born Oct. 24, 1988 in Rutherfordton, NC.[1723]

914. Sarah Vanna[8] **Wooten** (Emily Ruth[7] Hennings, Grady Laster[6], Mirtie Lee[5] Henning, William Turner[4] Hennings, Josiah Tyson[3] Henning, Christian C.[2], John Adam[1]) was born Dec. 12, 1957 in Winston-Salem, NC. She married **Martin Wayne Price** on Aug. 28, 1982 at East Bend United Methodist Church, East Bend, NC. He is the son of **Ernest Price**. Martin was born June 2, 1961 in Winston-Salem, NC.[1724]

Children of Sarah Wooten and Martin Price are:

1095 i.   **Sarah Elizabeth**[9] **Price** born June 24, 1988 in Charlotte, NC.[1725]

1096 ii. **Matthew Wayne Price** born Nov. 13, 1994 in Charlotte, NC.[1726]

917. Brian David[8] Hennings (Paul Eugene[7], Grady Laster[6], Mirtie Lee[5] Henning, William Turner[4] Hennings, Josiah Tyson[3] Henning, Christian C.[2], John Adam[1]) was born May 17, 1959 in Okinawa, Japan. He married **Elizabeth Ann Hurt** on May 21, 1982 in St. John Vianney, Omaha, NE. She is the daughter of **Robert Hurt** and **Violet Gravel**. Elizabeth was born Dec. 19, 1959 in Seward, NE.[1727]

Children of Brian Hennings and Elizabeth Hurt are:

1097 i. **Natalie Elizabeth[9] Hennings** born Nov. 16, 1987 in Harris Cty., Houston, TX.[1728]
1098 ii. **Madeline Marie Hennings** born Dec. 31, 1989 in DuPage Cty., Naperville, IL.[1729]

919. Russell Myers[8] Hennings (Grady Lee[7], Grady Laster[6], Mirtie Lee[5] Henning, William Turner[4] Hennings, Josiah Tyson[3] Henning, Christian C.[2], John Adam[1]) was born June 20, 1958 in NC. He married **Mary Margaret O'Brien** on Feb. 1, 1986 in Letterkenny, Donegul, Ireland. She is the daughter of **Patrick O'Brien** and **Vera Haughey**. Mary was born July 4, 1963 in Glasgow, Scotland.[1730]

Children of Russell Hennings and Mary O'Brien are:

1099 i. **Cara Marie[9] Hennings** born Feb. 27, 1989 in Winston-Salem, NC.[1731]
1100 ii. **Megan Dana Hennings** born July 19, 1993 in Letterkenny, Donegul, Ireland.[1732]

921. Karen Renee[8] Hennings (Alvis Ray[7], Grady Laster[6], Mirtie Lee[5] Henning, William Turner[4] Hennings, Josiah Tyson[3] Henning, Christian C.[2], John Adam[1]) was born July 17, 1958. She married **Dennis Dwayne Reece** on June 1, 1980 in East Bend Methodist Church, East Bend, NC. He was the son of **Fred Reece** and **Mary**

Denkins. Dennis was born April 1, 1957 in Forsyth Cty., NC.[1733]

Children of Karen Hennings and Dennis Reece are:

> 1101 i. **Justin Dwayne**[9] **Reece** born Nov. 3, 1981 in Winston-Salem, NC.[1734]
>
> 1102 ii. **Andrew Ian Reece** born Feb. 23, 1985 in Winston-Salem, NC.[1735]

923. Kevin Bennett[8] **Hennings** (Joe Bennett[7], Grady Laster[6], Mirtie Lee[5] Henning, William Turner[4] Hennings, Josiah Tyson[3] Henning, Christian C.[2], John Adam[1]) was born Sept. 10, 1960 in Winston-Salem, NC. He married **Janet Ryan Wooten** on Nov. 6, 1983 in East Bend, NC. She was the daughter of **Roger Wooten** and **Lydia Adams**. Janet was born Jan. 13, 1960 in Forsyth Cty., NC.[1736]

Child of Kevin Hennings and Janet Wooten is:

> 1103 i. **Sophia Noelle**[9] **Hennings** born March 26, 1998 in Winston-Salem, NC .[1737]

924. Joe Barrett[8] **Hennings** (Joe Bennett[7], Grady Laster[6], Mirtie Lee[5] Henning, William Turner[4] Hennings, Josiah Tyson[3] Henning, Christian C.[2], John Adam[1]) was born January 13, 1962 in Winston-Salem, NC. He married **Penny Gail Williams** on Oct. 21, 1984. Penny was born Aug. 29, 1963 in Forsyth County, NC.[1738]

Child of Joe Hennings and Penny Williams is:

> 1104 i. **Barrett J.**[9] **Hennings** born May 12, 1996 in Winston-Salem, NC.[1739]

925. Darren Zell[8] **Hennings** (Joe Bennett[7], Grady Laster[6], Mirtie Lee[5] Henning, William Turner[4] Hennings, Josiah Tyson[3] Henning, Christian C.[2], John Adam[1]) was born March 19, 1965 in Winston-Salem, NC. He married **(1) Amanda Kay Spillman** on Aug. 21,

1988. He married (2) **Catherine Elizabeth O'Brien** on April 8, 1995. She is the daughter of **Patrick Joseph O'Brien** and **June Long**. Catherine was born June 21, 1965 in St. Louis, MO.[1740]

Child of Darren Hennings and Catherine O'Brien is:

    1105 i.   **Chelsea Elizabeth**[9] **Miles** born May 26, 1991 in Onslow County, NC. She is Catherine's child by a previous marriage.[1741]

926. Brittley L.[8] **Hennings** (Joe Bennett[7], Grady Laster[6], Mirtie Lee[5] Henning, William Turner[4] Hennings, Josiah Tyson[3] Henning, Christian C.[2], John Adam[1]) was born Aug. 26, 1969 in Winston-Salem, NC. He married **Kendra Kristene Carter** on Oct. 8, 1994. She is the daughter of **Kenneth Carter** and **Virginia Steelman**. Kendra was born July 23, 1970 in Surry Cty., NC.[1742]

Child of Brittley Hennings and Kendra Carter is:

    1106 i.   **Bryson Ladd**[9] **Hennings** born April 2, 1997 in Winston-Salem, NC.[1743]

927. Jennifer Carol[8] **Murphy** (Ruby Carol[7] Hennings, Grady Laster[6], Mirtie Lee[5] Henning, William Turner[4] Hennings, Josiah Tyson[3] Henning, Christian C.[2], John Adam[1]) was born Nov. 10, 1960 in Winston-Salem, NC. She married **David Ray Phillips, Jr.** on May 22, 1983 at East Bend United Methodist Church, East Bend, NC.[1744] David was born Nov. 27, 1960 in Winston-Salem, NC.[1745]

Children of Jennifer Murphy and David Phillips are:

    1107 i.   **Courtney Carol**[9] **Phillips** born Aug. 30, 1990 in Winston-Salem, NC.[1746]
    1108 ii.   **Austin Ray Phillips** born June 2, 1995 in Winston-Salem, NC.[1747]

928. Heather Leigh[8] Murphy (Ruby Carol[7] Hennings, Grady Laster[6], Mirtie Lee[5] Henning, William Turner[4] Hennings, Josiah Tyson[3] Henning, Christian C.[2], John Adam[1]) was born Jan. 3, 1973 in Winston-Salem, NC. She married **Brent James Russell** on July 16, 1993 in East Bend Methodist Church, East Bend, NC. Brent is the son of **James Russell** and **Mae**.[1748]

Child of Heather Murphy and Brent Russell is:

> 1109　i.　**Jacob Lee[9] Russell** born July 6, 1998 in Mesa, AZ.[1749]

934. Tamala Dawn[8] Choplin (Joe Wesley[7], Irene Hope[6] Adams, Lela Greene[5] Henning, William Turner[4] Hennings, Josiah Tyson[3] Henning, Christian C.[2], John Adam[1]) was born Dec. 26, 1961 in Winston-Salem, NC. She married **Christopher Joe Leinbach** on Sept. 17, 1983. He was the son of **Bobby Leinbach** and **Robin Parnell**. Christopher was born Dec. 30.[1750]

Child of Tamala Choplin and Christopher Leinbach is:

> 1110　i.　**Brittany Olivia[9] Leinbach** born Jan. 25, 1986.[1751]

936. Kerry David[8] McDuffie (Carol Jean[7] Choplin, Irene Hope[6] Adams, Lela Greene[5] Henning, William Turner[4] Hennings, Josiah Tyson[3] Henning, Christian C.[2], John Adam[1]) was born May 30, 1958 in Lake Charles, LA. He married **Sharon Fulbright** on June 20, 1980. She was the daughter of **Otis Fulbright** and **Gertrude**. She was born in Mt. Vernon, MO.[1752]

Child of Kerry McDuffie and Sharon Fulbright is:

> 1111　i.　**Jennifer Lynn[9] McDuffie** born Oct. 8, 1981.[1753]

945. Melinda[8] Crews (Polly Ann[7] Smitherman, Robert Benbow[6], Ila Ladrone[5] Henning, William Turner[4] Hennings, Josiah Tyson[3] Henning, Christian C.[2], John Adam[1]) She married **Jerry Floyd**.[1754]

Children of Melinda Crews and Jerry Floyd are:

        1112 i.   **Tara[9] Floyd**. She married ____ Craig.[1755]

+   1113 ii.   **Lori Floyd**.[1756]

946. Jeff[8] Crews (Polly Ann[7] Smitherman, Robert Benbow[6], Ila Ladrone[5] Henning, William Turner[4] Hennings, Josiah Tyson[3] Henning, Christian C.[2], John Adam[1])[1757]

        1114 i.   **Matthew[9] Crews**.[1758]

948. Bo[8] Crews (Polly Ann[7] Smitherman, Robert Benbow[6], Ila Ladrone[5] Henning, William Turner[4] Hennings, Josiah Tyson[3] Henning, Christian C.[2], John Adam[1]) He married **Tessie**.[1759]

Children of Bo Crews and Tessie are:

        1115 i.   **Austin[9] Crews**.[1760]

        1116 ii.   **Dustin Crews**.[1761]

        1117 iii.   **Justin Crews**.[1762]

949. Thomas E.[8] Crews (Polly Ann[7] Smitherman, Robert Benbow[6], Ila Ladrone[5] Henning, William Turner[4] Hennings, Josiah Tyson[3] Henning, Christian C.[2], John Adam[1])[1763]

        1118 i.   **Brent[9] Crews**.[1764]

        1119 ii.   Jamie Crews.[1765]

955. Marty[8] Smitherman (Robert Burgess[7], Willie Jennings[6], Ila Ladrone[5] Henning, William Turner[4] Hennings, Josiah Tyson[3] Henning, Christian C.[2], John Adam[1])[1766]

Children of Marty Smitherman are:

  1120 i. **Nichole**[9] **Smitherman.**[1767]
  1121 ii. **Matthew Smitherman.**[1768]

956. Penny[8] **Smitherman** (Robert Burgess[7], Willie Jennings[6], Ila Ladrone[5] Henning, William Turner[4] Hennings, Josiah Tyson[3] Henning, Christian C.[2], John Adam[1]) She married _____ **Johnson.**[1769]

Child of Penny Smitherman and _____ Johnson.
  1122 i. **Deanna**[9] **Johnson.**[1770]

987. Cathy Lynn[8] **Conte** (Judith Ann[7] Welborn, Dixie LaVon[6] Binkley, Mattie White[5] Hennings, Lewis Hiram[4] Hennings, Josiah Tyson[3] Henning, Christian C.[2], John Adam[1]) was born April 30, 1964. She married **Dale Graham Houser III** on June 17, 1995. He was born Jan. 29, 1969.[1771]

Dale and Cathy adoped the following children on Nov. 22, 1998.[1772]

  1123 i. **Ashley Brook**[9] **Houser** born May 16, 1986.[1773]
  1124 ii. **Jenna Michelle Houser** born Aug. 27, 1987.[1774]
  1125 iii. **Haley Ann Houser** Dec. 24, 1988.[1775]

989. William Joe[8] **Weaver** (William Wesley[7], Violet Fannie[6] Henning, Eugene Walter[5] Hennings, Joseph Manasseh[4], Josiah Tyson[3] Henning, Christian C.[2], John Adam[1]) was born Oct. 24, 1958. He married **Tammy Plouch** in 1978. Tammy was born in 1958.[1776]

+ 1126 i. **Trishalyn Marie**[9] **Bursott** born Feb. 8, 1979.[1777]
+ 1127 ii. **Matthew William Bursott** born March 6, 1980.[1778]

990. Scott Wesley[8] Weaver (William Wesley[7],Violet Fannie[6] Henning, Eugene Walter[5] Hennings, Joseph Manasseh[4], Josiah Tyson[3] Henning, Christian C.[2], John Adam[1]) was born May 26, 1962. He married in 1981 to (1) **Dena** _____ in 1981. Dena was born Sept. 26. He later married (2) **Angela Sue McCann.** She was born Feb. 27, 1960.[1779]

Child of Scott Weaver and Dena is:

    1128 i.   **Tyson Wesley[9] Weaver** born Nov. 26, 1982.[1780]

Children of Scott Weaver and Angela McCann are:

    1129. i.   **Amanda Sue[9] McCann** born March 31, 1987.[1781]

    1130 ii.   **Brittany Michelle Weaver** born Nov. 20, 1992.[1782]

992. Robyn Annette[8] Bray (Nancy Elloise[7] Weaver, Violet Fannie[6] Henning, Eugene Walter[5] Hennings, Joseph Manasseh[4], Josiah Tyson[3] Henning, Christian C.[2], John Adam[1]) was born Feb. 26, 1958. She married[1783] **Fred Davis** on Feb. 3, 1978. Fred was born Nov. 7, 1958.

Children of Robyn Bray and Fred Davis are:

+   1131 i.   **Heather Annette[9] Davis**[1784] born March 14, 1981.

    1132 ii.   **Amber Elizabeth Davis** born May 8, 1984.[1785]

    1133 iii.   **Samantha Rene Davis** born March 26, 1987.[1786]

    1134 iv.   **Natalie Alane Davis** born May 4, 1990.[1787]

993. Alycen Elizabeth[8] Bray (Nancy Elloise[7] Weaver, Violet Fannie[6] Henning, Eugene Walter[5] Hennings, Joseph Manasseh[4], Josiah Tyson[3] Henning, Christian C.[2], John Adam[1]) was born Jan. 1, 1960.

She married **Jerald Kirk Hughes** in 1984. Jerald was born June 16, 1960.[1788]

Child of Alycen Bray and Jerald Hughes is:

    1135   i.   **Aubrey Elizabeth[9] Hughes** born March 15, 1999.[1789]

994. Josalyn Alane[8] Bray (Nancy Elloise[7] Weaver, Violet Fannie[6] Henning, Eugene Walter[5] Hennings, Joseph Manasseh[4], Josiah Tyson[3] Henning, Christian C.[2], John Adam[1]) was born Aug. 16, 1961. She married **(1) Ronald Lee Adams** on June 19, 1981. He was born July 5, 1958. She married **(2) Ronald Keith Conwell** on Dec. 3, 1986.[1790]

Children of Josalyn Bray and Ronald Adams are:

    1136   i.   **Tiffani Jalyn Adams** born Jan. 21, 1983.[1791]
    1137   ii.   **Mystee Dawn Adams** born Nov. 25, 1985.[1792]

Children of Josalyn Bray and Ronald Conwell are:

    1138   i.   **Ryan Truitt[9] Conwell** born July 31, 1993.[1793]
    1139   ii.   **Rachel Katherine Conwell** born Dec. 20, 1994.[1794]

995. Kristyn Eloise[8] Bray (Nancy Elloise[7] Weaver, Violet Fannie[6] Henning, Eugene Walter[5] Hennings, Joseph Manasseh[4], Josiah Tyson[3] Henning, Christian C.[2], John Adam[1]) was born Nov. 16, 1967. She married **(1) Donald James Bradshaw** on April 14, 1983. She married **(2) Tymothy Allen Van Arsdale** on Dec. 27, 1993. He was born March 6, 1970.[1795]

Children of Kristyn Bray and Donald Bradshaw are:

    1140   i.   **Jennifer Lani[9] Bradshaw** born Sept. 21, 1986.[1796]

1141   ii.   **Katherine Aron Bradshaw** born Aug. 9, 1989.[1797]

Children of Kristyn Bray and Tymothy Van Arsdale are:

1142   i.   **Kassandra Leigh[9] Van Arsdale** born July 20, 1994.[1798]

1143   ii.   **Tyler Owen Van Arsdale** born June 19, 1995.[1799]

997. Gregory Duane[8] Denault (Constance Gae[7] Henning, Laurence Walter[6], Eugene Walter[5] Hennings, Joseph Manasseh[4], Josiah Tyson[3] Henning, Christian C.[2], John Adam[1]) was born July 3, 1961. He married **Tami Piatt** on April, 1981. she was born Dec. 14, 1961.[1800]

Children of Gregory Denault and Tami Piatt are:

1144   i.   **Cory Scott[9] Denault** born July 28, 1987.[1801]

1145. ii.   **Shannon Reece Denault** born April 16, 1992.[1802]

1146. iii.   **Mitchell Gregoy Denault** born Nov. 18, 1993.[1803]

998. Douglas Scott[8] Denault (Constance Gae[7] Henning, Laurence Walter[6], Eugene Walter[5] Hennings, Joseph Manasseh[4], Josiah Tyson[3] Henning, Christian C.[2], John Adam[1]) was born Feb. 13, 1963. He married **Donna Hartung** in March, 1983. Donna was born Oct. 3, 1956.[1804]

Donna Hartung's children:

Robert Hartung born May 14, 1976.
Amy Hartung born Oct. 23, 1980.

Children of Douglas Denault and Donna Hartung are:

> 1147 i. **Neil Laurence[9] Denult** born Nov. 5, 1983.[1805]
> 1148 ii. **Nicholas Dane Denault** born Dec. 19, 1987.[1806]

999. Jeffrey Brian[8] Denault (Constance Gae[7] Henning, Laurence Walter[6], Eugene Walter[5] Hennings, Joseph Manasseh[4], Josiah Tyson[3] Henning, Christian C.[2], John Adam[1]) was born Jan. 14, 1964. He married **Heidi Staib** on Oct. 8, 1989. Heidi was born Nov. 22, 1966.[1807]

Child of Jeffrey Denault and Heidi Staib is:

> 1149 i. **Alexandra Elizabeth[9] Denault** born July 7, 1994.[1808]

1000. Lance Joseph[8] Denault (Constance Gae[7] Henning, Laurence Walter[6], Eugene Walter[5] Hennings, Joseph Manasseh[4], Josiah Tyson[3] Henning, Christian C.[2], John Adam[1]) was born June 22, 1967. He married **Dina Matchette** on Nov. 21, 1988.[1809]

Terry Steen born June 28, 1985 is Dina Matchette's son.

Children of Lance Denault and Dina Matchette are:

> 1150 i. **Brittany Renee[9] Denault** born April 29, 1988.[1810]
> 1151 ii. **Candace Lauren Denault** born June 23, 1989.[1811]
> 1152 iii. **Jacob Lance Denault** born Oct. 16, 1991.[1812]

1010. Tiffany[8] Henning (Eugene Russell[7], Eugene Russell[6], Eugene Walter[5] Hennings, Joseph Manasseh[4], Josiah Tyson[3] Henning, Christian C.[2], John Adam[1])[1813]

Child of Tiffany Henning is:

    1153   i.   Sequoia[9] Henning born Jan., 1992.[1814]

1011. Andrew[8] Henning (Eugene Russell[7], Eugene Russell[6], Eugene Walter[5] Hennings, Joseph Manasseh[4], Josiah Tyson[3] Henning, Christian C.[2], John Adam[1]) He married **Nicky**.[1815]

Children of Andrew Henning and Nicky are:

    1154   i.   **Jacob[9] Henning**.[1816]
    1155   ii.   **Joshua Henning**.[1817]
    1156   iii.   **George Henning**.[1818]

1014. Mary Ann[8] Nutter (Sally Ann[7] Henning, Eugene Russell[6], Eugene Walter[5] Hennings, Joseph Manasseh[4], Josiah Tyson[3] Henning, Christian C.[2], John Adam[1]) was born March 11, 1968.[1819]

Children of Mary Ann Nutter are:

    1157   i.   **Michael[9] Nutter** born Dec, 1984.[1820]
    1158   ii.   **Ashley Nutter** born Aug., 1989.[1821]

1015. Christine Marie[8] Nutter (Sally Ann[7] Henning, Eugene Russell[6], Eugene Walter[5] Hennings, Joseph Manasseh[4], Josiah Tyson[3] Henning, Christian C.[2], John Adam[1]) was born May 11, 1970.[1822]

Child of Christine Marie Nutter is:

    1159   i.   **Samantha[9] Nutter** born Nov., 1989.[1823]

1016. Sue Lynn[8] Nutter (Sally Ann[7] Henning, Eugene Russell[6], Eugene Walter[5] Hennings, Joseph Manasseh[4], Josiah Tyson[3] Henning, Christian C.[2], John Adam[1]) was born Feb. 6, 1974. She married **Mark Hopkins** in Nov., 1995.[1824]

Children of Sue Nutter and Mark Hopkins are:

> 1160 i.   **Aliana[9] Hopkins** born Jan., 1994.[1825]
> 1161 ii. **Russell Andrew Hopkins** born June, 1996. [1826]

1031. Timothy Gray[8] Davis (Patricia Elwood[7] Hennings, Thomas Elwood[6], Henry Thomas[5], Joseph Manasseh[4], Josiah Tyson[3] Henning, Christian C.[2], John Adam[1]) was born April 21, 1958. He married (1) **Teresa Rosanne Adams**. She was born Aug. 31, 1960. He married (2) **Aileen** on May 31, 1980. She was born Jan. 8, 1959. They divorced in Jan., 1990.[1827]

Children of Timothy Davis and Aileen are:

> 1162 i.   **Adam Gray[9] Davis** born July 21, 1982.[1828]
> 1163 ii. **Jedidiah Gray Davis** born Sept. 11, 1987.[1829]

1033. Janis Marie[8] Dorn (Judith Marie[7] Simmons, Helen Elizabeth[6] Hennings, Henry Thomas[5], Joseph Manasseh[4], Josiah Tyson[3] Henning, Christian C.[2], John Adam[1]) was born June 2, 1970. She married **Robert Harding Morgan** on June 3, 1989. He was born June 25, 1964.[1830]

Children of Janis Dorn and Robert Morgan are:

> 1164 i.   **Robert Harding[9] Morgan, Jr.** born Aug. 18, 1994.[1831]
> 1165 ii. **Connor Dorn Morgan** born March 31, 1997.[1832]

1058. Sheila Rene Jones[8] Mercer (Patricia Ann[7] Tollett, Clifford[6], Dora[5] Hester, Sarah Ann[4] Phillips, Martha A. E.[3] Henning, Adam[2], John Adam[1]) was born Sept. 9, 1960. She was adopted by Robert Mercer. She married **Roger A. Williamson** on March 2, 1984.[1833]

Children of Sheila Mercer and Roger Williamson are:

1166 i.   **Roger Adrian**[9] **Williamson** born Feb. 4, 1985.[1834]

1167 ii.   **Joel Robert Williamson** born June 14, 1986.[1835]

1168 iii. **Karisa Annette Williamson** born April 2, 1988.[1836]

1059. Kevin Jacob Jones[8] **Mercer** (Patricia Ann[7] Tollett, Clifford[6], Dora[5] Hester, Sarah Ann[4] Phillips, Martha A. E.[3] Henning, Adam[2], John Adam[1]) was born Jan. 7, 1963. He was adopted by Robert Mercer. Kevin married **Rene Van Derbaush** on Dec. 8, 1988.[1837]

Child of Kevin Mercer and Rene Van Derbaush is:

1169 i.   **Ean Robert Jones**[9] **Mercer** born June 16, 1989.[1838]

1061. Julie Annette[8] **Mercer** (Patricia Ann[7] Tollett, Clifford[6], Dora[5] Hester, Sarah Ann[4] Phillips, Martha A. E.[3] Henning, Adam[2], John Adam[1]) was born Dec. 8, 1972. She married **David Duane Graff** on Nov. 1, 1992.[1839]

Child of Julie Mercer and David Graff is:

1170 i.   **Christopher Duane**[9] **Graff** born Jan. 6, 1995.[1840]

1078. Melanie[8] **Higgins** (Dorothy Ann[7] Bullard, Guy Styers[6], Guy Styers[5], Martha Ophelia[4] Styers, Delilah Louise[3] Henning, Gabriel[2], John Adam[1]) was born July 23, 1977 in Morganton, NC. She married **Shane Abee** on Oct. 11, 1997.[1841]

Child of Melanie Higgins and Shane Abee is:

    1171   i.   **Jenna Michelle**[9] **Abee** born Aug. 12, 1998 in Morganton, NC.[1842]

1081. Paul Andrew[8] **Riehle** (Diane Sue[7] Pendleton, Mescal L.[6] Hill, Ethel Rosetta[5] Snipes, Lewis Edwin[4], Lauretta Elizabeth[3] Henning, Gabriel[2], John Adam[1]) was born Oct. 10, 1973 in Lafayette, IN. He married **Jennifer Marie Vaughn** on July 19, 1997 in Tippecanoe Cty., IN. She was the daughter of **Robert L. Vaughn**.[1843]

Child of Paul Riehle and Jennifer Vaughn is:

    1172   i   **Courtney Marie**[9] **Riehle** born Dec., 1997.[1844]

Generation No. 9

1113. Lori[9] **Floyd** (Melinda[8] Crews, Polly Ann[7] Smitherman, Robert Benbow[6], Ila Ladrone[5] Henning, William Turner[4] Hennings, Josiah Tyson[3] Henning, Christian C.[2], John Adam[1]) She married **David White**.[1845]

Child of Lori Floyd and David White is:

    1173   i.   **Ashton**[10] **White**.[1846]

1126. Trishalyn Marie[9] **Bursott** (William Joe[8] Weaver, William Wesley[7], Violet Fannie[6] Henning, Eugene Walter[5] Hennings, Joseph Manasseh[4], Josiah Tyson[3] Henning, Christian C.[2], John Adam[1]) was born Feb. 8, 1979. She married **Joey Hyche**.[1847]

Child of Trishalyn Bursott and Joey Hyche is:

    1174   i.   **Khrystafer Drake**[10] **Hyche** born Nov. 16, 1997.[1848]

1127. Matthew William[9] Bursott (William Joe[8] Weaver, William Wesley[7], Violet Fannie[6] Henning, Eugene Walter[5] Hennings, Joseph Manasseh[4], Josiah Tyson[3] Henning, Christian C.[2], John Adam[1]) was born March 6, 1980. He married **Diane West** on Oct. 31, 1998. Diane was born in Nov., 1980.[1849]

Child of Matthew Bursott and Diane West is:

    1175   i.   **Elizabeth Ann[10] Bursott** born May 18, 1999.[1850]

1131. Heather Annette[9] Davis (Robyn Annette[8], Nancy Elloise[7] Weaver, Violet Fannie[6] Henning, Eugene Walter[5] Hennings, Joseph Manasseh[4], Josiah Tyson[3] Henning, Christian C.[2], John Adam[1]) was born March 14, 1981. She married **Billy Joe Hruska** on April 17, 1999. He was born in 1978.[1851]

Child of Heather Davis and Billy Joe Hruska is:

    1176   i.   **Billy Joe[10] Hruska III** born May 6, 1999.[1852]

Addendum I

233. Lee[5] Massengale (Bettie Jean[4] Phillips, Martha A. E.[3] Henning, Adam[2], John Adam[1]) was born 1894 in Lupton, TN, died 1935 in Spokane, WA.[1853] He married **Bertha Squires** in 1921.[1854]

Children of Lee Massengale and Bertha Squires are:

    1177   i.   **Orval[6] Massengale.**[1855]
    1178   ii.   **Arnold Massengale.**[1856]
    1179   iii.   **Mary Edna Massengale.**[1857]
    1180   iv.   **Earl Junior Massengale.**[1858]

Addendum II

319. Geraldine[6] "Jerry" Cline (Raymond Arthur[5], Pleas David[4], Eli[3], Mary Anna[2] Henning, John Adam[1]) was born March 24, 1931 in Forsyth Cty., NC. Married **Robert Abraham Brinegar, Jr.** on March 3, 1950 in Forsyth Cty., NC. Robert "Buddy" was born Nov. 10, 1932 in Forsyth Cty., NC.[1859]

+	1181	i.	**Robert Kevin[7] Brinegar** born April 6, 1951 in Forsyth Cty., NC.[1860]
	1182	ii.	**Paul Alexander Brinegar** born March 9, 1953, died March 9, 1953 in Forsyth Cty., NC.[1861]
+	1183	iii.	**David Keith Brinegar** born Nov. 8, 1954 in Forsyth Cty., NC.[1862]
+	1184	iv.	**Tammy Melia Brinegar** born March 5, 1960 in Forsyth Cty., NC.[1863]

1181. Robert Kevin[7] Brinegar (Geraldine[6] Cline, Raymond Arthur[5], Pleas David[4], Eli[3], Mary Anna[2] Henning, John Adam[1]) was born April 6, 1951 in Forsyth Cty., NC. He married **Rebecca Sue Wall** on Nov. 15, 1969. They later divorced. Rebecca was born March 28, 1951 in Forsyth Cty., NC. She was the daughter of **Donald Wall** and **Jeannie Ingram**.[1864]

+	1185	i.	**Rebecca Suzanne[8] Brinegar** was born Feb. 18, 1972.[1865]
	1186	ii.	**Jennifer Gayle Brinegar** was born July 25, 1975 in Forsyth Cty., NC.[1866]

1183. David Keith[7] Brinegar (Geraldine[6] Cline, Raymond Arthur[5], Pleas David[4], Eli[3], Mary Anna[2] Henning, John Adam[1]) was born Nov. 8, 1954 in Forsyth Cty., NC. He married **(1) Joyce Diane Hayes**. Then he married **(2) Sally Ann Harding Dunn** on Nov. 18, 1974 in Jackson, MS. Sally was born Feb. 8, 1955 in Shannon Cty., MO. Then David married **(3) Judith Ellen Carte** on Aug. 1, 1980. Judith was born May 11, 1956 in Kanawa Cty., W. VA. Her father was **Russell**

Carte and her mother was Mary Chapman.[1867]

Child of David Keith Brinegar and Sally Ann Harding Dunn is:

> 1187 i. **Kenneth Matthew[8] Brinegar** born Oct. 7, 1975 in Las Vegas, NV.[1868]

Child of David Keith Brinegar and Judith Ellen Carte is:

> 1188 i. **Alex Gerald[8] Brinegar** was born July 20, 1989 in Chatham Cty., NC.[1869]

1184. Tammy Melia[7] Brinegar (Geraldine[6] Cline, Raymond Arthur[5], Pleas David[4], Eli[3], Mary Anna[2] Henning, John Adam[1]) was born March 5, 1960 in Forsyth Cty., NC. She married **(1) Michael Anthony Muto** on Oct. 7, 1960. Married **(2) Kevin Reece Lamm** on June 1, 1985 in Wake Cty., NC.[1870]

> 1189 i. **Megan Angela[8] Lamm** born Aug. 21, 1986.[1871]

1185. Rebecca Suzanne[8] Brinegar (Robert Kevin[7] Brinegar, Geraldine[6] Cline, Raymond Arthur[5], Pleas David[4], Eli[3], Mary Anna[2] Henning, John Adam[1]) was born Feb. 17, 1972 in Forsyth Cty., NC. She married Sept., 1994 to **Richard McDowell** in Forsyth Cty., NC.[1872]

Child of Rebecca Suzanne Brinegar is:

> 1190 i. **Richard Joshua[9] Brinegar** born June 20, 1993 in Guilford Cty., NC.[1873]

Child of Rebecca Suzanne Brinegar and Richard McDowell is:

> 1191 i. **Lauren Elizabeth[9] McDowell** born Dec. 28, 1994 in Guilford Cty., NC.[1874]

The Henning Family

Abraham Lincoln often quoted the following lines from *Hamlet:*

There's a divinity that shapes our ends,
Rough-hew them how we will.

The Henning Family

1.Adelaid L. Fries, Douglas LeTell Rights, Minnie J. Smith, and Kenneth
Hamilton (eds.), Records of the Moravians in North Carolina (Raleigh, NC:
Edwards & Broughton Printing Co., 1954), Vol. VIII, pp. 3718-19.
2.Annette Fuller, "City's Growth Influenced by Hessians," Winston-Salem Journal,
4 Sept. 1979, p. 24.
3.Will of John Adam Henning dated Nov. 17, 1823, Stokes County, NC (Raleigh:
State Dept. of Archives & History). Here after referred to as the Will of John Adam
Henning.
4.1820 Stokes County, NC Census, p. 1.
5.Alan Willis, "In a Little Woodsy Knoll . . .", The Sentenel, 3 April 1981, p. 2.
6.Adelaid L. Fries, Douglas LeTell Rights, Minnie J. Smith, and Kenneth
Hamilton (eds.), Records of the Moravians in North Carolina (Raleigh, NC:
Edwards & Broughton Printing Co., Vol. IV, p. 1687.
7.Willis.
8.Patsy Moore Ginns, Rough Weather Makes Good Timber, (Chapel Hill:
University of North Carolina Press, 1977), p. 171.
9.Fuller.
10.Phronica P. Hill, 1137 South 11th St., Noblesville, IN 46060, letter dated Jan.
30, 1987.
11.Jeffrey Smith Coltrane, Jr., 4813 Meadow Hill Rd., Winston-Salem, NC 27106.
12.Journal of the Genealogical Society of Rockingham & Stokes Counties North
Carolina, Vol. V, Issue 4, No. 18, March, 2000, p. 717.
13.Stokes County, NC Index to Real Estate Conveyances, Grantees, Reel
C.090.40148, NC State Archives, Jones St., Raleigh, NC.
14.Adelaid L. Fries, Douglas LeTell Rights, Minnie J. Smith, and Kenneth
Hamilton (eds.), Records of the Moravians in North Carolina Raleigh, NC:
Edwards & Broughton Printing Co., Vol. VIII, pp. 3718-19.
15.Will of John Adam Henning.
16.Ibid.
17.Ibid.
15.Ibid.
16.Ibid.
17.Ibid.
18.Ibid.
19.Ibid.
20.Ibid.
21.Ibid.
22.Ibid.
23.Ibid.
24.Ibid.
25.Jerry Cline Brinegar, 1490 Norwich Rd., Winston-Salem, NC 27107, notes
Sept, 1999.
26.1850 Forsyth County, NC Census, dwelling 940, family 954, p. 262.

27.Fries, Vol. IX, pp. 4943-4945.
28.Coltrane.
29.Brinegar, note dated March 11, 1999.
30.Forsyth County, NC Will Book, p. 126, Dec., 1858, Will of Catherine Heckerdorn.
31.Stokes County, NC Bastardy Bonds dated 1842, NC State Archives, Jones St., Raleigh, NC.
32.Carl C. Hoots, Cemeteries of Yadkin County, North Carolina, (Spartanburg, SC: The Reprint Co., 1985), p. 153.
33.Irene Choplin, 2901 Stockton St., Winston-Salem, NC 27107, Family Group Sheet.
34.Ibid.
35.Brinegar, letter dated Feb. 12, 1987.
36.1850 Forsyth County, NC Census, dwelling 1185, family 1202.
37.Stokes County, NC Bastardy Bonds dated March 23, 1812 and June 11, 1818, NC State Archives, Jones St., Raleigh, NC.
38.Kay Fulp Hauser, 3186 Friendship Rd., Germanton, NC 27019, e-mail dated Feb. 16, 1999.
39.Ibid.
40.Ibid.
41.Ibid.
42.Ibid.
43.Ibid.
44.Ibid.
45.Will of John Adam Henning.
46.1850 Forsyth County, NC Census, dwelling 1224, family 1239.
47.Brinegar, notes Sept., 1999.
48.Stokes County, NC Bastardy Bonds, dated March 23, 1812 and June 11, 1818, NC State Archives, Jones St., Raleigh, NC.
49.1850 Forsyth County, NC Census, dwelling 1185, family 1202.
50.1860 Forsyth County, NC Census, dwelling 2252, family 2133, Belews Creek Township.
51.Brinegar, Family Group Sheet, Jan. 31, 1987.
52.Will of John Adam Henning.
53.Brinegar.
54.Ibid.
55.Stokes County, NC Marriage Bond dated Sept. 4, 1821 to Joseph Sailor & Susanna Henning, #000141266.
56.Brinegar.
57.Stokes County, NC Marriage Bond dated Sept. 4, 1821 to Joseph Sailor & Susanna Henning, #000141266.
58.Brinegar.
59.Ibid.

60.Fries, et. al., Vol. VIII, p. 3730.
61.Brinegar.
62.Ibid.
63.Ibid.
64.Ibid.
65.Will of John Adam Henning.
66.Hoots, p. 153.
67.Charles Edgar "Ed" Hennings, 1004 Elderwood Place, Greensboro, NC 27410. Hereafter shown as Ed Hennings.
68.Hoots, p. 153.
69.Ibid.
70.Ibid., p. 310.
71.Donald W. Stanley, ed., Forsyth County, N. C. Cemetery Records, (Winston-Salem, NC: Hunter Publishing Co., 1978) Vol. V, p. 992.
72.Brinegar, letter dated Aug. 8, 1987.
73.Brinegar, notes dated Sept., 1999.
74.Will of John Adam Henning.
75.Dora Henning Hereford, The Henning Family, p. 1.
76.Family Tree Maker's World Archives, CD-ROM, #8.
77.Hereford, p. 1.
78.Ibid.
79.Ibid.
80.Ibid.
81.Ibid., p. 2.
82.Anderson County, TN Marriages, July 5, 1885 James Bagley to Sarah Hennings, 1838 to 1912, Microfilm V233-1.
83.1850 Surry County, NC Census, dwelling 1212, family 1218, South Division, p. 244.
84. Hereford, p. 2.
85.Family Tree Maker's World Archives, CD-ROM, #8.
86.Julie Painter Pittman, 1462 Waterman Rd., Rosalia, WA 99170, genealogy.
87.Hereford, p. 2.
88.Will of John Adam Henning.
89.Choplin.
90.Brinegar, notes dated July 2, 1999.
91.Ibid., notes dated Sept., 1999.
92.Stokes County, NC Index to Real Estate Conveyances, Grantees, Reel C.090.40148, NC State Archives, Jones St., Raleigh, NC.
93.The Forsyth County Genealogical Society Journal, Vol. I, No. II, Winter, 1983, p. 60.
94.Stanley, 1978, Vol. V, p. 992
95.Ruth F. Shore, 6975 Shallowford Rd., Lewisville, NC 27023, Family Group Sheet, April, 1999.

96.Stanley, 1977, Vol. III, p. 593.

97.Hill.

98.1860 Yadkin County, NC Census, dwelling 257, family 247, Forbush Post Office, p. 268.

99.Ibid.

100.Choplin.

101.1880 Yadkin County, NC Census, dwelling 167, Family 167, Forbush Township, p. 19.

102.1860 Yadkin County, NC Census, dwelling 257, family 247, Forbush Post Office, p. 268.

103.Will of John Adam Henning.

104.1860 Forsyth County, NC Census, dwelling 2252, family 2133, Belews Creek Township.

105.Brinegar, Family Group Sheet, Feb. 12, 1987.

106.1860 Forsyth County, NC Census, dwelling 2252, family 2133, Belews Creek Township.

107.Stanley, 1978, Vol. V, p. 1256.

108.Brinegar, notes dated July 2, 1999.

109.1860 Forsyth County, NC Census, dwelling 2252, family 2133, Belews Creek Township.

110.Ibid.

111.Ibid.

112.Ibid.

113.Ibid.

114.Stanley, 1978, Vol. IV, p. 807.

115.Stokes County, NC Marriage Bond dated Sept. 23, 1833 to Nancy Klien & William Conrad, #000137919.

116.Hauser.

117.Stanley, 1978, Vol. IV, p. 821.

118.Brinegar, letter dated Feb. 12, 1987.

119.Ibid.

120.1850 Forsyth County, NC Census, dwelling 1185, family 1202.

121.Ibid.

122.Ibid.

123.Ibid.

124.Ibid.

125.Hauser, e-mail dated Feb. 16, 1999.

126.Ibid.

127.Ibid.

128.Ibid.

129.Ibid.

130.Kenneth G. Hamilton, ed., <u>Records of the Moravians in North Carolina</u>, (Raleigh, NC: State Department of Archives and History, 1969), Vol. XI, p. 5755.

131.Hauser, e-mail dated Feb. 16, 1999.
132.Ibid.
133.Ibid.
134.Brinegar, letter dated March 30, 1988.
135.1850 Forsyth County, NC Census, dwelling 1190, family 1206.
136.Brinegar, notes Sept., 1999.
137.Stanley, 1978, Vol. IV, p. 813.
138.1860 Forsyth County, NC Census, dwelling 494, family 459, Yadkin Township, Winston Post Office.
139.Brinegar.
140.1860 Forsyth County, NC Census, dwelling 494, family 459, Yadkin Township, Winston Post Office.
141.Stanley, 1976, Vol. II, p. 391.
142.1860 Forsyth County, NC Census, dwelling 494, family 459, Yadkin Township, Winston Post Office.
143.1870 Forsyth County, NC Census, dwelling 154, family 154, Vienna Township, Vienna Post Office, p. 20.
144.Ibid.
145.Ibid.
146.Stanley, 1978, Vol. IV, p. 813.
147.Brinegar.
148.Stanley, 1978, Vol. IV, p. 813.
149.Forsyth County, NC Marriage Licenses, 1907-1908, Reel C.038.60015, NC State Archives, Jones St., Raleigh, NC.
150.Stanley, 1976, Vol. II, p. 434.
151.Stanley, 1978, Vol. IV, p. 812.
152.Forsyth County, NC Marriage Licenses, 1907-1908, Reeel C.038.60015, NC State Archives, Jones St., Raleigh, NC.
153.1850 Forsyth County, NC Census, dwelling 1185, family 1202.
154.Davidson County, NC Marriage Bond dated January 17, 1840 to Edmond Wood & Rashel [sp.] Hennings, #000037714.
155.1850 Forsyth County, NC Census, dwelling 1185, family 1202.
156.Will of John Adam Henning.
157.1850 Forsyth County, NC Census, dwelling 1185, family 1202.
158.Ibid.
159.Ibid.
160.Ibid.
161.1860 Forsyth County, NC Census, dwelling 2252, family 2133, Belews Creek Township.
162.Brinegar, Family Group Sheet, Jan. 31, 1987.
163.Will of John Adam Henning.
164.Stokes County, NC Bastardy Bonds, July 31, 1840 for Elizabeth Henning, NC State Archives, Jones St., Raleigh, NC.

165.Ibid.
166.Brinegar, Family Group Sheet dated March 11, 1999.
167.1850 Forsyth County, NC Census, dwelling 1224, family 1239.
168.Hoots, p. 153.
169.NC Death Certificate, Vol. 241, p. 231, NC State Archives, Jones St., Raleigh, NC.
170.Hoots, p. 153.
171.1880 Yadkin County, NC Census, dwelling 233, family 233, Liberty Township, p. 25.
172.Hoots, p. 153.
173.Brinegar, letter dated Nov. 17, 1998.
174.Hoots, p. 153.
175.Brinegar.
176.1860 Yadkin County, NC Census, dwelling 310, family 296, Forbush Post Office, p. 271.
177.Ibid.
178.Stanley, 1978, Vol. IV, p. 881.
179.1860 Yadkin County, NC Census, dwelling 310, family 296, Forbush Post Office, p. 271.
180.Ibid.
181.1870 Yadkin County, NC Census, dwelling 241, family 241, Forbush Township, Huntsville Post Office, p. 34.
182.Hoots, p. 310.
183.Hennings, Ed.
184.The Forsyth County Genealogical Society Journal, Vol. I, No. II, Winter, 1983, p. 60.
185.Hoots, p. 310.
186.Ibid., p. 11.
187.Ibid., p. 310.
188.Stanley, 1978, Vol. V, p. 992.
189.Ibid.
190.1850 Forsyth County, NC Census, dwelling 1421, family 1436, p. 294.
191.Hamilton, ed., 1969, Vol. XI, p. 6143.
192.Winston-Salem Journal, Sat, Oct. 11, 1930, Obituary.
193.John Robert Bullard, Sr., (deceased) Wyman Rd., Winston-Salem, NC, telephone conversation March 5, 1987.
194.Forsyth County, NC Estate Records, 1930, Paul Jackson Henning, NC State Archives, Jones St., Raleigh, NC.
195.Winston-Salem Journal, Sat., Oct. 11, 1930, Obituary.
196.Ibid., Sun., Oct. 12, 1930, Obituary.
197.Hereford, p. 4.
198.Yadkin County, NC Marriage Bond dated Sept. 28, 1854 to Martha E. Henings[sp.] to Lewis B. Phillips, NC State Archives, Jones St., Raleigh, NC.

199.Hereford, p. 1.
200.Pittman.
201.Hereford, p. 4.
202.Ibid., p. 8.
203.Ibid., p. 1.
204.Anderson County, TN Marriage 1838 to 1912, V233-1, dated Dec. 13, 1865 to A. G. Henning & N. A. Galbreath.
205.Hereford, p. 2.
206.Ibid., p. 1.
207.Pittman.
208.Hereford, p. 12.
209.Ibid., p. 15.
210.Ibid.
211.Pittman.
212.Hereford, Obituary.
213.1850 Surry County, NC Census, dwelling 1212, family 1218, South Division, p. 244.
214.Pittman.
215.Ibid.
216.Hereford, p. 2.
217.Anderson County, TN Marriages, 1838 to 1912, V233-1, dated Dec. 3, 1882 to John Henning & Annie Wright.
218.Pittman.
219.Ibid.
220.Ibid.
221.Family Tree Maker's World Archives, CD #8.
222.Ibid.
223.1860 Anderson County, TN Census, dwelling 435, family 435, Robertsville Post Office, p. 62.
224.Pittman.
225.Anderson County, TN Marriages, 1838 to 1912, V233-1, dated Oct. 11, 1874 to Santford Henning & Elizabeth F. Johnson.
226.Hereford, p. 2.
227.Anderson County, TN Marriages, 1838 to 1912, V233-1, dated Feb. 9, 1888 to Santford Henning to Happy Elizabeth Hooks.
228.Hereford, p. 2.
229.Ibid., p. 16.
230.1880 Anderson County, TN Census, dwelling 84, family 86, 9th Civil District, p. 9.
231.Hereford, p. 16.
232.Ibid.
233.Pittman.
234.Ibid.

235.Ibid.
236.Ibid.
237.Ibid.
238.Ibid.
239.Hereford, p. 25.
240.Broderbund Family Archives, #110, Vol. 2, Ed. 5, Social Security Death Index, Internal Ref. #1.112.5.38161.148.
241.Pittman.
242.1860 Anderson County, TN Census, dwelling 435, family 435, Robertsville Post Office, p. 62.
243.Anderson County, TN Marriages, 1838 to 1912, V233-1, dated Aug. 4, 1881 to William Gabriel Henning & Betty Tunnel/Roberts.
244.Pittman.
245.Ibid.
246.Stanley, 1978, Vol. V, p. 992.
247.Forsyth County, NC Marriage Bond issued Sept. 4, 1859 to Nathaniel R. Styers & Delilah Louise Henning, NC State Archives, Jones St., Raleigh, NC.
248.Estate papers for Nathaniel Richard Styers dated Oct. 7, 1864, Forsyth Cty., NC, NC State Archives, Jones St., Raleigh, NC.
249.Stanley, 1978, Vol. IV, p. 846.
250.Ibid, 1978, Vol. V, p. 996.
251.Forsyth County, NC Marriage Bond issued on Oct. 18, 1866 to Edward T. Henning and Delilah Louise Henning Styers, NC Archives, Jones St., Raleigh, NC.
252.Stanley, 1978, Vol. 5, p. 992.
253.Hill, letter dated Sept. 19, 1986.
254.Shore.
255.Susan J. Gall, 232 Shawnee St., S.W., Winston-Salem, NC 27127, e-mail dated Oct. 1, 1998.
256.Shore.
257.Ibid.
258.Stanley, 1977, Vol. III, p. 593.
259.Brinegar, letter dated March 7, 1988.
260.Stanley, 1977, Vol. III, p. 593.
261.The Forsyth County Genealogical Society Journal, Vol. V., No. 3, Spring, 1987, pp. 54-56.
262.Ibid.
263.Ibid.
264.Ibid.
265.Stanley, 1978, Vol. V, p. 1174.
266.The Forsyth County Genealogical Society Journal, Vol. V, No. 3, Spring, 1987, pp. 54-56.
267.Ibid.
268.Ibid.

269.Ibid.
270.Stanley, 1977, Vol. III, p. 603.
271.Hill.
272.Pam Pendleton, 2019 W. 450 S., Lafayette, IN 47905.
273.Hill.
274.Ibid.
275.Rita Hineman Townsend, Hutchins-Hutchens, Descendants of Strangeman Hutchins, p. 2207.
276.Choplin.
277.Ibid.
278.Choplin.
279.1880 Yadkin County, NC Census, dwelling 167, family 167, Forbush Township, p. 19.
280.Choplin, letter dated June 4, 1984 to Jeffrey Coltrane, Jr.
281.1880 Yadkin County, NC Census, dwelling 167, family 167, Forbush Township, p. 19.
282.Ibid.
283.Stanley, 1978, Vol. IV, p. 821.
284.Brinegar, notes dated July 2, 1999.
285.Stanley, 1978, Vol. IV, p. 821.
286.Ibid.
287.Brinegar, notes dated July 2, 1999.
288.Ibid.
289.Hauser, e-mail dated Feb. 16, 1999.
290.Brenda Nance Adams, e-mail dated June 18, 1999.
291.Hauser, e-mail dated Feb. 16, 1999.
292.Hauser, e-mail dated Feb. 16, 1999.
293.Hauser, printout dated Sept., 1999.
294.Ibid.
295.Hauser, e-mail dated Feb. 16, 1999.
296.Ibid.
297.Ibid
298.Ibid.
299.Broderbund Family Archive #110, Vol. 1, Ed. 5, Social Security Death Index, Internal Ref. #1.111.5.45359.170.
300.Hauser, e-mail dated Feb. 16, 1999.
301.Ibid.
302.Ibid.
303.Ibid.
304.Stanley, 1978, Vol. IV, p. 812.
305.Ibid., p. 992.
306.Brinegar, letter dated Aug. 8, 1987.
307.Ibid.

308. Broderbund Family Archive #110, Vol. 1, Ed. 5, Social Security Death Index, Internal Ref. #1.111.5.45359.170.
309. Forsyth County, NC Marriage Licenses, 1916, Reel C.038.60022, NC State Archives, Jones St., Raleigh, NC.
310. Stanley, 1976, Vol. II, p. 391.
311. Ibid.
312. Forsyth County, NC Marriage Licenses, 1909, Reel C.038.60016, NC State Archives, Jones St., Raleigh, NC.
313. Stanley, 1976, Vol. II, p. 391.
314. Ibid.
315. Forsyth County, NC Marriage Licenses, 1912, Reel C.038.60018, NC State Archives, Jones St., Raleigh, NC.
316. Brinegar, Family Group Sheet dated March 11, 1999.
317. Brinegar, Family Group Sheet dated Jan. 31, 1987.
318. Ibid.
319. Brinegar, Family Group Sheet dated March 11, 1999.
320. Ibid.
321. Ibid.
322. Ibid.
323. Ibid.
324. Ibid.
325. Ibid.
326. Ibid.
327. Ibid.
328. Ibid.
329. Ibid.
330. Stokes County, NC Bastardy Bonds, December 11, 1843, NC State Archives, Jones St., Raleigh, NC.
331. NC Birth and Death Index, 1906-1911, Vol. 296, p. 342, NC State Archives, Jones St., Raleigh, NC.
332. Brinegar, Family Group Sheet dated March 11, 1999.
333. The Heritage of Surry County, NC, (Winston-Salem, NC: Hunter Publishing Co., 1983), Vol. I, Item 716, p. 542.
334. Brinegar, Family Group Sheet dated March 11, 1999.
335. Hoots, p. 153.
336. 1880 Yadkin County, NC Census, dwelling 233, family 233, Liberty Township, p. 25.
337. Hoots, p. 153.
338. Ibid., p. 212.
339. Ibid., p. 153.
340. 1880 Yadkin County, NC Census, dwelling 233, family 233, Liberty Township, p. 25.
341. 1910 Yadkin County, NC Census, dwelling 282, Supervisor's District 144.

342.Ibid.
343.Ibid.
344.Ibid.
345.Ibid.
346.Ibid.
347.1920 Yadkin County, NC Census, dwelling 220, family 221, Reel T625-1324.
348.1910 Yadkin County, NC Census, dwelling 282, Supervisor's District 144.
349.Ibid.
350.Ibid.
351.Ibid.
352.Ibid.
353.Stanley, 1978, Vol. IV, p. 881.
354.Death Certificate of John Kenyon Henning, Vol. 905, p. 257, NC State Archives, Jones St., Raleigh, NC.
355.Robert E. Henning, 214 Tabor View Ln., Winston-Salem, NC 27106, Family Work Sheet, 1992.
356.Stanley, 1978, Vol. IV, p. 881.
357.Ibid.
358.Broderbund Family Archive #110, Vol. 1, Ed. 5, Social Security Death Index, Internal Ref. #1.111.5.105640.65.
359.Stanley, 1978, Vol. IV, p. 881.
360.Forsyth County, NC Marriage Licenses, 1915, Forsyth County Court House, Winston-Salem, NC.
361.Broderbund Family Archives #110, Vol. 1, Ed. 5, Social Security Death Index, Internal Ref. #1.111.5.105634.152.
362.Ibid., Internal Ref. #1.111.5.105646.24.
363.Hoots, p. 310.
364.Brinegar, letter dated Aug. 8, 1987.
365.Hoots, p. 310.
366.1920 Yadkin County, NC Census, East Bend Township, p. 201.
367.Stanley, 1977, Vol. III, p. 597.
368.Hennings, Ed, Family Group Sheet dated March 10, 1999.
369.Hoots, p. 311.
370.Choplin.
371.Ibid.
372.Hennings, Ed, Family Group Sheet dated March 10, 1999.
373.Ibid.
374.Ibid.
375.Hoots, p. 11.
376.Choplin.
377.Ibid.
378.The Heritage of Yadkin County, North Carolina, Hunter Publishing Co., Winston-Salem, NC, 1981, Item 232, p. 214.

379.Choplin.

380.Hoots, p. 11.

381.Hennings, Ed, Family Group Sheet dated March 10, 1999.

382.Choplin.

383.Hennings, Ed, fax dated April 8, 1999.

384.Hoots, p. 11.

385.Broderbund Family Archive #110, Vol. 2, Ed. 5, Social Security Death Index, Internal Ref. #1.112.5.44116.64.

386.Hennings, Ed., fax dated April 19, 1999.

387.Brinegar, letter dated Aug. 8, 1987.

388.Hoots, p. 310.

389.Death Certificate, Vol. 1065, p. 335, NC State Archives, Jones St., Raleigh, NC.

390.Hennings, Ed, e-mail dated March 19, 1999.

391.1920 Yadkin County, NC Census, dwelling 240, family 241, East Bend Township, p. 201, Reel T625-1324.

392.Broderbund Family Archive #110, Vol. 1, Ed. 5, Social Security Death Index, Internal Ref. #1.111.5.105635.177.

393.Ibid.

394.Hoots, p. 310.

395.Ibid.

396.Ibid.

397.Choplin.

398.1920 Yadkin County, NC Census, dwelling 225, family 226, East Bend Township, p. 200.

399.Choplin.

400.Hennings, Ed, Family Group Sheet dated March 10, 1999.

401.Pittman.

402.Hereford, p. 4.

403.Ibid.

404.Ibid.

405.Pittman.

406.Ibid.

407.Ibid.

408.Ibid.

409.Hereford, p. 5.

410.Ibid., p. 6.

411.Broderbund Family Archive #110, Vol. 1, Ed. 5, Social Security Death Index, Internal Ref. #1.111.5.106956.108.

412.Hereford, p. 8.

413.Pittman.

414.Broderbund Family Archive #110, Vol. 1, Ed. 5, Social Security Death Index, Internal Ref. #1.111.5.129212.41.

415.Ibid., Internal Ref. #1.111.5.116010.78.
416.Hereford, p. 8.
417.Ibid.
418.Ibid.
419.Pittman.
420.Broderbund Family Archive #110, Vol. 2, Ed. 5, Social Security Death Index, Internal Ref. #1.112.5.7989.181.
421.Pittman.
422.Hereford, p. 11.
423.Ibid.
424.Ibid.
425.Broderbund Family Archive #110, Vol. 1, Ed. 5, Social Security Death Index, Internal Ref. #1.111.5.80294.9.
426.Pittman.
427.Ibid.
428.Hereford, p. 12.
429.Ibid.
430.Ibid.
431.Broderbund Family Archive #110, Vol. 2, Ed. 5, Social Security Death Index, Internal Ref. #1.112.5.57260.133.
432.Ibid., Vol. 1, Ed. 5, Internal Ref. #1.111.5.105631.40.
433.Hereford, p. 14.
434.Pittman.
435.Hereford, p. 14.
436.Pittman.
437.Broderbund Family Archive #110, Vol. 1, Ed. 5, Social Security Death Index, Internal Ref. #1.111.5.67899.15.
438.1880 Anderson County, TN Census, dwelling 84, family 86, 9th Civil District, p. 9.
439.Pittman.
440.Hereford, p. 16.
441.Ibid.
442.Broderbund Family Archive #110, Vol. 1, Ed. 5, Social Security Death Index, Internal Ref. #1.111.5.105636.13.
443.Pittman.
444.Broderbund Family Archive #110, Vol. 1, Ed. 5, Social Security Death Index, Internal Ref. #1.111.5.105642,175.
445.Pittman.
446.Ibid.
447.Ibid.
448.Ibid.
449.Ibid.
450.Ibid.

451.Hereford, p. 18.
452.Broderbund Family Archive #110, Vol. 2, Ed. 5, Social Security Death Index, Internal Ref. #1.112.5.48036.80.
453.Hereford, Obituary.
454.Pittman.
455.Broderbund Family Archive #110, Vol. 1, Ed. 5, Social Security Death Index, Internal Ref. #1.111.5.105638.58.
456.Ibid., Internal Ref. #1.111.5.105646.114.
457.Hereford, p. 22.
458.Hereford, Obituary.
459.Pittman.
460.Hereford, p. 23.
461.Pittman.
462.Ibid.
463.Hereford, Obituary.
464.Pittman.
465.Ibid.
466.Ibid.
467.Ibid.
468.Hereford, p. 25.
469.Pittman.
470.Broderbund Family Archive #110, Vol. 1, Ed. 5, Social Security Death Index, Internal Ref. #1.111.5.106136.
471.Pittman.
472.Broderbund Family Archive #110, Vol. 1, Ed. 5, Social Security Death Index, Internal Ref. #1.111.5.106137.29.
473.Ibid., Internal Ref. #1.111.5.106137.130.
474.Pittman.
475.Ibid.
476.Hereford, p. 27.
477.Pittman.
478.Ibid.
479.Stanley, 1978, Vol. IV, p. 846.
480.Forsyth County, NC Marriage Licenses, 1870-1879, Reel C.038.60005, NC State Archives, Jones St., Raleigh, NC.
481.Stanley, 1978, Vol. IV, p. 846.
482.Ophelia Conrad Fordham, 1936 Gaston St., Winston-Salem, NC 27103, letter dated April 5, 1987.
483.Stanley, 1978, Vol. V, p. 1083.
484.Treva Bullard Miller Jennings, 1819 Country Club Dr., High Point, NC 27260, letter dated March 24, 1987. Mrs. Jennings is now deceased.
485.Lynn G. Ester, 685 Nighthawk Rd., Lynchburg, VA 24504.

486.Charlotte Observer, Dec. 31, 1981, Obituary, no page number was given in the clipping sent by Dorothy Bullard.
487.Broderbund Family Archive #110, Vol. 1, Ed. 5, Social Security Death Index, Internal Ref. #1.111.5.40142.21.
488.Coltrane, Family Group Sheet dated March 7, 1987.
489.Ibid.
490.Ibid.
491.Ibid.
492.Ibid.
493.Ibid.
494.Ibid.
495.Ibid.
496.Susan J. Gall, 323 Shawnee St., SW, Winston-Salem, NC 27127, genealogy, 1998.
497.Ruth F. Shore, 6975 Shallowford Rd., Lewisville, NC 27023, Family Group Sheet, May, 1999.
498.Broderbund Family Archive #110, Vol. 1, Ed. 5, Social Security Death Index, Internal Ref. #1.112.5.74205.64.
499.Shore Family Group Sheet dated May, 1999.
500.Broderbund Family Archive #110, Vol. 1, Ed. 5, Social Security Death Index, Internal Ref. #1.112.5.74197.60.
501.Shore Family Group Sheet dated May, 1999.
502.Coltrane, Family Group Sheet dated March 7, 1987.
503.Shore, Family Group Sheet dated May, 1999.
504.Gall, genealogy.
505.Shore, Family Group Sheet dated May, 1999.
506.Ibid.
507.Ibid.
508.Ibid.
509.Stanley, 1977, Vol. III, p. 592.
510.Ibid., p. 593.
511.Ibid.
512.Ibid.
513.The Forsyth County Genealogical Society Journal, Vol. V, No. 3, Spring, 1987, pp. 54-56.
514.Ibid.
515.Ibid.
516.Ibid.
517.Ibid.
518.Ibid.
519.Broderbund Family Archive #110, Vol. 1, Ed. 5, Social Security Death Index, Internal Ref. #1.111.5.24440.57.

520.The Forsyth County Genealogical Society Journal, Vol. V, No. 3, Spring, 1987, pp. 54-56.
521.Pam Pendleton, 2019 W. 450 S. Lafayette, IN 47905, genealogy Oct., 1998.
522.Ibid.
523.The Forsyth County Genealogical Society Journal, Vol. V, No. 3, Spring, 1987, pp. 54-56.
524.Pendleton.
525.Phronica P. Hill, 1137 S. 11th St., Noblesville, IN 46060, letter dated Sept. 19, 1986.
526.Ibid.
527.Broderbund Family Archive #110, Vol. 1, Ed. 5, Social Security Death Index, Internal Ref. #1.111.5.77764.175.
528.Adams.
529.Ibid.
530.Hauser, e-mail dated Feb. 16, 1999.
531.Ibid.
532.Ibid.
533.Ibid.
534.Ibid.
535.Ibid.
536.Ibid.
537.Ibid.
538.Ibid.
539.Ibid.
540.Ibid.
541.Ibid.
542.Ibid.
543.Ibid.
544.Ibid.
545.Brinegar, letter dated Aug. 8, 1987.
546.Forsyth County, NC Marriage Licenses, 1913, Reel C.038.60019, NC State Archives, Jones St., Raleigh, NC.
547.Broderbund Family Archive #110, Vol. 1, Ed. 5, Social Security Death Index, Internal Ref. #1.111.5.45392.26.
548.Stanley, 1976, Vol. II, p. 371.
549.Brinegar, letter dated Aug. 8, 1987.
550.Ibid., Family Group Sheet dated March 11, 1999.
551.Ibid.
552.Ibid.
553.Ibid., notes dated July 2, 1999.
554.Ibid., Family Group Sheet dated March 11, 1999.
555.Jeffrey L. Ferguson, 3935 Chilton Dr., Winston-Salem, NC 27106, e-mail Jan. 10, 2000.

556.Ibid., e-mail dated July 30, 1999.
557.Broderbund Family Archive #110, Vol. 2, Ed. 5, Social Security Death Index, Internal Ref. #1.112.5.7181.99.
558.Ibid., Vol. 1, Internal Ref. #1.111.5.105657.176.
559.Ferguson, e-mail received Aug. 14, 1999.
560.Ibid.
561.Henning, Robert, Family Group Sheet dated 1992.
562.Broderbund Family Archive #110, Vol. 1, Ed. 5, Social Security Death Index, Internal Ref. #1.111.5.11546.10.
563.Ibid., Internal Ref. #1.111.5.11546.13.
564.Ibid., Internal Ref. #1.111.5.105646.24.
565.Henning, Robert, letter dated March 10, 1992.
566.Broderbund Family Archive #110, Vol. 1, Ed. 5, Social Security Death Index, Internal Ref. #1.111.5.105649.36.
567.Joem Rivers Davis Henning, 1012 Shaker Ct., Winston-Salem, NC 27104, Family Group Sheet dated March 5, 1992.
568.Stanley, 1977, Vol. III, p. 597.
569.Hennings, Ed., Family Group Sheet dated March 10, 1999.
570.Choplin.
571.Forsyth County, NC Marriage Licenses, 1934, Reel C.038.60042, NC State Archives, Jones St., Raleigh, NC.
572.Broderbund Family Archive #110, Vol. 1, Ed. 5, Social Security Death Index, Internal Ref. #1.111.5.105638.122.
573.Ibid., Internal Ref. #1.111.5.105639.142.
574.Choplin.
575.Stanley, 1977, Vol. III, p. 597.
576.Death Certificate, Vol. 850, p. 221, NC State Archives, Jones St., Raleigh, NC.
577.Stanley, 1977, Vol. III, p. 592.
578.Choplin.
579.Hennings, Ed, fax dated April 8, 1999.
580.Broderbund Family Archive #110, Vol. 1, Ed. 5, Social Security Death Index, Internal Ref. #1.111.5.48575.85.
581.Stanley, 1977, Vol. III, p. 592.
582.NC Birth & Death Index, 1906-1911, Vol. 444, p. 393, NC State Archives, Jones St., Raleigh, NC.
583.Broderbund Family Archive #110, Vol. 1, Ed. 5, Social Security Death Index, Internal Ref. #1.111.5.105648.192.
584.Ibid., Vol. 2, Internal Ref. #1.112.5.33696.0.
585.Hennings, Ed, fax dated April 8, 1999.
586.Ibid., Family Group Sheet dated March 10, 1999.
587.Hoots, p. 311.
588.Winston-Salem Journal, Obituary, Fri., April 3, 1999.

589.Choplin.

590.Broderbund Family Archive #110, Vol. 1, Ed. 5, Social Security Death Index, Internal Ref. #1.111.5.102732.50.

591.Choplin.

592.Broderbund Family Archive #110, Vol. 1, Ed. 5, Social Security Death Index, Internal Ref. #1.112.5.6771.33.

593.Hennings, Ed, Family Group Sheet dated March 10, 1999.

594.Ibid.

595.Choplin.

596.Ibid.

597.Ibid.

598.Ibid.

599.Ibid.

600.Ibid.

601.Ibid.

602.Ibid.

603.Broderbund Family Archive #110, Vol. 1, Ed. 5, Social Security Death Index, Internal Ref. #1.111.5.105631.133.

604.Ibid., Internal Ref. #1.111.5.130561.130.

605.Choplin.

606.Ibid.

607.Hennings, Ed, Family Group Sheet dated March 10, 1999.

608.Choplin.

609.Broderbund Family Archive #110, Vol. 2, Ed. 5, Social Security Death Index, Internal Ref. #1.112.5.80406.14.

610.Henning, Ed., Family Group Sheet dated March 10, 1999.

611.Broderbund Family Archive #110, Vol. 2, Ed. 5, Social Security Death Index, Internal Ref. #1.112.5.80406.133.

612.Choplin.

613.Hennings, Ed, Family Group Sheet dated March 10, 1999.

614.Betty S. Collins, 411 Thurston St., Winston-Salem, NC 27103 notes postmarked May 13, 1999.

615.Choplin.

616.Hennings, Ed, Family Group Sheet dated March 10, 1999.

617.Ibid.

618.Choplin.

619.Henning, Ed, Family Group Sheet dated March 10, 1999.

620.Choplin.

621.Ibid.

622.Ibid.

623.Hennings, Ed, Family Group Sheet dated March 10, 1999.

624.Ibid, fax dated April 19, 1999.

625.Choplin.

626.Ibid.
627.Hennings, Ed, fax dated April 19, 1999.
628.Ibid.
629.Ibid.
630.Ibid.
631.Choplin.
632.Broderbund Family Archive #110, Vol. 1, Ed. 5, Social Security Death Index, Internal Ref. #1.111.5.105631.1331.
633.Choplin.
634.Hoots, p. 11.
635.Ibid.
636.Forsyth County, NC Marriage Licenses, 1938, Reel C.038.60046, NC State Archives, Jones St., Raleigh, NC.
637.Ruth Earlene Hennings Speas, 1827 Butner Mill Rd., East Bend, NC 27018.
638.Varnon, p. 55.
639.Choplin.
640.Varnon, p. 56.
641.Choplin.
642.Philip Christoph Vogler Memorial, Inc. Newsletter, Vol. 5, No. 3, Sept., 1991, p. 6.
643.Speas, Aug., 1999.
644.Hennings, Ed, Family Group Sheet dated March 10, 1999.
645.Choplin.
646.Hennings, Ed, Family Group Sheet dated March 10, 1999.
647.Ibid., fax dated April 8, 1999.
648.Ibid.
649.Choplin.
650.Brinegar, letter dated April 8, 1987.
651.Choplin.
652.Ibid.
653.Ibid.
654.Ibid.
655.Ibid.
656.Broderbund Family Archive #110, Vol. 1, Ed. 5, Social Security Death Index, Internal Ref. #1.111.5.115704.29.
657.Hennings, Ed, Family Group Sheet dated March 10, 1999.
658.Ibid.
659.Ibid.
660.Ibid.
661.Hoots, p. 11.
662.Choplin.
663.Hoots, p. 11.
664.Choplin.

665.Ibid.
666.Ibid.
667.Ibid.
668.Ibid.
669.Broderbund Family Archive #110, Vol. 2, Ed. 5, Social Security Death Index, Internal Ref. #1.112.5.44116.64.
670.Varnon, p. 56.
671.Hennings, Ed, fax dated April 19, 1999.
672.Choplin.
673.Broderbund Family Archive #110, Vol. 2, Ed. 5, Social Security Death Index, Internal Ref. #1.111.5.20872.45.
674.Hennings, Ed, fax dated April 19, 1999.
675.Ibid.
676.Ibid.
677.Ibid.
678.Ibid.
679.Ibid.
680.Ibid.
681.Choplin.
682.Ibid.
683.Ibid.
684.Ibid.
685.Broderbund Family Archive #110, Vol. 1, Ed. 5, Social Security Death Index, Internal Ref. #1.111.5.105635.177.
686.Hennings, Ed, Family Group Sheet dated March 10, 1999.
687.Violet Fannie Henning Weaver, Rt. 1, Box 99, Glenwood, AR 71943, Aug., 1999.
688.Connie Henning Bland, 164 W. 1st St., Manteno, IL 60950.
689.Ibid.
690.Ibid.
691.Weaver.
692.Broderbund Family Archive #110, Vol. 1, Ed. 5, Social Security Death Index, Internal Ref. #1.111.5.105633.176.
693.Hennings, Ed, Family Group Sheet dated March 10, 1999.
694.Ibid., notes dated May 15, 1999.
695.Ibid.
696.Patsy Simmons, 5312 Bent Tree Ct., Pfafftown, NC 27040, letter dated Jan. 13, 1990.
697.Hennings, Ed, fax dated March 21, 1999.
698.Ibid., Family Group Sheet dated July 11, 1999.
699.Ibid.
700.Ibid.
701.Ibid.

702.Ibid.
703.Ibid.
704.Hoots, p. 310.
705.Hennings, Ed, fax dated April 8, 1999.
706.Ibid.
707.Ibid.
708.Ibid.
709.Choplin.
710.Broderbund Family Archive #110, Vol. 1, Ed. 5, Social Security Death Index, Internal Ref. #1.111.5.111689.110.
711.Hennings, Ed, fax dated April 8, 1999.
712.Choplin.
713.Hennings, Ed, fax dated April 8, 1999.
714.Ibid, Family Group Sheet dated March 10, 1999.
715.Ibid.
716.Ibid.
717.Ibid.
718.Ibid.
719.Choplin.
720.Hennings, Ed, Family Group Sheet dated March 10, 1999.
721.Choplin.
722.Herefored, p. 4.
723.Ibid.
724.Ibid., p. 5.
725.Pittman.
726.Ibid.
727.Ibid.
728.Broderbund Family Archive #110, Vol. 2, Ed. 5, Social Security Death Index, Internal Ref. #1.112.5.96808.135.
729.Pittman.
730.Hereford, p. 5.
731.Ibid.
732.Ibid.
733.Broderbund Family Archive #110, Vol. 1, Ed. 5, Social Security Death Index, Internal Ref. #1.111.5.106956.108.
734.Hereford, p. 6.
735.Ibid., p. 7.
736.Ibid.
737.Ibid.
738.Ibid.
739.Broderbund Family Archive #110, Vol. 1, Ed. 5, Social Security Death Index, Internal Ref. #1.111.5.129212.41.
740.Pittman.

741.Broderbund Family Archive #110, Vol. 1, Ed. 5, Social Security Death Index, Internal Ref. #1.111.5.116010.78.
742.Pittman.
743.Broderbund Family Archive #110, Vol. 1, Ed. 5, Social Security Death Index, Internal Ref. #1.111.5.115992.131.
744.Pittman.
745.Ibid.
746.Hereford, p. 9.
747.Hereford, p. 9.
748.Ibid.
749.Ibid., p. 10.
750.Broderbund Family Archive #110, Vol. 1, Ed. 5, Social Security Death Index, Internal Ref. #1.111.5.80294.9.
751.Hereford, p. 11.
752.Ibid., p. 11.
753.Broderbund Family Archive #110, Vol. 1, Ed. 5, Social Security Death Index, Internal Ref. #1.111.5.80306.122.
754.Hereford, p. 12.
755.Ibid.
756.Ibid.
757.Broderbund Family Archive #110, Vol. 2, Ed. 5, Social Security Death Index, Internal Ref. #1.112.5.94181.84.
758.Hereford, p. 13.
759.Ibid.
760.Ibid.
761.Ibid.
762.Broderbund Family Archive #110, Vol. 2, Ed. 5, Social Security Death Index, Internal Ref. #1.112.5.57260.133.
763.Hereford, p. 13.
764.Pittman.
765.Ibid.
766.Ibid.
767.Ibid.
768.Broderbund Family Archive #110, Vol. 1, Ed. 5, Social Security Death Index, Internal Ref. #1.111.5.67899.15.
769.Ibid., Internal Ref. #1.111.5.67898.199.
770.Pittman.
771.Ibid.
772.Ibid.
773.Ibid.
774.Ibid.
775.Ibid.
776.Ibid.

777.Ibid.

778.Hereford, Obituary.

779.Hereford, p. 18.

780.Pittman.

781.Hereford, p. 18.

782.Broderbund Family Archive #110, Vol. 2, Ed. 5, Social Security Death Index, Internal Ref. #1.112.5.48036.80.

783.Hereford, p. 18.

784.Broderbund Family Archive #110, Vol. 2, Ed. 5, Social Security Death Index, Internal Ref. #1.112.5.48012.671.

785.Hereford, p. 19.

786.Ibid.

787.Ibid.

788.Broderbund Family Archive #110, Vol. 1, Ed. 5, Social Security Death Index, Internal Ref. #1.111.5.105639.162.

789.Pittman.

790.Hereford, p. 20.

791.Pittman.

792.Broderbund Family Archive #110, Vol. 1, Ed. 5, Social Security Death Index, Internal Ref. #1.111.5.105646.114.

793.Hereford, p. 21.

794.Ibid.

795.Ibid.

796.Ibid.

797.Ibid.

798.Pittman.

799.Hereford, p. 22.

800.Ibid.

801.Pittman.

802.Hereford, p. 22.

803.Ibid.

804.Ibid.

805.Ibid., p. 23.

806.Pittman.

807.Hereford, p. 23.

808.Pittman.

809.Ibid.

810.Ibid.

811.Ibid.

812.Ibid.

813.Ibid.

814.Ibid.

815.Ibid.

816.Ibid.
817.Ibid.
818.Ibid.
819.Hereford, Wedding Announcement.
820.Pittman.
821.Ibid.
822.Ibid.
823.Hereford, p. 25.
824.Ibid.
825.Ibid.
826.Ibid.
827.Ibid.
828.Ibid.
829.Ibid.
830.Ibid.
831.Broderbund Family Archive #110, Vol. 1, Ed. 5, Social Security Death Index, Internal Ref. #1.111.5.106137.130.
832.Hereford, p. 26.
833.Ibid.
834.Ibid.
835.Ibid.
836.Broderbund Family Archive #110, Vol. 1, Ed. 5, Social Security Death Index, Internal Ref. #1.111.5.147239.129.
837.Hereford, p. 27.
838.Ibid.
839.Ibid.
840.Margaret L. Hartle, 1020 Miller St., Winston-Salem, NC 27103, letter dated Dec. 28, 1987.
841.Forsyth County, NC Marriage Licenses, 1898-1899, Reel C.038.60010, NC State Archives, Jones St., Raleigh, NC.
842.Hartle.
843.Ibid.
844.Ibid.
845.Ibid.
846.Ibid.
847.Ibid.
848.Ophelia Conrad Fordham, 1936 Gaston St., Winston-Salem, NC 27103, letter dated April 5, 1987.
849.Ibid.
850.Ibid.,
851.Stanley, 1978, Vol. V, p. 1083.
852.Forsyth County, NC Marriage Licenses, 1910-1911, Reel C.038.60017, NC State Archives, Jones St., Raleigh, NC.

853.Broderbund Family Archive #110, Vol. 1, Ed. 5, Social Security Death Index, Internal Ref. #1.111.5.32870.149.

854.Ibid., Internal Ref. #1.111.5.32873.172.

855.Ibid., Vol. 2, Internal Ref. #1.112.5.21011.90.

856.Jennings, letter dated March 24, 1987.

857.Forsyth County, NC Marriage Licenses, 1920, Reel C.038.60026, NC State Archives, Jones St., Raleigh, NC.

858.Jennings.

859.Broderbund Family Archive #110, Vol. 1, Ed. 5, Social Security Death Index, Internal Ref. #1.111.5.119666.31.

860.Lynn Griffith Ester, 685 Nighthawk Rd., Lynchburg, VA 24504.

861.Dorothy Early Bullard, 500 Lenoir Rd., Apt. 224, Morganton, NC 28655, letter dated Aug. 4, 1986.

862.Funeral bulletin, Vogler's Funeral Home, Reynolda Rd., Winston-Salem, NC dated April 6, 1998.

863.Ester.

864.Charlotte Observer, dated Dec. 31, 1981, Obituary. No page number listed. Newspaper clipping from Dorothy E. Bullard.

865.Broderbund Family Archive #110, Vol. 1, Ed. 5, Social Security Death Index, Internal Ref. #1.111.5.32873.20.

866.May Evangeline Moore Bullard's ancestry chart given to Dorothy E. Bullard, mailed Oct. 31, 1985.

867.Ibid.

868.Who's Who in the South, and Southwest, 1967-1968,1 (Chicago, IL: Marquis Who's Who, 1967), p. 138.

869.Broderbund Family Archive #110, Vol. 1, Ed. 5, Social Security Death Index, Internal Ref. #1.111.5.40142.21.

870.Forsyth County, NC Marriage Licenses, 1918, NC State Archives, Jones St., Raleigh, NC.

871.Stanley, 1976, Vol. III, p. 517.

872.Bullard, John Robert, Sept. 27, 1985.

873.Ibid.

874.Broderbund Family Archive #110, Vol. 1, Ed. 5, Social Security Death Index, Internal Ref. #1.111.5.40143.124.

875.Coltrane, Family Group Sheet dated March 7, 1987.

876.Ibid.

877.Ibid.

878.Ibid.

879.Ibid.

880.Ibid.

881.Ibid.

882.Ibid., letter dated March 3, 2000.

883.Ibid.

884.Ibid.
885.Ibid.
886.Ibid.
887.Ibid.
888.Gall.
889.Ibid.
890.The Forsyth County Genealogical Society Journal, Vol. V, No. 3, Spring, 1987, pp. 54-56.
891.Stanley, 1977, Vol. III, 592.
892.Ibid.
893.Broderbund Family Archive #110, Vol. 1, Ed. 5, Social Security Death Index, Internal Ref. #1.111.5.24438.21.
894.The Forsyth County Genealogical Society Journal, Vol. V, No. 3, Spring, 1987, pp. 54-56.
895.Pendleton, Oct., 1998.
896.Ibid.
897.Ibid.
898.Ibid.
899.Ibid.
900.Ibid.
901.Ibid.
902.Ibid.
903.Ibid.
904.Ibid.
905.Ibid.
906.Broderbund Family Archive #110, Vol. 1, Ed. 5, Social Security Death Index, Internal Ref. #1.111.5.107995.44.
907.Pendleton, Oct., 1998.
908.Ibid.
909.Ibid.
910.Ibid.
911.Broderbund Family Archive #110, Vol. 1, Ed. 5, Social Security Death Index, Internal Ref. #1.111.5.108304.98.
912.Pendleton, Oct., 1998.
913.Ibid.
914.Ibid.
915.Ibid.
916.Hauser, e-mail dated Feb. 16, 1999.
917.Ibid.
918.Ibid.
919.Ibid.
920.Ibid.
921.Ibid.

922.Ibid.
923.Ibid.
924.Ibid.
925.Ibid.
926.Ibid.
927.Ibid.
928.Ibid.
929.Ibid.
930.Ibid.
931.Ibid.
932.Brinegar, Family Group Sheet dated March 11, 1999.
933.Ibid.
934.Ibid.
935.Ibid.
936.Ibid.
937.Ibid.
938.Ibid., notes dated July 2, 1999.
939.Ibid.
940.Ibid.
941.Ibid.
942.Ibid.
943.Ibid., Family Group Sheet dated March 11, 1999.
944.Broderbund Family Archive #110, Vol. 1, Ed. 5, Social Security Death Index, Internal Ref. #1.111.5.10014.6.
945.Brinegar, notes dated July 2, 1999.
946.Ibid.
947.Ibid.
948.Ibid.
949.Ibid.
950.Ibid.
951.Ibid.
952.Brinegar, notes dated July 2, 1999.
953.Broderbund Family Archive #110, Vol. 2, Ed. 5, Social Security Death Index, Internal Ref. #1.112.5.7181.99.
954.Ferguson, e-mail dated Aug. 14, 1999.
955.Ibid.
956.Henning, Joem, March 5, 1992.
957.Ibid.
958.Ibid.
959.Ibid.
960.Hennings, Ed, fax dated April 8, 1999.
961.Broderbund Family Archive #110, Vol. 1, Ed. 5, Social Security Death Index, Internal Ref. #1.111.5.36481.38.

962.Hennings, Ed., fax dated April 8, 1999.
963.Broderbund Family Archive #110, Vol. 1, Ed. 5, Social Security Death Index, Internal Ref. #1.111.5.48575.85.
964.Choplin.
965.Ibid.
966.Ibid.
967.Broderbund Family Archive #110, Vol. 1, Ed. 5, Social Security Death Index, Internal Ref. #1.111.5.105648.192.
968.Hennings, Ed., fax dated April 8, 1999.
969.Ibid.
970.Ibid.
971.Ibid.
972.Ibid.
973.Broderbund Family Archive #110, Vol. 2, Ed. 5, Social Security Death Index, Internal Ref. #1.112.5.33696.0.
974.Ibid., Internal Ref. #1.112.5.33731.2.
975.Choplin.
976.Ibid.
977.Hennings, Ed, fax dated April 8, 1999.
978.Broderbund Family Archive #110, Vol. 1, Ed. 5, Social Security Death Index, Internal Ref. #1.111.5.8795.33.
979.Choplin.
980.Ibid.
981.Ibid.
982.Ibid.
983.Winston-Salem Journal, Obituary dated Fri., April 3, 1999.
984.Hennings, Ed, fax dated April 8, 1999.
985.Ibid., Family Group Sheet dated May 15, 1999.
986.Ibid.
987.Ibid.
988.Ibid.
989.Ibid.
990.Ibid.
991.Hennings, Ed, fax dated March 10, 1999.
992.Ibid., fax dated April 29, 1999.
993.Choplin.
994.Ibid.
995.Ibid.
996.Ibid.
997.Hennings, Ed, Family Group Sheet dated March 10, 1999.
998.Ibid., fax dated April 29, 1999.
999.Choplin.
1000.Ibid.

1001.Ibid.
1002.Ibid.
1003.Hennings, Ed, Family Group Sheet dated March 10, 1999.
1004.Ibid.
1005.Choplin.
1006.Ibid.
1007.Ibid.
1008.Ibid.
1009.Broderbund Family Archive #110, Vol. 1, Ed. 5, Social Security Death Index, Internal Ref. #1.111.5.43087.23.
1010.Choplin.
1011.Ibid.
1012.Ibid.
1013.Ibid.
1014.Choplin.
1015.Ibid.
1016.Ibid.
1017.Ibid.
1018.Ibid.
1019.Broderbund Family Archive #110, Vol. 1, Ed. 5, Social Security Death Index, Internal Ref. #1.111.5.66201.91.
1020.Ibid., Internal Ref. #1.111.5.66200.192.
1021.Choplin.
1022.Hennings, Ed, Family Group Sheet dated March 10, 1999.
1023.Collins.
1024.Choplin.
1025.Ibid.
1026.Ibid.
1027.Ibid.
1028.Broderbund Family Archive #110, Vol. 2, Ed. 5, Social Security Death Index, Internal Ref. #1.112.5.80406.133.
1029.Collins.
1030.Ibid.
1031.Ibid.
1032.Ibid.
1033.Hennings, Ed, Family Group Sheet dated March 10, 1999.
1034.Collins.
1035.Ibid.
1036.Hennings, Ed, Family Group Sheet dated March 10, 1999.
1037.Collins.
1038.Hennings, Ed, Family Group Sheet dated March 10, 1999.
1039.Collins.
1040.Ibid.

1041.Choplin.
1042.Ibid.
1043.Ibid.
1044.Ibid.
1045.Ibid.
1046.Ibid.
1047.Ibid.
1048.The Heritage of Yadkin County, North Carolina (Winston-Salem, NC: Hunter Publishing Co., 1981) Item 535, p. 406.
1049.Choplin.
1050.Ibid.
1051.The Heritage of Yadkin County, North Carolina (Winston-Salem, NC: Hunter Publishing Co., 1981) Item 535, p. 406.
1052.Ibid.
1053.Choplin.
1054.Ibid.
1055.Ibid.
1056.Ibid.
1057.Hennings, Ed, fax dated April 8, 1999.
1058.Ibid.
1059.Ibid.
1060.Ibid.
1061.Ibid., fax dated April 20, 1999.
1062.Choplin.
1063.Ibid.
1064.Ibid.
1065.Ibid.
1066.Hennings, Ed, fax dated April 19, 1999.
1067.Choplin.
1068.Ibid.
1069.Ibid.
1070.Varnon, p. 56.
1071.Ibid.
1072.Philip Christoph Vogler Memorial, Inc. Newsletter, Vol. 5, No. 3, Sept., 1991, p. 6.
1073.Speas.
1074.Ibid.
1075.Ibid.
1076.Ibid.
1077.Ibid.
1078.Hennings, Ed, fax dated April 8, 1999.
1079.Ibid., Family Group sheet dated March 10, 1999.
1080.Ibid.

1081.Matthews.
1082.Hennings, Ed, notes dated may 15, 1999.
1083.Matthews.
1084.Varnon, p. 57.
1085.Ibid.
1086.Ibid.
1087.Ibid.
1088.Ibid.
1089.Ibid.
1090.Ibid.
1091.Ibid.
1092.Ibid.
1093.Ibid.
1094.Hennings, Ed, notes dated May 15, 1999.
1095.Varnon, p. 57.
1096.Ibid.
1097.Ibid.
1098.Ibid.
1099.Ibid.
1100.Matthews.
1101.Varnon, p. 57.
1102.Hennings, Ed, notes dated May 15, 1999.
1103.Matthews.
1104.Hennings, Ed, notes dated May 15, 1999.
1105.Ibid.
1106.Varnon, p. 57.
1107.Ibid.
1108.Ibid.
1109.Ibid.
1110.Hennings, Ed, fax dated April 19, 1999.
1111.Ibid.
1112.Ibid.
1113.Ibid.
1114.Violet Fannie Henning Weaver, Rt. 1, Box 99, Glenwood, AR 71943, Aug., 1999.
1115.Connie Henning Bland, 164 W. 1st St., Manteno, IL 60950.
1116.Weaver.
1117.Ibid.
1118.Bland.
1119.Ibid.
1120.Ibid.
1121.Ibid.
1122.Ibid.

1123.Ibid.
1124.Ibid.
1125.Ibid.
1126.Ibid.
1127.Ibid.
1128.Ibid.
1129.Ibid.
1130.Ibid.
1131.Ibid.
1132.Ibid.
1133.Ibid.
1134.Ibid.
1135.Weaver.
1136.Bland.
1137.Ibid.
1138.Ibid.
1139.Hennings, Ed, Family Group Sheet dated July 11, 1997.
1140.Ibid.
1141.Ibid.
1142.Ibid.
1143.Ibid.
1144.Ibid.
1145.Ibid.
1146.Ibid.
1147.Ibid.
1148.Ibid.
1149.Ibid.
1150.Ibid.
1151.Ibid.
1152.Ibid.
1153.Ibid.
1154.Ibid.
1155.Ibid.
1156.Ibid.
1157.Ibid., fax dated April 8, 1999.
1158.Ibid.
1159.Ibid.
1160.Ibid., notes dated May 15, 1999.
1161.Ibid., fax dated April 8, 1999.
1162.Ibid.
1163.Ibid.
1164.Ibid., Family Group Sheet dated March 10, 1999.
1165.Ibid.

1166.Ibid.
1167.Pittman.
1168.Hereford, p. 4.
1169.Ibid., p. 5.
1170.Ibid.
1171.Ibid.
1172.Broderbund Family Archive #110, Vol. 1, Ed. 5, Social Security Death Index, Internal Ref. #1.111.5.106950.195.
1173.Pittman.
1174.Hereford, p. 5.
1175.Ibid.
1176.Ibid., p. 6.
1177.Ibid.
1178.Broderbund Family Archive #110, Vol. 2, Ed. 5, Social Security Death Index, Internal Ref. #1.112.5.96808.135.
1179.Hereford, p. 6.
1180.Pittman.
1181.Ibid.
1182.Ibid.
1183.Ibid.
1184.Hereford, p. 7.
1185.Ibid.
1186.Ibid.
1187.Ibid.
1188.Ibid.
1189.Ibid.
1190.Ibid.
1191.Pittman.
1192.Hereford, p. 7.
1193.Ibid.
1194.Ibid., p. 8.
1195.Ibid.
1196.Ibid.
1197.Ibid.
1198.Ibid.
1199.Ibid., p. 9.
1200.Broderbund Family Archive #110, Vol. 1, Ed. 5, Social Security Death Index, Internal Ref. #1.111.5.35232.126.
1201.Hereford, p. 9.
1202.Ibid.
1203.Ibid.
1204.Ibid.
1205.Ibid., p. 10.

1206.Ibid.
1207.Ibid.
1208.Ibid.
1209.Ibid., p. 11.
1210.Ibid.
1211.Ibid.
1212.Broderbund Family Archive #110, Vol. 1, Ed. 5, Social Security Death Index, Internal Ref. #1.111.5.80306.122.
1213.Hereford, p. 12.
1214.Ibid.
1215.Ibid.
1216.Ibid.
1217.Ibid.
1218.Ibid.
1219.Ibid.
1220.Ibid.
1221.Ibid., p. 13.
1222.Ibid.
1223.Ibid.
1224.Ibid.
1225.Ibid.
1226.Ibid.
1227.Ibid.
1228.Ibid.
1229.Ibid.
1230.Ibid.
1231.Ibid.
1232.Ibid., p. 14.
1233.Ibid., p. 13.
1234.Ibid.
1235.Ibid.
1236.Ibid., p. 14.
1237.Ibid.
1238.Ibid.
1239.Ibid.
1240.Pittman.
1241.Hereford, p. 14.
1242.Ibid.
1243.Pittman.
1244.Ibid.
1245.Ibid.
1246.Ibid.
1247.Ibid.

1248.Ibid.
1249.Ibid.
1250.Ibid.
1251.Ibid.
1252.Ibid.
1253.Ibid.
1254.Ibid.
1255.Ibid.
1256.Ibid.
1257.Ibid.
1258.Ibid.
1259.Ibid.
1260.Ibid.
1261.Ibid.
1262.Ibid.
1263.Ibid.
1264.Ibid.
1265.Ibid.
1266.Ibid.
1267.Ibid.
1268.Ibid.
1269.Ibid.
1270.Ibid.
1271.Ibid.
1272.Ibid.
1273.Ibid.
1274.Ibid.
1275.Ibid.
1276.Ibid.
1277.Hereford, p. 20.
1278.Ibid.
1279.Ibid.
1280.Ibid., p. 21.
1281.Ibid.
1282.Ibid., p. 22.
1283.Ibid.
1284.Ibid.
1285.Ibid.
1286.Ibid.
1287.Ibid.
1288.Ibid.
1289.Ibid., p. 23.
1290.Ibid.

1291.Ibid.
1292.Ibid.
1293.Pittman.
1294.Ibid.
1295.Ibid.
1296.Ibid.
1297.Ibid.
1298.Ibid.
1299.Ibid.
1300.Ibid.
1301.Ibid.
1302.Ibid.
1303.Ibid.
1304.Ibid.
1305.Ibid.
1306.Ibid.
1307.Ibid.
1308.Ibid.
1309.Ibid.
1310.Ibid.
1311.Hereford, p. 27.
1312.Ibid.
1313.Hartle.
1314.Ibid.
1315.Ibid.
1316.Ibid.
1317.Ibid.
1318.Ibid.
1319.Ibid.
1320.Ibid.
1321.Ibid.
1322.Ibid.
1323.Ibid.
1324.Ibid.
1325.Winston-Salem Journal, July 24, 1990, Obituary, p. 18.
1326.Fordham.
1327.Ibid.
1328.Broderbund Family Archive #110, Vol. 2, Ed. 5, Social Security Death Index, Internal Ref. #1.112.5.21011.90.
1329.Bullard, John Robert.
1330.Broderbund Family Archive #110, Vol. 2, Ed. 5, Social Security Death Index, Internal Ref. #1.112.5.21015.65.
1331.Bullard, John Robert.

1332.Ibid.
1333.Broderbund Family Archive #110, Vol. 1, Ed. 5, Social Security Death Index. Internal Ref. 1.111.5.119666.31.
1334.Jennings.
1335.Ibid.
1336.Ibid.
1337.Bullard, Dorothy Early.
1338.Forsyth County, NC Marriage Licenses, 1931-1949, Reel C.038.60086, NC State Archives, Jones St., Raleigh, NC.
1339.Bullard, Dorothy Early.
1340.Ibid.
1341.Ibid.
1342.Forsyth County, NC Marriage Licenses, 1931-1949, Reel C.038.60086, NC State Archives, Jones St., Raleigh, NC.
1343.Ruth Joye T. Bullard, c/o Springwood Care Ctr., 5755 Shattalon Rd., Winston-Salem, NC 27105, letter dated March 6, 1987.
1344.Bullard, Ruth Joye T.
1345.Ibid.
1346.Ibid.
1347.Lynn Griffith Ester, 685 Nighthawk Rd., Lynchburg, VA 24504-4224.
1348.Bullard, Hoke Vogler.
1349.Ibid.
1350.Ibid.
1351.Ibid.
1352.Ibid.
1353.Coltrane, Family Group Sheet dated March 7, 1987.
1354.Ibid.
1355.Ibid.
1356.Ibid.
1357.Ibid.
1358.Ibid.
1359.Ibid.
1360.Ibid.
1361.Pendleton.
1362.Ibid.
1363.Ibid.
1364.Ibid.
1365.Ibid.
1366.Ibid.
1367.Ibid.
1368.Ibid.
1369.Ibid.
1370.Ibid.

1371.Ibid.
1372.Ibid.
1373.Ibid.
1374.Ibid.
1375.Ibid.
1376.Ibid.
1377.Hill, e-mail dated March 10, 2000.
1378.Pendleton.
1379.Ibid.
1380.Broderbund Family Archive #110, Vol. 1, Ed. 5, Social Security Death Index, Internal Ref. #1.111.5.108304.98.
1381.Pendleton.
1382.Ibid.
1383.Ibid.
1384.Ibid.
1385.Ibid.
1386.Ibid.
1387.Ibid.
1388.Ibid.
1389.Ibid.
1390.Ibid.
1391.Ibid.
1392.Ibid.
1393.Ibid.
1394.Hauser, e-mail dated Feb. 16, 1999.
1395.Ibid.
1396.Ibid.
1397.Broderbund Family Archive #110, Vol. 1, Ed. 5, Social Security Death Index, Internal Ref. #1.111.5.102725.52.
1398.Ibid.
1399.Ibid.
1400.Ibid.
1401.Ibid.
1402.Ibid.
1403.Ibid.
1404.Brinegar, notes dated July 2, 1999.
1405.Ibid.
1406.Ibid.
1407.Ibid.
1408.Ibid.
1409.Ibid.
1410.Ibid.
1411.Ibid.

1412.Ibid.
1413.Ibid.
1414.Ibid.
1415.Ibid.
1416.Ibid.
1417.Ibid.
1418.Ibid.
1419.Ibid.
1420.Ibid.
1421.Ibid.
1422.Ibid.
1423.Ibid.
1424.Ibid.
1425.Ibid.
1426.Ibid.
1427.Ibid.
1428.Ibid.
1429.Ibid.
1430.Ibid.
1431.Ibid.
1432.Ibid.
1433.Ibid.
1434.Ibid.
1435.Ibid.
1436.Ibid.
1437.Ibid.
1438.Ibid.
1439.Ibid.
1440.Henning, Joem Davis.
1441.Ibid.
1442.Ibid.
1443.Ibid.
1444.Hennings, Ed, fax dated April 8, 1999.
1445.Ibid.
1446.Ibid.
1447.Choplin.
1448.Ibid.
1449.Ibid.
1450.Ibid.
1451.Ibid.
1452.Ibid.
1453.Ibid.
1454.Ibid.

1455.Ibid.
1456.Ibid.
1457.Mark Armstrong, Henning Family Reunion, Stony Knoll Methodist Church, East Bend, NC, Aug. 1, 1999.
1458.Ibid.
1459.Ibid.
1460.Ibid.
1461.Hennings, Ed, Family Group Sheet dated May 15, 1999.
1462.Anne Wooten Teeling, 9111 Arbon Park Dr., Dallas, TX 75243, Dec., 1998.
1463.Ibid.
1464.Ibid.
1465.Ibid.
1466.Ibid.
1467.Hennings, Ed, Family Group Sheet dated May 15, 1999.
1468.Ibid.
1469.Ibid.
1470.Ibid.
1471.Ibid.
1472.Ibid.
1473.Ibid.
1474.Ibid.
1475.Ibid.
1476.Ibid.
1477.Ibid.
1478.Ibid.
1479.Ibid.
1480.Ibid.
1481.Ibid.
1482.Ruby Hennings Murphy, 2325 Flint Hill Rd., East Bend, NC, Family Group Sheet dated March 19, 1999.
1483.Ibid.
1484.Ibid.
1485.Choplin.
1486.Ibid.
1487.Ibid.
1488.Ibid.
1489.Ibid.
1490.Ibid.
1491.Ibid.
1492.Ibid.
1493.Ibid.
1494.Ibid.
1495.Ibid.

1496.Ibid.
1497.Ibid.
1498.Ibid.
1499.Ibid.
1500.Ibid.
1501.Ibid.
1502.Ibid.
1503.Ibid.
1504.Ibid.
1505.Ibid.
1506.Ibid.
1507.Collins.
1508.Ibid.
1509.Ibid.
1510.Ibid.
1511.Ibid.
1512.Ibid.
1513.Ibid.
1514.Ibid.
1515.Ibid.
1516.Ibid.
1517.Ibid.
1518.Ibid.
1519.Ibid.
1520.Ibid.
1521.Ibid.
1522.Ibid.
1523.Ibid.
1524.Ibid.
1525.Choplin.
1526.Ibid.
1527.Ibid.
1528.Ibid.
1529.Ibid.
1530.Ibid.
1531.Ibid.
1532.Ibid.
1533.Ibid.
1534.Ibid.
1535.Ibid.
1536.Ibid.
1537.Hennings, Ed, fax dated April 8, 1999.
1538.Ibid.

1539.Ibid.
1540.Ibid.
1541.Ibid.
1542.Ibid.
1543.Ibid.
1544.Ibid.
1545.Varnon, p. 56.
1546.Ibid.
1547.Ibid.
1548.Ibid.
1549.Ibid., p. 57.
1550.Ibid.
1551.Ibid.
1552.Matthews.
1553.Ibid.
1554.Ibid.
1555.Varnon, p. 57.
1556.Hennings, Ed, notes dated May 15, 1999.
1557.Ibid.
1558.Ibid.
1559.Varnon, p. 57.
1560.Matthews.
1561.Varnon, p. 57.
1562.Matthews.
1563.Ibid.
1564.Ibid.
1565.Ibid.
1566.Ibid.
1567.Ibid.
1568.Ibid.
1569.Ibid.
1570.Hennings, Ed, fax dated April 19, 1999.
1571.Ibid.
1572.Weaver.
1573.Ibid.
1574.Ibid.
1575.Ibid.
1576.Ibid.
1577.Ibid.
1578.Ibid.
1579.Ibid.
1580.Ibid.
1581.Ibid.

1582.Ibid.
1583.Bland.
1584.Ibid.
1585.Ibid.
1586.Ibid.
1587.Ibid.
1588.Ibid.
1589.Ibid.
1590.Ibid.
1591.Ibid.
1592.Ibid.
1593.Ibid.
1594.Ibid.
1595.Ibid.
1596.Ibid.
1597.Ibid.
1598.Ibid.
1599.Ibid.
1600.Ibid.
1601.Ibid.
1602.Ibid.
1603.Ibid.
1604.Ibid.
1605.Ibid.
1606.Ibid.
1607.Ibid.
1608.Ibid.
1609.Ibid.
1610.Ibid.
1611.Ibid.
1612.Ibid.
1613.Ibid.
1614.Ibid.
1615.Ibid.
1616.Ibid.
1617.Ibid.
1618.Ibid.
1619.Ibid.
1620.Ibid.
1621.Ibid.
1622.Ibid.
1623.Ibid.
1624.Ibid.

1625.Ibid.
1626.Hennings, Ed, Family Group Sheet updated July 11, 1997.
1627.Ibid.
1628.Ibid.
1629.Ibid.
1630.Ibid.
1631.Ibid.
1632.Ibid.
1633.Ibid.
1634.Ibid.
1635.Ibid.
1636.Ibid.
1637.Ibid.
1638.Ibid.
1639.Ibid.
1640.Ibid.
1641.Ibid.
1642.Ibid.
1643.The Heritage of Yadkin County, North Carolina, Hunter Publishing Co.,
Winston-Salem, NC, 1981, Item 536, p. 406.
1644.Ibid.
1645.Hennings, Ed, fax dated April 8, 1999.
1646.Ibid.
1647.Ibid.
1648.Ibid., Family Group Sheet dated March 10, 1999.
1649.Ibid.
1650.Ibid.
1651.Ibid.
1652.Ibid.
1653.Ibid.
1654.Ibid.
1655.Hereford, p. 4.
1656.Ibid.
1657.Ibid.
1658.Ibid.
1659.Ibid.
1660.Ibid.
1661.Ibid.
1662.Hereford, p. 5.
1663.Ibid.
1664.Ibid.
1665.Ibid.
1666.Ibid.

1667.Pittman.
1668.Ibid.
1669.Ibid.
1670.Ibid.
1671.Ibid.
1672.Ibid.
1673.Ibid.
1674.Ibid.
1675.Ibid.
1676.Ibid.
1677.Ibid.
1678.Ibid.
1679.Ibid.
1680.Ibid.
1681.Hereford, p. 10.
1682.Ibid.
1683.Ibid.
1684.Ibid.
1685.Ibid., p. 13.
1686.Ibid.
1687.Ibid.
1688.Ibid.
1689.Ibid.
1690.Pittman.
1691.Ibid.
1692.Ibid.
1693.Ibid.
1694.Ibid.
1695.Ibid.
1696.Ibid.
1697.Fordham, information dated April 5, 1987.
1698.Winston-Salem Journal, obituary dated July 24, 1990, p. 18.
1699.Bullard, Dorothy Early, letter dated Aug. 4, 1986.
1700.Ibid.
1701.Bullard, Ruth Joye Tuttle Bullard, letter dated March 6, 1987.
1702.Ibid.
1703.Ibid.
1704.Pendleton.
1705.Ibid.
1706.Ibid.
1707.Ibid.
1708.Ibid.
1709.Ibid.

1710.Ibid.
1711.Ibid.
1712.Ibid.
1713.Ibid.
1714.Hauser, e-mail dated Feb. 16, 1999.
1715.Ibid.
1716.Brinegar, notes dated July 2, 1999.
1717.Teeling.
1718.Ibid.
1719.Ibid.
1720.Ibid.
1721.Ibid.
1722.Ibid.
1723.Ibid.
1724.Ibid.
1725.Ibid.
1726.Ibid.
1727.Hennings, Ed, Family Group Sheet dated May 15, 1999.
1728.Beth Hennings, 1667 Bow Tree Dr., West Chester, PA.
1729.Ibid.
1730.Hennings, Ed, Family Group Sheet dated May 15, 1999.
1731.Ibid
1732.Ibid.
1733.Ibid.
1734.Ibid.
1735.Ibid.
1736.Ibid.
1737.Ibid.
1738.Ibid.
1739.Ibid.
1740.Ibid.
1741.Ibid.
1742.Ibid.
1743.Ibid.
1744.Murphy.
1745.Jennifer Murphy Phillips, 2417 Flint Hill Rd., East Bend, NC, Family Group
Sheet dated March 19, 1999.
1746.Ibid.
1747.Ibid.
1748.Murphy.
1749.Heather Murphy Russell, 3430 N. Mtn. Ridge Rd., Mesa, AZ, Family Group
Sheet dated March 19, 1999.
1750.Choplin.

1751.Ibid.
1752.Ibid.
1753.Ibid.
1754.Collins.
1755.Ibid.
1756.Ibid.
1757.Ibid.
1758.Ibid.
1759.Ibid.
1760.Ibid.
1761.Ibid.
1762.Ibid.
1763.Ibid.
1764.Ibid.
1765.Ibid.
1766.Ibid.
1767.Ibid.
1768.Ibid.
1769.Ibid.
1770.Ibid.
1771.Hennings, Ed, fax dated April 19, 1999.
1772.Ibid.
1773.Ibid.
1774.Ibid.
1775.Ibid.
1776.Weaver.
1777.Ibid.
1778.Ibid.
1779.Ibid.
1780.Ibid.
1781.Ibid.
1782.Ibid.
1783.Ibid.
1784.Ibid.
1785.Ibid.
1786.Ibid.
1787.Ibid.
1788.Ibid.
1789.Ibid.
1790.Ibid.
1791.Ibid.
1792.Ibid.
1793.Ibid.

1794.Ibid.
1795.Ibid.
1796.Ibid.
1797.Ibid.
1798.Ibid.
1799.Ibid.
1800.Bland.
1801.Ibid.
1802.Ibid.
1803.Ibid.
1804.Ibid.
1805.Ibid.
1806.Ibid.
1807.Ibid.
1808.Ibid.
1809.Ibid.
1810.Ibid.
1811.Ibid.
1812.Ibid.
1813.Ibid.
1814.Ibid.
1815.Ibid.
1816.Ibid.
1817.Ibid.
1818.Ibid.
1819.Ibid.
1820.Ibid.
1821.Ibid.
1822.Ibid.
1823.Ibid.
1824.Ibid.
1825.Ibid.
1826.Ibid.
1827.Hennings, Ed, Family Group Sheet updated July 11, 1997.
1828.Ibid.
1829.Ibid.
1830.Ibid.
1831.Ibid.
1832.Ibid.
1833.Pittman.
1834.Ibid.
1835.Ibid.
1836.Ibid.

1837.Ibid.
1838.Ibid.
1839.Ibid.
1840.Ibid.
1841.Bullard, Dorothy Early, letter dated Sept. 9, 1998.
1842.Ibid.
1843.Pendleton.
1844.Ibid.
1845.Collins.
1846.Ibid.
1847.Weaver.
1848.Ibid.
1849.Ibid.
1850.Ibid.
1851.Ibid.
1852.Ibid.
1853.Ibid.
1854.Hereford, p. 9.
1855.Pittman.
1856.Ibid.
1857.Ibid.
1858.Ibid.
1859.Brinegar, notes dated July 2, 1999.
1860.Ibid.
1861.Ibid.
1862.Ibid.
1863.Ibid.
1864.Ibid.
1865.Ibid.
1866.Ibid.
1867.Ibid.
1868.Ibid.
1869.Ibid.
1870.Ibid.
1871.Ibid.
1872.Ibid.
1873.Ibid.
1874.Ibid.

Index of Names

240

Michael Lynn: 147
Scott Allen: 148
Tamala Dawn: 146, 173
Wesley Clark: 102
William Herman: 146
Church -
    Robert: 9
Clapper -
    Marilyn Janeen: 134
    Melvin: 133
Clark -
    Harley: 63
    Henrietta: 63
Cline -
    Annie Laura: 36
    Augustine C.: 17, 37
    Augustine S.: 37
    Carlton Clinton: 38
    Charles Christian: 16, 35
    Charlie: 95
    Charlie Earnest: 35, 58
    Clarence: 37
    Dallas David: 39
    Early: 18
    Edwin: 9
    Eli: 8, 16, 61
    Elizabeth: 9, 18
    Everett Odell: 37, 60
    Everett Odell, Jr.: 60
    Flossie Irene: 38
    Fredrick Garson: 96
    Geraldine (aka: Jerry): 4, 6,
    8, 61, 97, 185
    Gladys: 58
    Grady Oscar: 38
    Gurney Lee: 38
    Henry: 8
    Howard O.: 60
    Howard Olin: 36, 59
    Irma: 6, 95
    Isaac: 17
    J. Harrison: 18
    James Nathan: 16, 35, 36
    James Raymond: 96
    Jamie B.: 37
    Jennie: 16
    Juluis: 16
    Karen: 96
    Karl: 36
    Katherine: 38
    Laura: 17
    Lewis W.: 17
    Lisetta Catherine: 16

    Maggie: 35
    Margaret Jean: 96
    Martha Jane: 37
    Mattie: 16
    Mattie Beatrice: 36, 58
    Maude: 36
    Melvina (aka: Ellen): 17
    Mertie: 36
    Myrtle Louise: 38
    Nancy: 8, 15
    Nellie Larue: 61, 96
    Nellie Mae: 38
    Norris: 96
    Peter: 7, 8, 16, 17
    Peter S.: 17, 36
    Peter Solomon: 8, 15
    Phyllis Kathleen: 96
    Pleas David: 17, 37, 61
    Raymond Arthur: 38, 60
    Raymond Arthur, Jr.: 61, 96
    Rex: 60
    Richard: 17
    Rosa J.: 37
    Ruth: 60
    Sanford: 17
    Sarah: 17
    Solomon: 15, 16
    Stella: 37
    Sudie: 36
    Susan Irene: 96, 138
    Uriah W.: 19
    Virginia Dare: 38
    Walter B.: 37
    Wilma Dane: 60
Cochran -
    Benjamin J.: 127
    Maggie: 127
    Terry: 127
Coe -
    Velma: 72
Colbert -
    John S.: 11
Colehour -
    Joann: 156
Collins -
    Candi Lee: 162
    Claude: 162
    Claudia Ann: 162
    Edward Lee: 105
    Edward Lee, Jr.: 105
    Herman L.: 146
    Kathleen Ruth: 162
    Katie Rose: 150

Kenneth Gordon: 162
Mitchell Van: 105, 149
Ronald David: 162
Roxie Olivia: 146
Coltrane -
Clara Augusta: 89
Cora Fannie: 90
Edith Elena: 90
Emma Bell: 133
Helen Eaton: 133
Hugh William: 24, 89
Jeffrey H.: 88
Jeffrey Smith: 89, 132
Jeffrey Smith, Jr.: 3, 5, 6,
13, 18, 19, 23, 133
Pearl Lutency: 89
Robert McKinley: 133
Ruby Belle: 89
Sarah Elizabeth: 133
Velna Snow: 89
Virginia Hall: 133
William Jackson: 133
William McKindry: 88
Combs -
Debra Sue: 154
Conrad -
Augustine E. B.: 15
Catharine A.: 15
Clementine R.: 15
Emily S.: 15
Ethel Conrad: 86
Eugene Moore: 1
Felicia: 15
George: 93
Georgia Marie: 93, 136
Julia A.: 15, 34
Laura Ophelia: 86, 129
Lela: 91
Louisa M.: 15
Permelia M.: 15
Phillip: 98
Robert Arthur: 98
Victor: 98
W. W.: 59
Walter W.: 85
William: 15, 16
Conte -
Cathy Lynn: 154, 175
Peter Frank: 154
Conwell -
Rachel Katherine: 177
Ronald Keith: 177
Ryan Truitt: 177

Cook -
Carolyn: 68
Kenneth Ray: 116
Ray Harding: 116
Virginia: 119
Cornelius -
Christy: 107
Denise: 107
Leon Turner: 100
Lesta Wilmouth: 100
Luther Weldon: 67
Marsha R.: 108
Ralph Weldon: 67
Richard Gray: 67, 107
Ricky: 107
Robert Joe: 68
Ruby Gail: 68, 107
Sharon R.: 108
William Earl: 68, 108
William: 67
Cornelli -
Teresa: 97
Cornwallis -
General Charles: 1, 2
Cotton -
Patricia Ann: 154
Craft -
Sam: 24
Craig -
_____: 174
Amy: 150
Bradley: 150
Christopher: 150
William: 150
Cranfield -
Rachel: 74
Crews -
Austin: 174
Bo: 148, 174
Brent: 174
Dustin: 174
Jamie: 174
Jeff: 148, 174
Justin: 174
Lynn: 148
Matthew: 174
Melinda: 148, 174
Tessie: 173
Thomas E. Jr.: 148, 174
Thomas E., Sr.: 148
Crotts -
Jeff: 104

Crowe -
Carl: 118
Ethel Clementine: 26
James: 118
Crowley -
Dr. James: 117
Milford: 117
Culp -
Carl: 123
Cummings -
Mary: 38
Curtis -
Lula: 28
Dahlbert -
Thelma Irene: 80
Dahlstrom -
Marion: 117
Dail -
R. M.: 25
Dancy -
Freeman: 24
Darling -
Janice Valene: 80
Davenport -
Jane Elizabeth: 17, 61
Davis -
Adam Gray: 181
Aileen: 181
Amber Elizabeth: 176
Arvon Martin: 160
Bobby Gray: 101, 158
Cara Jean: 160
Claude: 26
Denise: 142
Edith: 28
Fred: 176
George Terry: 106
Gladys Louise: 62
Heather Annette: ; 176, 184
James Thurmon: 62
Jedidiah Gray (aka: Jed): 181
Joem Rivers: 98
John Wesley: 98
Martha Agness: 57
Martha Edna: 108
Natalie Alane: 176
Samantha Renee: 176
Timothy Gray (aka: Tim):
159, 181
Day -
Irene: 104

Deasy -
Craig Roberts: 122
James E.: 121
James Scott: 121
Kathryn Campbell: 121
Deeds -
Donna: 125
Deets -
John: 22
Deitz -
Charity: 10
John: 10, 22
Nancy: 10, 30
Denault -
Alexandra Elizabeth: 179
Brittany Renee: 179
Candace Lauren: 179
Cory Scott: 178
Douglas Scott: 155, 178
Duane: 155
Gregory Duane: 155, 178
Jacob Lance: 179
Jeffrey Brian: 155, 179
Lance Joseph: 155, 179
Marc Eugene: 155
Mitchell Gregory: 178
Neil Laurence: 179
Nicholas Dane: 179
Shannon Reece: 178
Denkins -
Mary Ruth: 171
Denny -
Sarah: 58
Dilworth -
Eliza: 57
George: 24
Mary E.: 57
Robert: 57
Dittus -
Virlin: 113
Doepper -
Carol Jean: 146
Doll -
Elizabeth: 15
Donough -
Dorothy: 112
Dorn -
Janis Marie: 159, 181
Jay Russell: 159
John Allen: 159

Franz -
  Brian: 120
  John A.: 78
  Leroy: 120
  Mary Iris: 78, 120
  Randall: 120
  Robert Leroy: 78, 120
French -
  Rose: 27
Fry -
  J.A.B.: 85
Fritzgerald -
  A. H.: 86
  Elizabeth: 86
  Lillian G.: 86
Fulbright -
  Gertrude: 173
  Otis: 173
  Sharon: 173
Fulk -
  Aaron: 58
  Augustus Danial (aka:
  Guster): 35
  Betty: 152
  Charles Robert: 59
  Charles Russell: 58
  Cornelia: 35
  Curtis Glenn: 94
  David Glenn: 137
  Herman Glenn (aka: Fulk):
  59, 94
  Howard Elmer: 58
  Larry: 94
  Maebelle: 54
  Michael Glenn: 137
  Oscar Odell: 59. 93
  Ray Rufus: 58, 93
Fulp -
  David: 137
  Hazel Cornelia: 59, 94
  Herman Glenn, Jr.: 95, 137
  Lisa: 137
  Martha Kay: 95, 136
  Michael: 137
  Mildred Marie: 59, 93
Fulton -
  Betsy: 94
Furches -
  Brian: 138
  Derrick: 139, 168
  Randall: 138
  Richard: 138

Scott: 168
Galbraith -
  Anna: 26
Galbreath -
  N. Ann: 25
Gay -
  James E. III: 129
Geasland -
  Frances Louise Lula: 49
Gehring -
  Charlene: 117
Gentry -
  ____: 149
  Patty Inez: 132
George -
  Amanda: 36
  Ellen W.: 17
  James: 19
  Levi: 19
  Rebecca: 35
Gibbons -
  Dale: 126
  Elmer: 126
  Jeanel: 126
  Neva: 82
Gibson -
  Viola Florence: 94
  Willie: 94
Googe -
  Ann Victoria: 116, 161
  Arthur Lee (aka: Bill): 116
  Jordan: 161
  Stephen Lee: 116, 161
  William L. (aka: Bill): 161
Gordon -
  Minnie: 18
Gossett -
  ____: 109
Gough -
  Barbara: 150
  James: 42
  Rose Anna Augusta: 42
  Tom: 24
Graff -
  Christopher Duane: 182
  David Duane: 182
Graham -
  Joseph: 1
Gravel -
  Violet June: 170

Gray -
  Robert Charles: 129
Green -
  April: 151
  James S.: 106
  Jason: 150
  John Sandford: 106
  Michael: 106, 150
  Paula: 150
  Tara: 151
  Tony: 106, 150
Greene -
  Albert: 129
Gregor -
  Anna: 80
Greider -
  Brother: 23, 30
Griffith -
  Lynn Edna: 132
  William Enoch: 132
  William Simpson: 132
Groce -
  Mary: 35
  Nancy: 110
Groover -
  Juliette: 92
Grubbs -
  Anna Lynn: 89
  Frieda Marie: 60
Grun -
  ___: 101
Hadranyi -
  Paul Peter: 89
Hake -
  Gladys: 51
Halbrook -
  ___: 23
Hale -
  Charles Arthur: 163
  Craig: 163
  Jenny Sue: 163
Hampton -
  Charity Faith: 153
  Charles Ray: 110, 152
  Jerry Wayne: 110
  Johnny: 110
  Kevin Ray: 153
Hanson -
  Alfred: 117
  C.H.: 52
  Joyce E.: 84

Nancy: 117
Harrell -
  Clifton: 69
  Pearl O.: 69
  William Consie: 69
Hartle -
  Margaret Lona (aka: Peggy): 129
  Pauline Pearce (aka: Polly): 129
  Ruth Louise: 129
  Thorne Cornelius: 129
  Thorne Cornelius (aka: Thornie): 129
Hartung -
  Amy: 178
  Donna: 178
  Robert: 178
Harvey -
  James S.: 166
  Steven Burt: 166
Hasket -
  Max: 91
Haughey -
  Vera: 170
Hauser -
  Cuthbert Toso: 136
  Cuthbert Toso, Jr.: 136
  Debbie: 101
  Greta: 101
  Jessica Lynn: 168
  John Anderson: 101
  John Wesley: 64
  Kay: 8, 15, 136
  Legusta: 35
  Nelle Augusta: 65, 101
  Rhonda Kay: 137
  Rodney Toso: 137, 168
  Ruth: 71
  Steve: 101
  Turner Wesley: 44, 65, 101, 114
Hawks -
  Wanda: 110
Hayes -
  Florence: 81
  Joyce Diane: 185
Heckerdom -
  Catherine: 6

261

William Turner Hennings
and his wife,
Rose Anna Augusta Gough
Photo courtesy of Charles Edgar Hennings.

Lewis Hiram Hennings
and his wife,
Martha Jane Speer
Photo courtesy of Charles Edgar Hennings.

Archibald G. Henning
1839 - 1921
Photo courtesy of Steven Wayne Henning.

John Reuben Smith, daughter Cora Bell, wife Mary Lutency Styers Smith holding daughter Mamie.

Photo courtesy of Guy Styers Bullard, Jr.

Martha Ophelia Styers Bullard and her husband,
Jonathan Wesley Bullard.

Photo courtesy of Guy Styers Bullard, Jr.

Gathering of the Santford Henning families at the home of Julius Henning in 1925

Front row: Oren Henning, Julius Henning, Fayet Henning, Santford Henning, Anna Henning Squires, Lloyd Squires, Elias Davis, Ruth Henning. **Second row:** Nola Henning, Dave Henning, Mamie Henning, Everett Henning, Lee Hereford, Dora Henning Hereford; standing behind Lee; Edith Henning, Tom Henning holding son James Henning, Jessie Henning, Edith Henning, Margaret Henning. **Back row:** Vena Henning, Fred Henning, George Henning, Hazel Henning, Lula Henning, John Henning, Dan Henning, Clarence Henning. *Photo courtesy of Julie Painter Pittman.*

James Carroll Simmons and his wife, Helen Henning Simmons. December, 1999. *Photo courtesy of Charles Edgar Hennings.*

Earlene Hennings Speas and her husband, Melvin S. Speas. December, 1999. *Photo courtesy of Charles Edgar Hennings.*

George Joseph Hennings, and his wife Bonnie Smith Hennings, December, 1999. *Photo courtesy of Charles Edgar Hennings.*

Mary Anna Routh Hennings and her husband, Charles Edgar Hennings, December, 1999. *Photo courtesy of Charles Edgar Hennings.*

Delilah Henning and her sister, Lauretta Elizabeth Henning Snipes.
Photo courtesy of Guy Styers Bullard, Jr.

Henry Thomas Hennings and his wife, Emma Sophronia Binkley Hennings, ca. 1950. *Photo courtesy of Charles Edgar Hennings.*

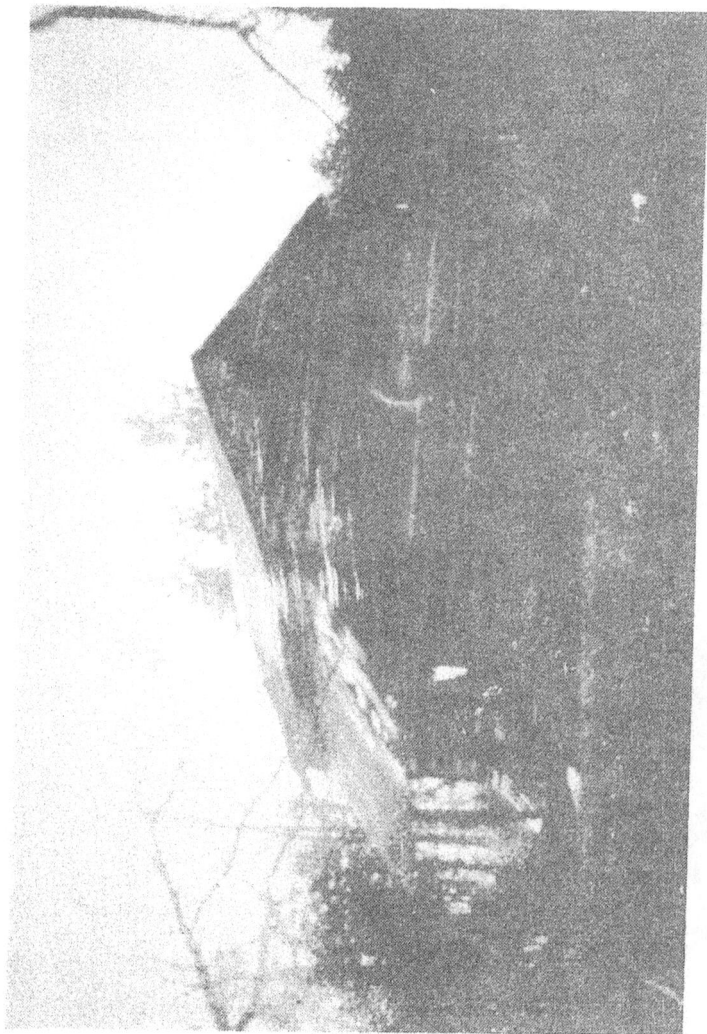

Log house built by John Adam Henning. Located on Sherborne Dr., Forsyth County, Pfafftown, NC. Cabin was dismantled and moved from the site some years ago. Present location unknown. *Photo courtesy of William Arthur Henning.*

Beulah Louise Bullard Cashion

1897-1976

Henry Thomas Henning(s)
1894-1963
Photo courtesy of Charles Edgar Hennings.

Rebecca Estelle Bullard Griffith
1924-1976

Rebecca Estelle Bullard Griffith
1924-1976

Hoke Vogler Bullard and his wife. May Evangeline
Moore Bullard.

Photo courtesy Guy Styers Bullard, Jr.

Julius Adam Henning and his wife, Marnie Ellis Fox
Henning, with their children Vena Anna Henning
(left) and Nola Jane Henning (right).

Photo courtesy of Julie Painter Pittman.

Paul Jackson Henning
1867-1930
Photo courtesy Dr. John M. Bullard

Edward T. Henning and his wife.
Delilah Henning Styers Henning
Photo courtesy Guy Styers Bullard, Jr.

Lavina Melvina Henning and her daughter,
Carrie Mae Henning
Photo courtesy of Jerry Cline Brinegar.

Emma Sophronia Binkley
wife of Henry Thomas Henning
Photo courtesy Charles Edgar Hennings.

Emma Sophronia Binkley
wife of Henry Thomas Henning
Photo courtesy Charles Edgar Hennings.

Julia Anna Hennings Hoots
1900-1967
Photo courtesy Charles Edgar Hennings.

Guy Styers Bullard. Sr.
1891-1983

Guy Styers Bullard, Sr.
1891-1983

www.ingramcontent.com/pod-product-compliance
Lightning Source LLC
Chambersburg PA
CBHW061717270326
41928CB00011B/2014